IMAGES
of America

CRANFORD

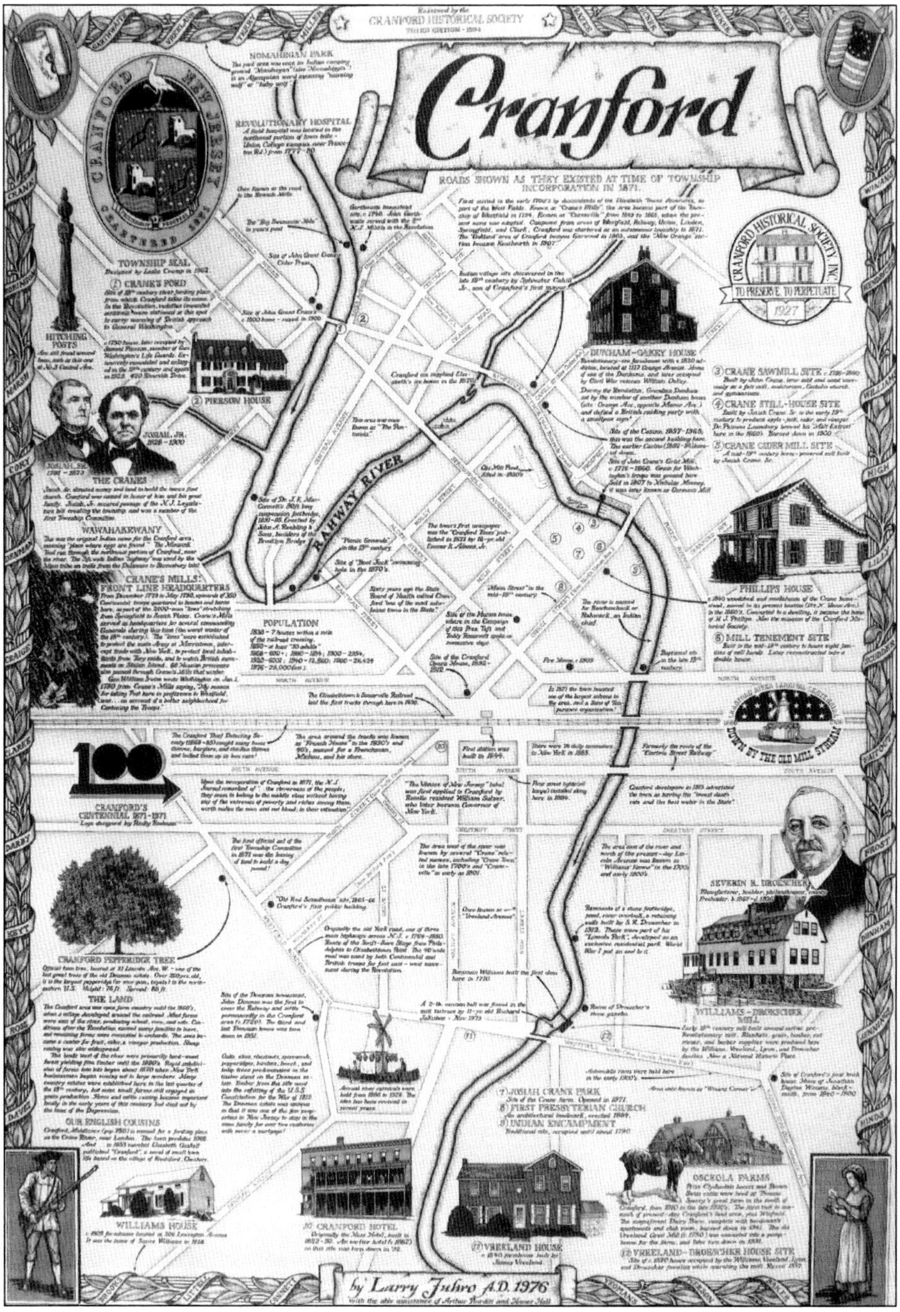

A MAP OF HISTORIC CRANFORD. Graphic artist and local historian Larry Fuhro researched and illustrated this poster map for the United States Bicentennial in 1976. As the graphic illustrates, Cranford has a long and colorful history dating back to before the Revolution. Through the years the town has been known as Crane's Mills, Crane Town, Craneville, and finally Cranford. In 1871, the year the township was incorporated, the new town "fathers" offered the State of New Jersey $200,000 and 20 acres of prime riverside land as an inducement to relocate the state capital to Cranford. One wonders what Cranford would be like today if the offer had been accepted.

IMAGES
of America

CRANFORD

Robert Fridlington and Lawrence Fuhro

ARCADIA
PUBLISHING

ISBN 978-0-7385-3924-9

Published by Arcadia Publishing
Charleston, South Carolina

Printed in the United States of America

Library of Congress Catalog Card Number: 2005931420

For all general information contact Arcadia Publishing at:
Telephone 843-853-2070
Fax 843-853-0044
E-mail sales@arcadiapublishing.com
For customer service and orders:
Toll-Free 1-888-313-2665

Visit us on the Internet at www.arcadiapublishing.com

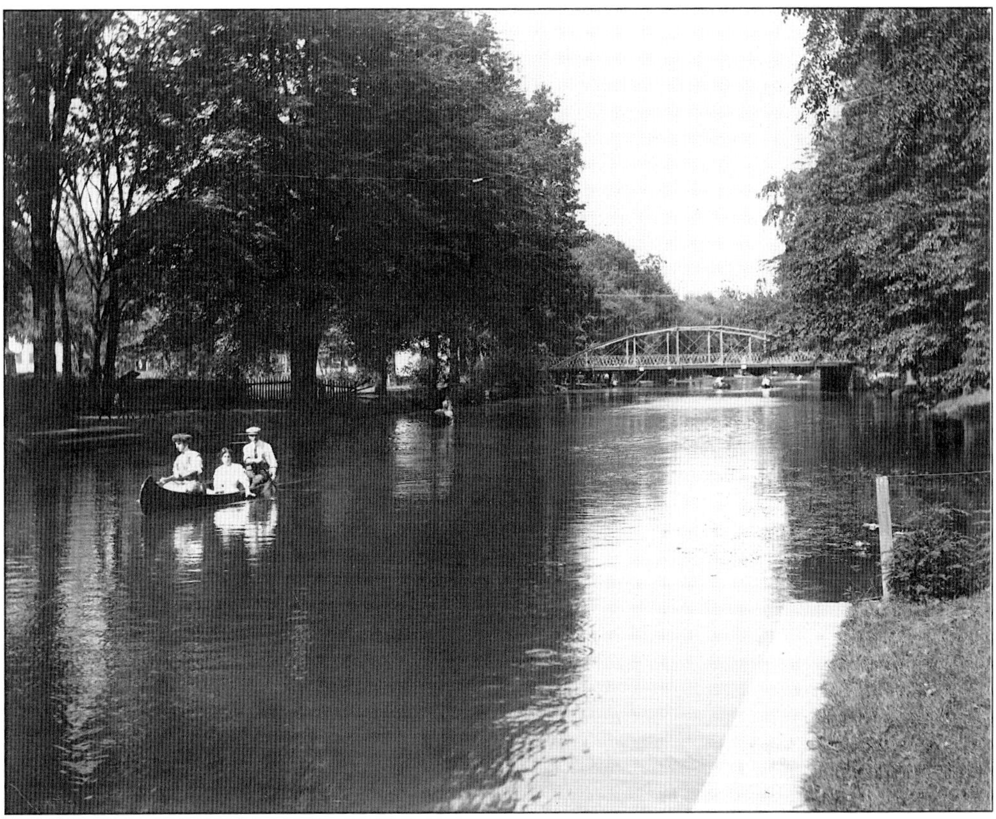

Contents

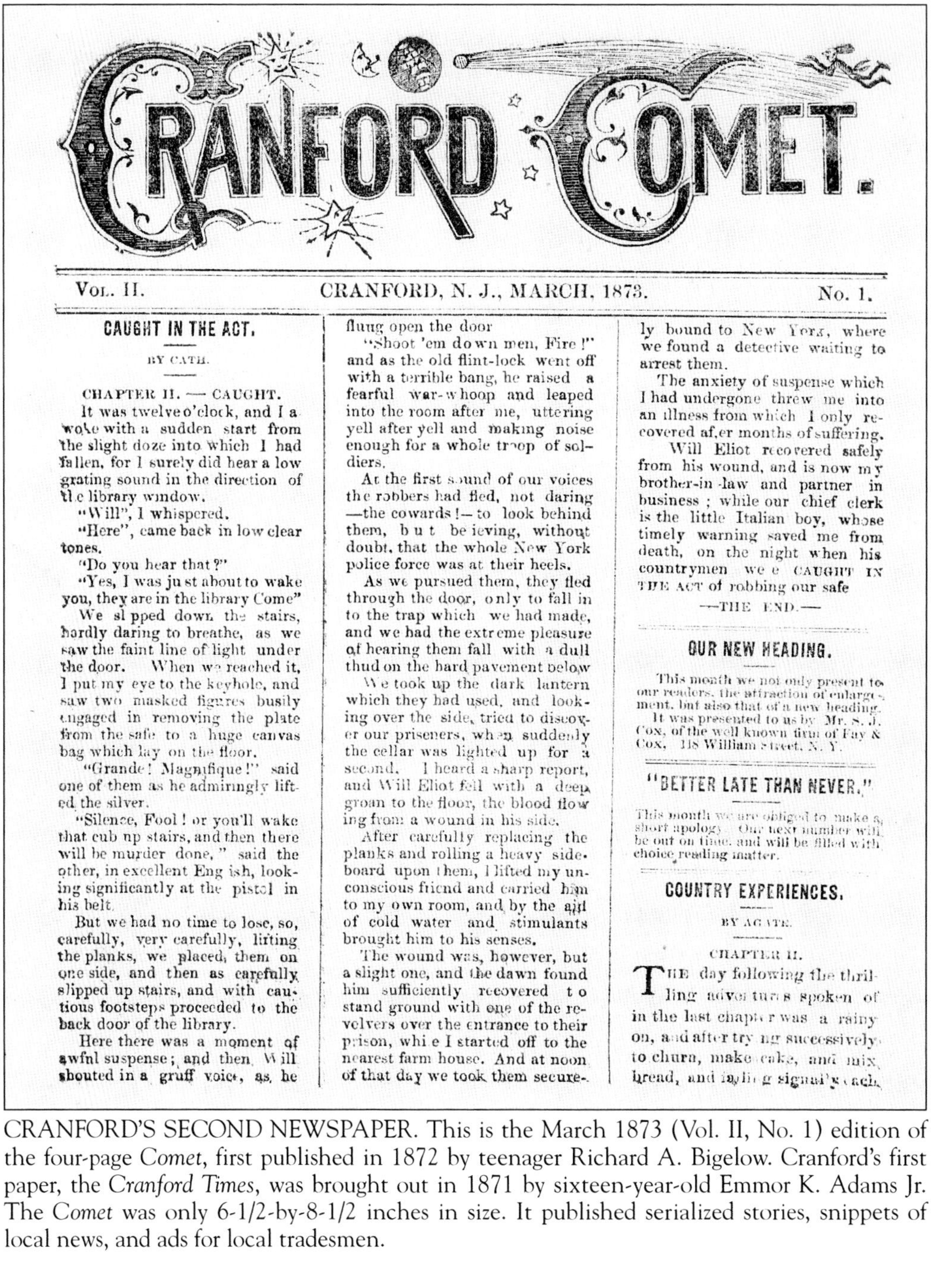

CRANFORD COMET.

VOL. II. CRANFORD, N. J., MARCH, 1873. No. 1.

CAUGHT IN THE ACT.

BY CATH.

CHAPTER II. — CAUGHT.

It was twelve o'clock, and I awoke with a sudden start from the slight doze into which I had fallen, for I surely did hear a low grating sound in the direction of the library window.

"Will", I whispered.

"Here", came back in low clear tones.

"Do you hear that?"

"Yes, I was just about to wake you, they are in the library Come"

We slipped down the stairs, hardly daring to breathe, as we saw the faint line of light under the door. When we reached it, I put my eye to the keyhole, and saw two masked figures busily engaged in removing the plate from the safe to a huge canvas bag which lay on the floor.

"Grande! Magnifique!" said one of them as he admiringly lifted the silver.

"Silence, Fool! or you'll wake that cub up stairs, and then there will be murder done," said the other, in excellent English, looking significantly at the pistol in his belt.

But we had no time to lose, so, carefully, very carefully, lifting the planks, we placed them on one side, and then as carefully slipped up stairs, and with cautious footsteps proceeded to the back door of the library.

Here there was a moment of awful suspense; and then Will shouted in a gruff voice, as he flung open the door

"Shoot 'em down men, Fire!" and as the old flint-lock went off with a terrible bang, he raised a fearful war-whoop and leaped into the room after me, uttering yell after yell and making noise enough for a whole troop of soldiers.

At the first sound of our voices the robbers had fled, not daring—the cowards!—to look behind them, but believing, without doubt, that the whole New York police force was at their heels.

As we pursued them, they fled through the door, only to fall in to the trap which we had made, and we had the extreme pleasure of hearing them fall with a dull thud on the hard pavement below

We took up the dark lantern which they had used, and looking over the side, tried to discover our priseners, when suddenly the cellar was lighted up for a second. I heard a sharp report, and Will Eliot fell with a deep groan to the floor, the blood flowing from a wound in his side.

After carefully replacing the planks and rolling a heavy sideboard upon them, I lifted my unconscious friend and carried him to my own room, and by the aid of cold water and stimulants brought him to his senses.

The wound was, however, but a slight one, and the dawn found him sufficiently recovered to stand ground with one of the revolvers over the entrance to their prison, while I started off to the nearest farm house. And at noon of that day we took them securely bound to New York, where we found a detective waiting to arrest them.

The anxiety of suspense which I had undergone threw me into an illness from which I only recovered after months of suffering.

Will Eliot recovered safely from his wound, and is now my brother-in-law and partner in business; while our chief clerk is the little Italian boy, whose timely warning saved me from death, on the night when his countrymen were CAUGHT IN THE ACT of robbing our safe

—THE END.—

OUR NEW HEADING.

This month we not only present to our readers, the attraction of enlargement, but also that of a new heading. It was presented to us by Mr. S. J. Cox, of the well known firm of Fay & Cox, 118 William street, N. Y.

"BETTER LATE THAN NEVER."

This month we are obliged to make a short apology. Our next number will be out on time, and will be filled with choice reading matter.

COUNTRY EXPERIENCES.

BY AGATHA.

CHAPTER II.

THE day following the thrilling adventures spoken of in the last chapter was a rainy on, and after trying successively to churn, make cake, and mix bread, and ... signal ... each

CRANFORD'S SECOND NEWSPAPER. This is the March 1873 (Vol. II, No. 1) edition of the four-page *Comet*, first published in 1872 by teenager Richard A. Bigelow. Cranford's first paper, the *Cranford Times*, was brought out in 1871 by sixteen-year-old Emmor K. Adams Jr. The *Comet* was only 6-1/2-by-8-1/2 inches in size. It published serialized stories, snippets of local news, and ads for local tradesmen.

Introduction

In 1996 Cranford will celebrate its 125th year as a township. An anniversary of this sort is a time for parties and parades, but it is also a time for reminiscence and reflection. To commemorate this anniversary, we have compiled this Cranford family album.

When the New Jersey Legislature created the Township of Cranford on March 17, 1871, the area was overwhelmingly rural, but the little village on the Rahway River was growing. It already had two churches (a Presbyterian and a Methodist), a schoolhouse, a saloon, and a chapter of the Sons of Temperance. The village had originally been known as Crane's Mills, and later as Craneville. When sophisticated ex-urbanites from New York and Brooklyn began moving to the village after the Civil War, they wanted a name that sounded a little more dignified, so the town became Cranford.

Much has changed since those early days. Outlying neighborhoods have broken away and established their own identities, as Garwood, Kenilworth, and Winfield. The rest of Cranford has grown beyond the fondest dreams of those early real estate promoters who attached their stars and their fortunes to the town's success. This collection of photographs, some only recently discovered and most published for the first time, records some of that change. But this is not a typical pictorial history. It is a Cranford family album, and the selection of photographs has been personal, affectionate, and even sentimental. What we have tried to do is show some of the people, places, and events that have made Cranford what it is today. If a bit of the special look and texture of Cranford's past shines through, or if this book in any way helps to create a sense of place, it will have served its purpose.

Happy Birthday Cranford!

Robert Fridlington and Lawrence Fuhro
August 1995

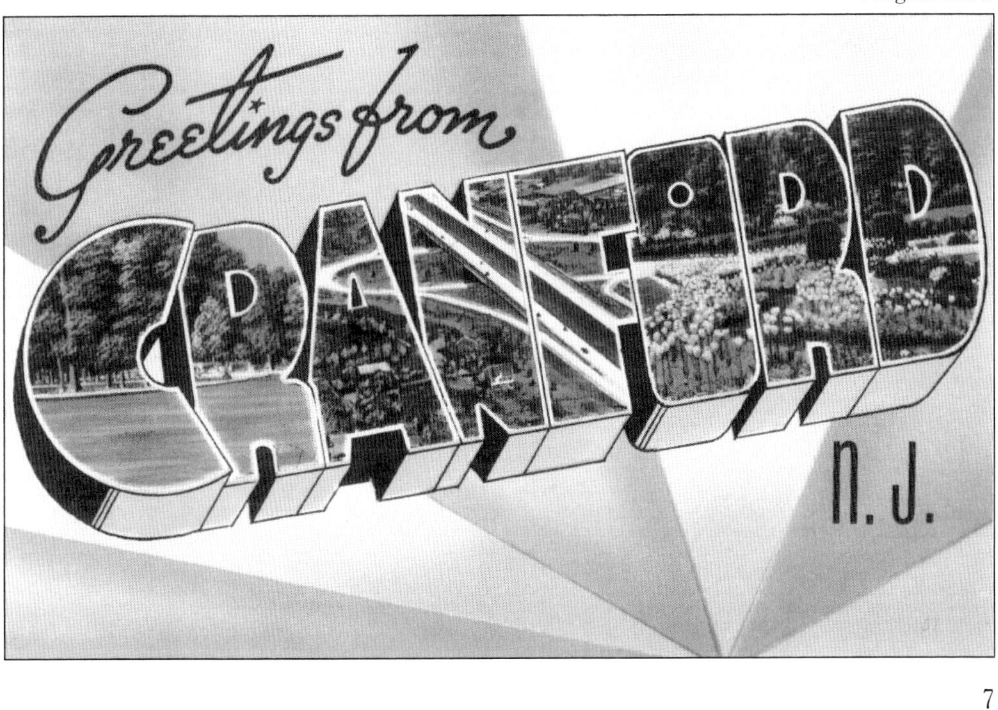

Acknowledgments

Like anyone who puts a book together, we have profited from the kindness and help of many people. Our heaviest debt is to the trustees of the Cranford Historical Society, who made the Society's photograph files available to us. We also are indebted to Pat Pavlak, the Society's Curator, who was a constant source of encouragement. The librarians of the Cranford Public Library, especially Linda Keller, Bonnie Goldstein, Martha Konczal, and Library Director John Malar, offered indispensable assistance, and all exhibited patience beyond measure.

William Harris, Maribeth Lisnock, Frederick Rizkalla, and William Tyree were generous with their time and graciously answered our many questions. Herb Ditzel III, John Dreyer, Tim Shaheen, Addie Vogel, and Police Chief Harry Wilde lent us photographs and provided essential information. Lillian Jones and Bertha Tyree not only unearthed some rare photographs, but they led us through some byways of Cranford's past that too long have been ignored. We owe them a special thanks.

Finally, there are a number of people who are no longer around to receive our thanks. These are the many men and women, now almost all forgotten, who took these wonderful photographs. To all of them, of course, we are deeply grateful.

One

Down by the Old Mill Stream

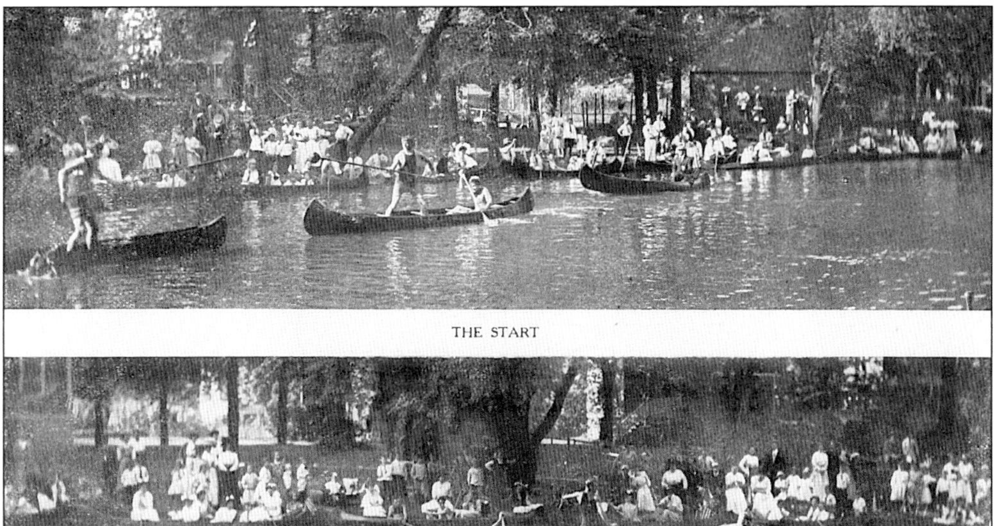

THE START

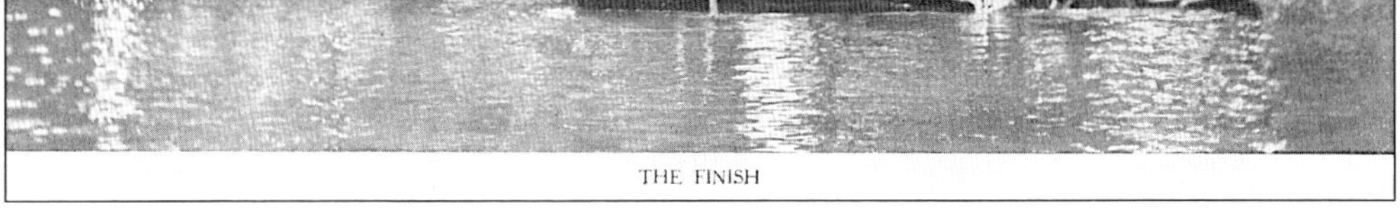

THE FINISH

A CANOE-TILTING MATCH ON THE RAHWAY, 1910. The river always played a central role in Cranford's development. An old Cranford real estate promotion put it this way: "No visitor can help but be enraptured by this pretty, homelike town with its winding, cool river, where, in the midst of peaceful semi-rural life, the tired businessman can play under the canopy of blue skies . . ." It was not only the tired businessman who played. Here, the spectators cheer on their teams in a canoe-tilting contest in 1910. Canoe regattas and river carnivals became synonymous with the way of life along the Rahway in Cranford.

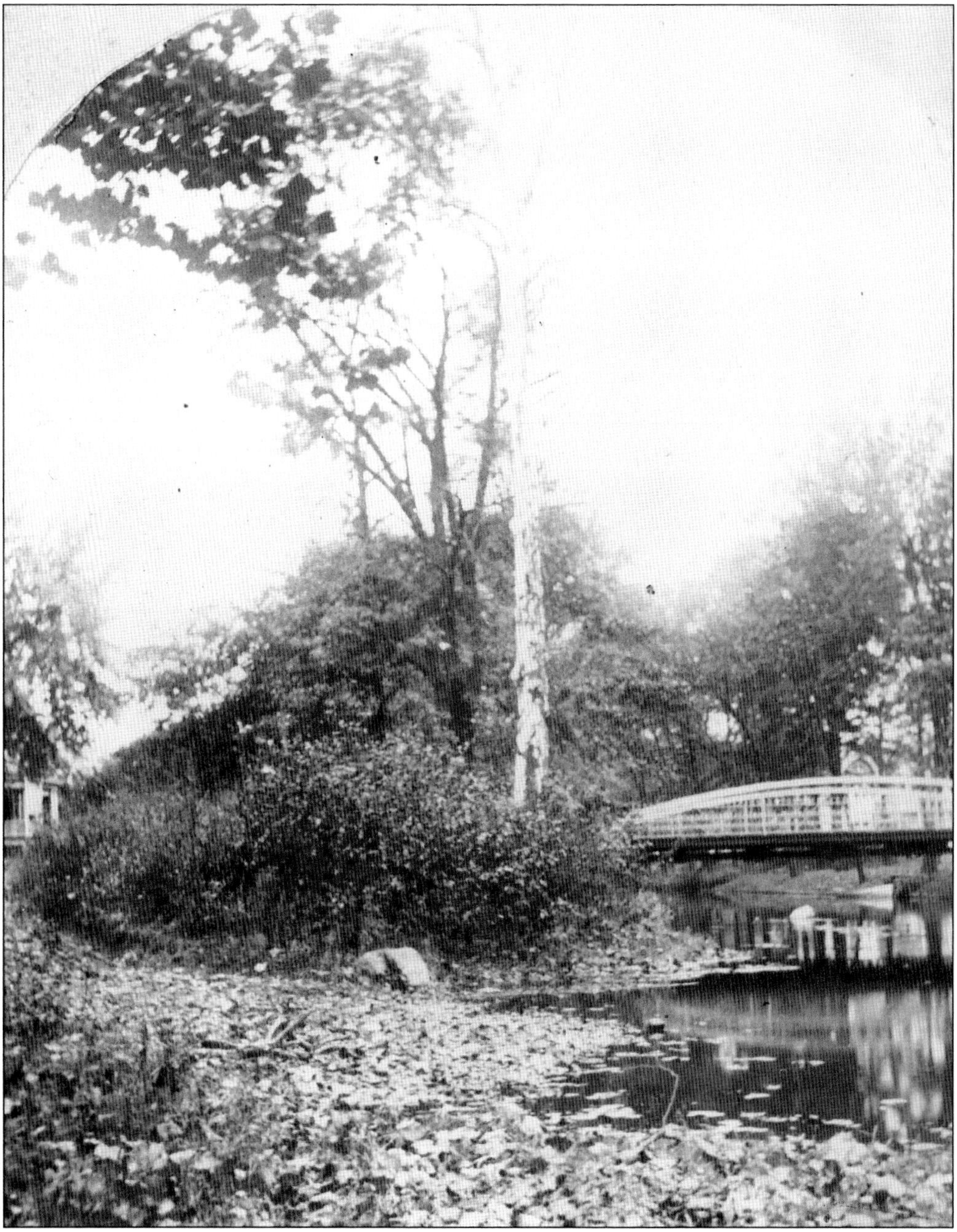

THE PLACE FROM WHICH CRANFORD TAKES ITS NAME, *c.* 1890. This is half of a *c.* 1890 stereo view picturing Crane's Ford at Riverside Drive and Springfield Avenue. Local tradition has it that during the American Revolution soldiers were posted here to warn George Washington's forces at Morristown of a British approach. The boulder seen in this view was later used to mount a plaque to memorialize the ford. Today the riverbank at the site, which is across from Memorial Park, is built up high above the water.

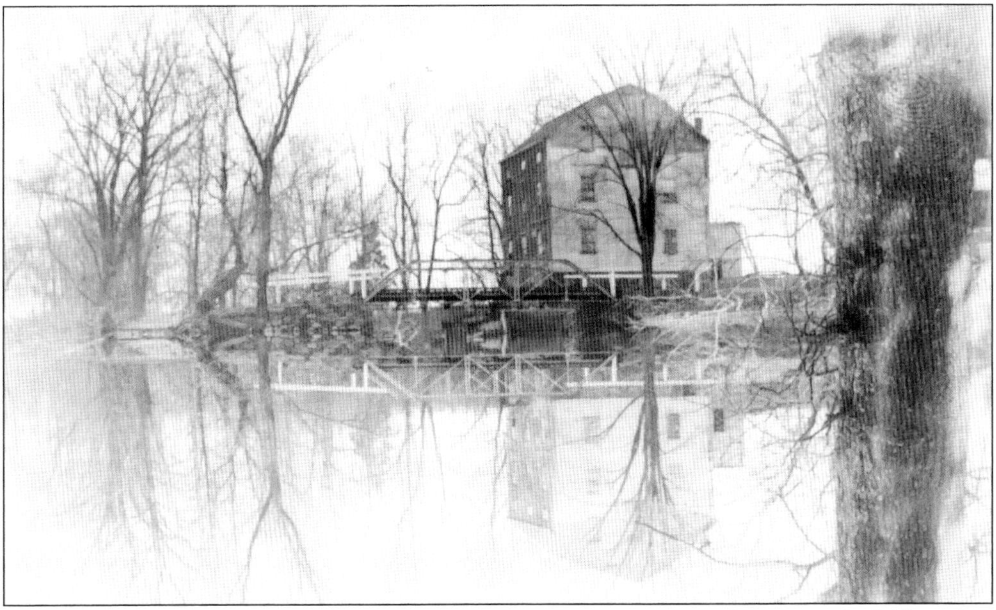

ONE OF VREELAND'S MILLS IN 1890. One of Vreeland's two mills in Cranford (the other is at Lincoln and High), this three-story gristmill once stood on the Rahway River near what is now the junction of Raritan Road, Centennial Avenue, and the Parkway. Built in the early 1700s by the Vreelands, it was known in the late nineteenth century as Clark's Mill. It was one of eleven mills that once existed along the Rahway.

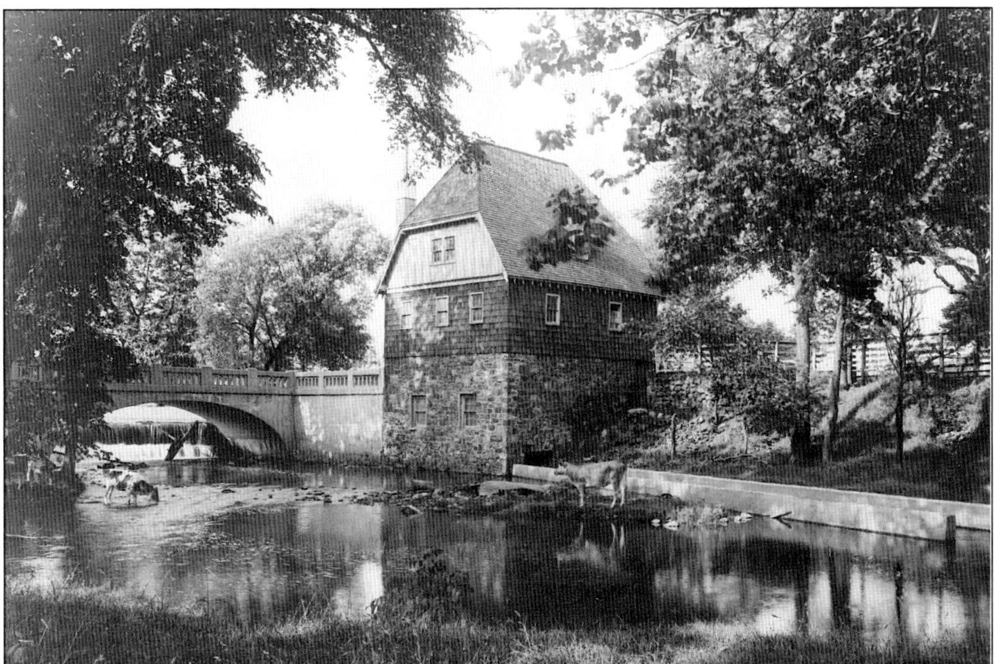

THE SAME MILL, 1913. This is the same building in the above photograph, only twenty-three years later. Thomas Sperry converted and modernized the old mill to serve as the pump house for Osceola Farms, where he bred prize Clydesdale horses and Brown Swiss cattle.

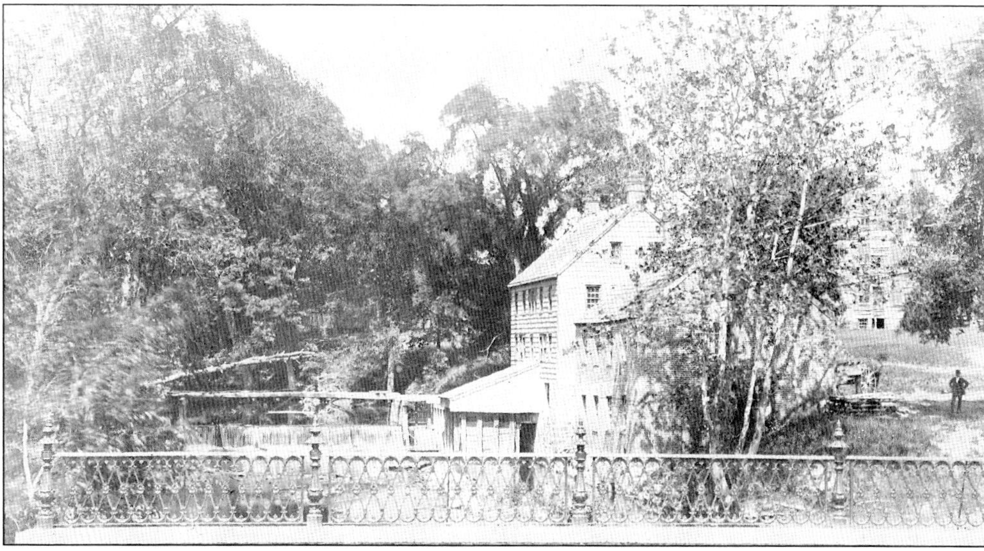

VREELAND'S OTHER MILL, 1890. These twin mill buildings were joined together and greatly altered between 1910 and 1919 by Severin R. Droescher, resulting in the mill seen today. Originally built in the eighteenth century, the mill has been owned or operated by the Williams, Vreeland, Chandler, Lyon, and Droescher families. Note the beautiful iron handrail on the High Street bridge.

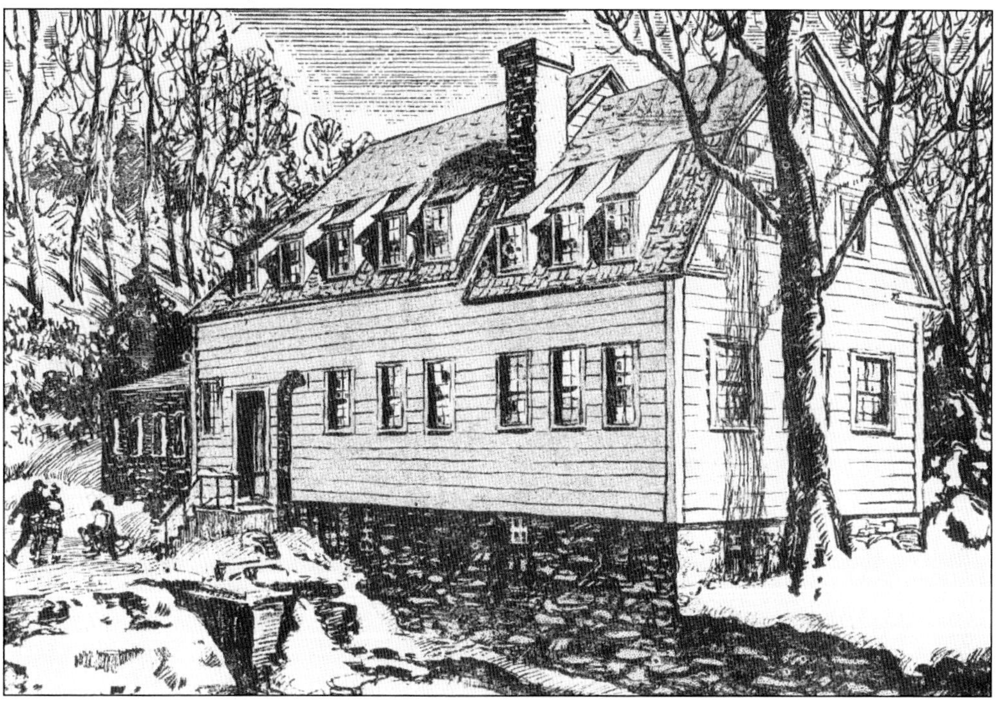

A DRAWING OF DROESCHER'S MILL MADE IN 1945. Cranford artist Leslie Crump, who designed the Cranford Township Seal, made this drawing of the mill and the frozen river. Known today as the Williams-Droescher Mill, it is located at 343 Lincoln Avenue East, and is in the National Register of Historic Places. Business and professional offices now occupy this last remaining mill on the Rahway River.

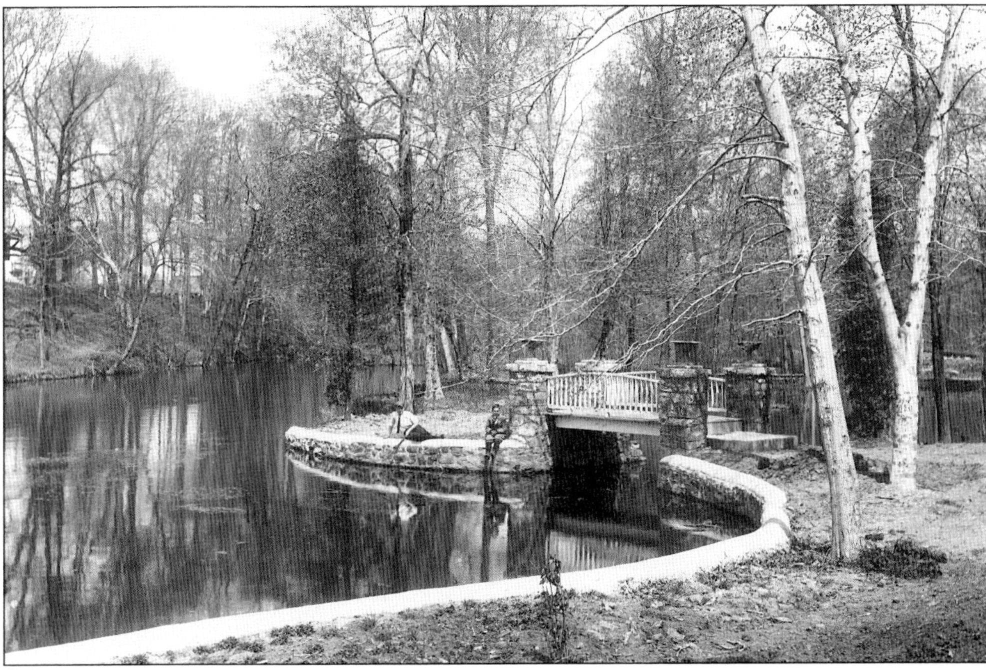

THE LINCOLN PARK BRIDGE, c. 1913. A few years before World War I, German-born Severin R. Droescher began his exclusive Lincoln Park residential development along the Rahway River north of Lincoln Avenue. The anti-German sentiment that accompanied America's entry into World War I destroyed Droescher's plan for the residential park.

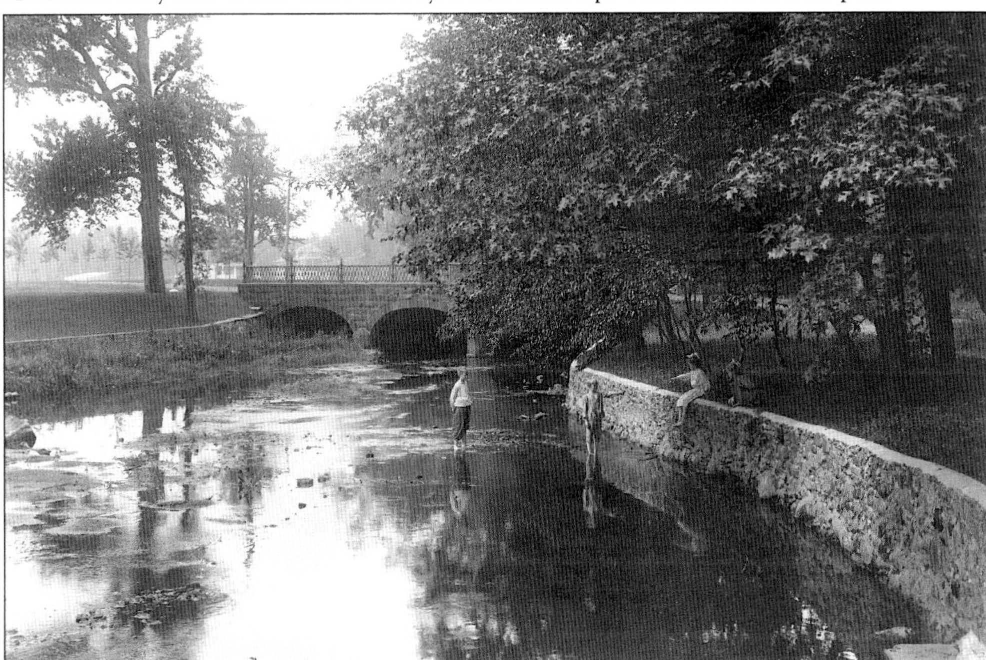

HUNTING CRAWDADS, c. 1900. Kicking off one's shoes and wading in the river is only half the fun. These two boys show the demure young ladies some of the wonderful things that can be found in the river between the High Street bridge and Droescher's Mill.

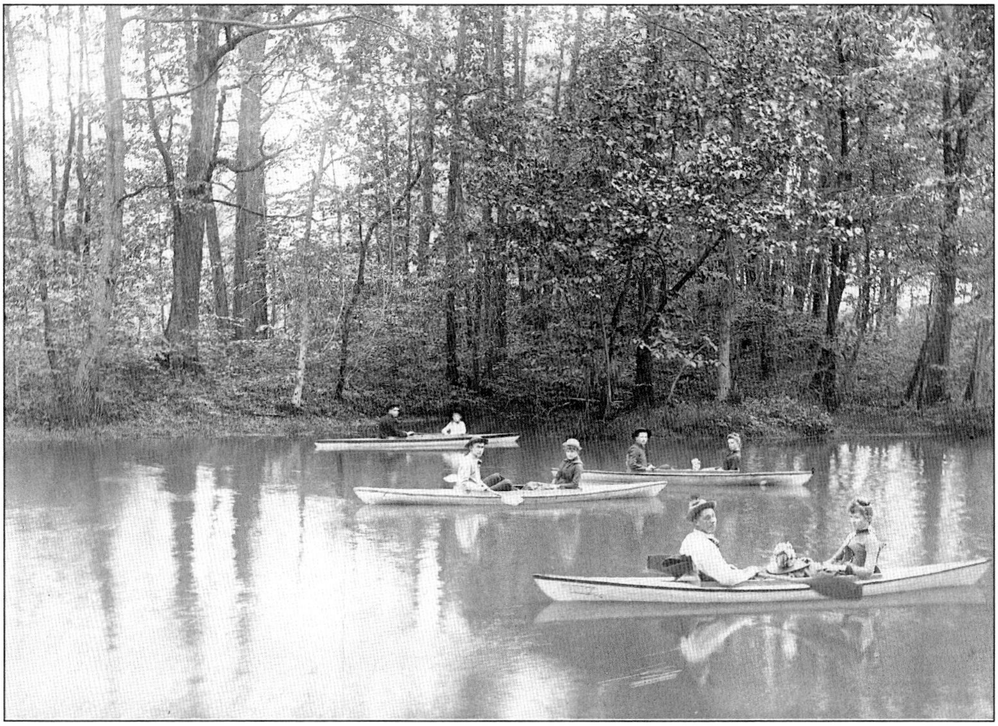

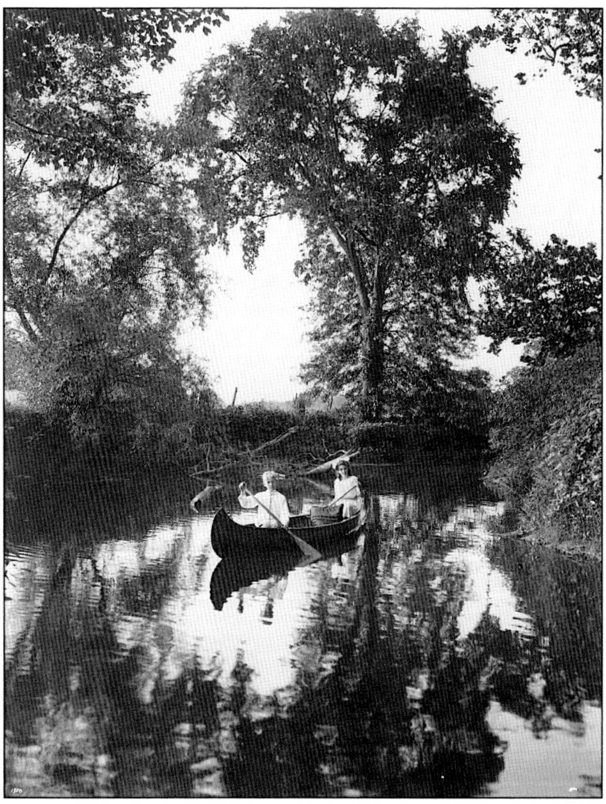

DOUBLES ON THE RAHWAY, c. 1885. As one can see in this picture, canoes were not the only recreational craft on the river in nineteenth-century Cranford. A New York City newspaper, *The Advocate*, said on September 16, 1886, that "Cranfordians are worshippers of a water nymph."

A LAZY DAY ON THE RIVER, c. 1900. According to the 1886 prospectus of the Cranford River Improvement Association: "Water is to the landscape what music is to the soul; and we have a river which, with its meandering course and wooded banks, challenges human skill to rival."

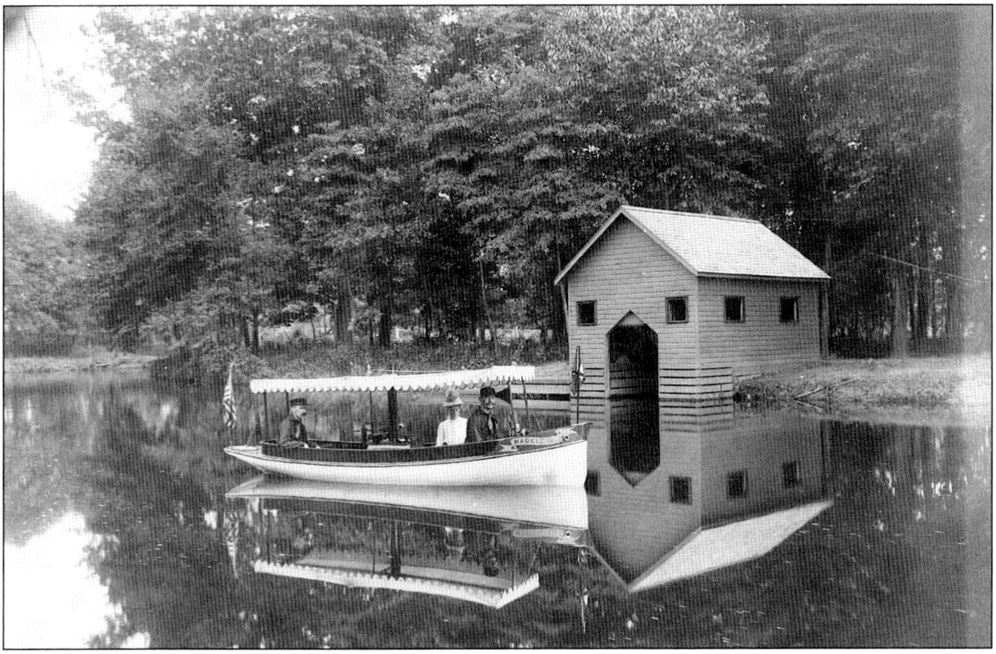

STEAMING DOWN THE RAHWAY, 1889. The best-known boat plying Cranford waters was the steam launch *Madeleine*, owned by Emmor K. Adams Jr. Here we see Adams at the helm taking Lucy Madeleine Miller and Winfield Scott Stevenson for an afternoon cruise on the Rahway. Adams and Miss Miller were married in 1896.

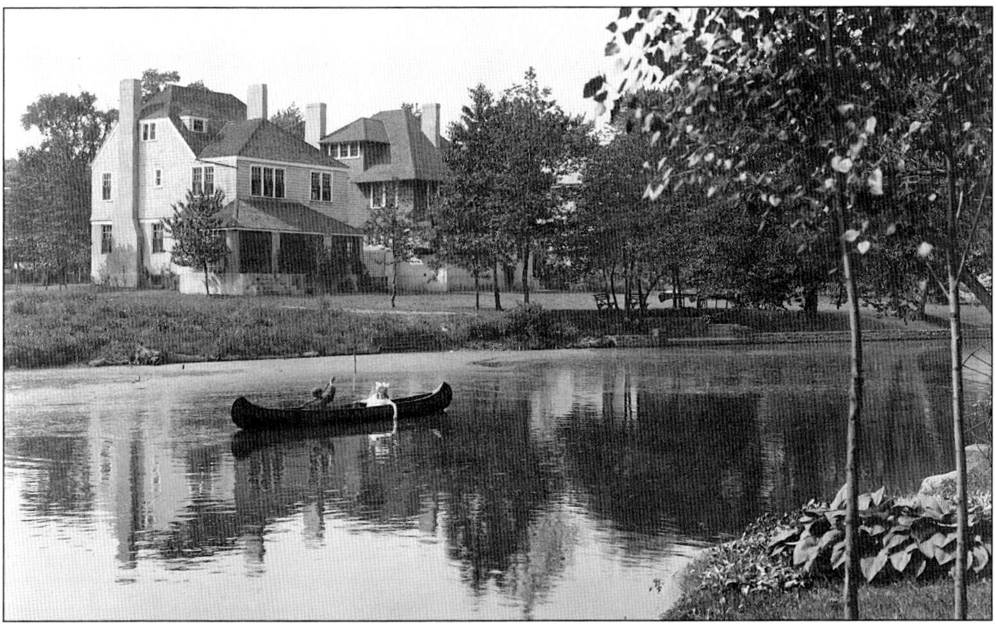

A DATE WITH HIS BEST GIRL? The paddler in this *c.* 1910 photograph can hardly see over the sides of his canoe. Decked out in a white dress and hair ribbon, his best girl (sister?) trails her hand in the mirror-like waters. This all took place on the Rahway, between Eastman Street and Springfield Avenue, looking west toward Central Avenue. Notice how remarkably modern the homes in the background appear.

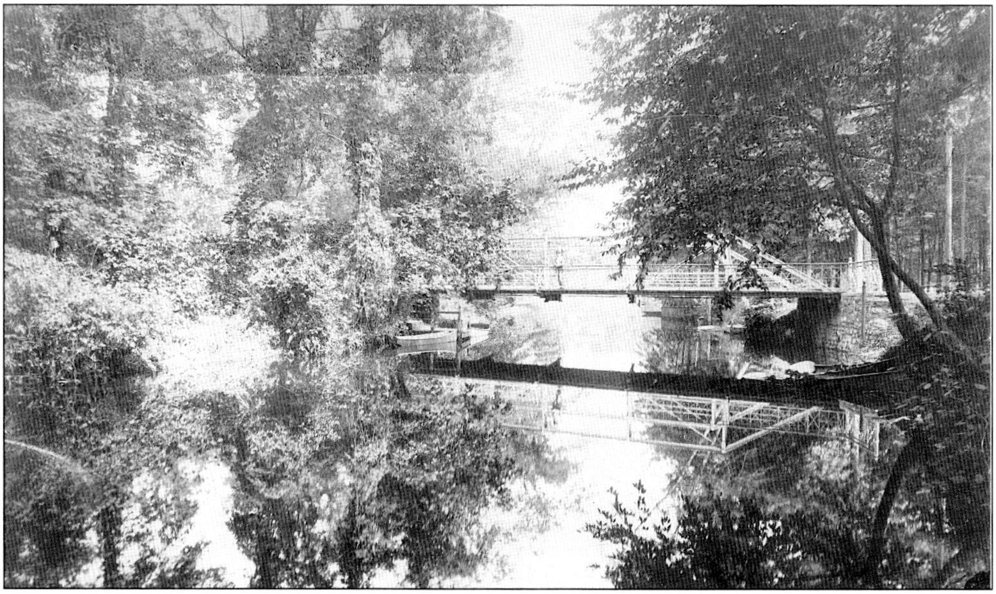

THE NORTH UNION AVENUE BRIDGE, 1894. It is hard to tell which is up and which is down in this reflective picture. The old, decorative, white-painted iron bridge was replaced in the early twentieth century. Great mature trees and verdant growth characterized the river in the late nineteenth century. The Rahway was an angler's paradise, attracting fishermen from miles around.

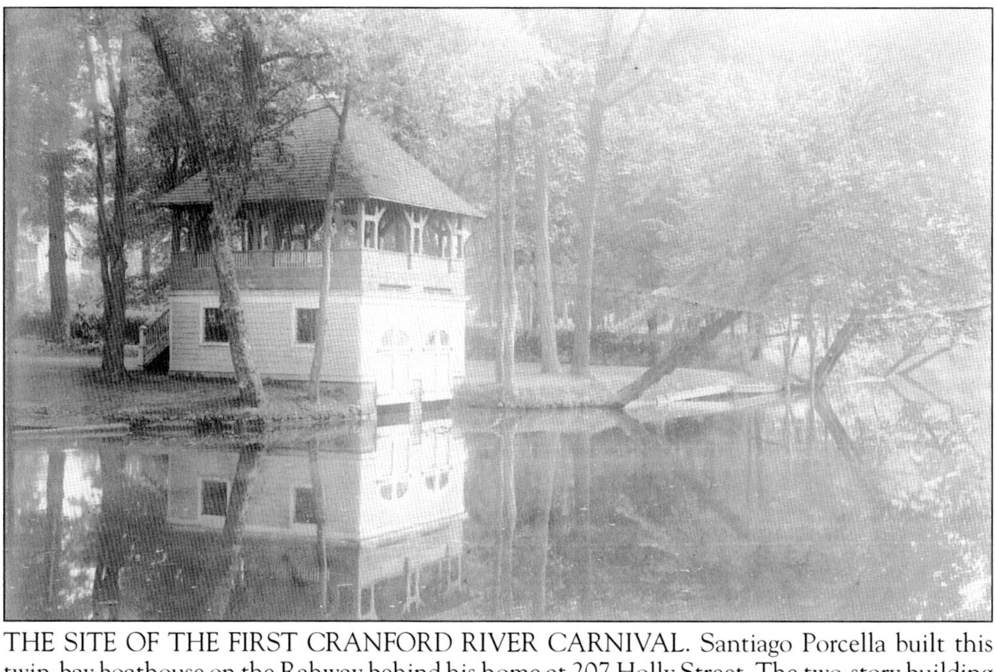

THE SITE OF THE FIRST CRANFORD RIVER CARNIVAL. Santiago Porcella built this twin-bay boathouse on the Rahway behind his home at 207 Holly Street. The two-story building had an open pavilion on the second floor. One summer evening in 1886, Mr. Porcella launched canoes lighted with Japanese lanterns from this spot. The scene so impressed neighbors that the event was enlarged and held every year. The boathouse, seen in this 1887 photograph, served as the reviewing stand.

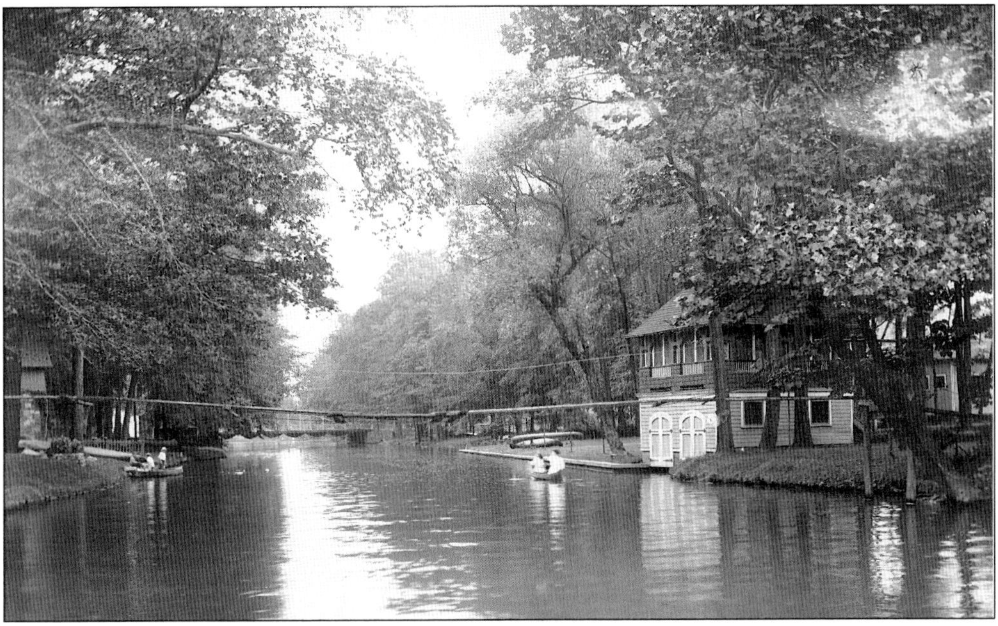

MOORE'S SUSPENSION BRIDGE, 1895. The thin line through the center of this picture is a footbridge suspended from steel cables. Originally built for Dr. J.K. MacConnell by John A. Roebling & Sons (builders of the Brooklyn Bridge), the bridge was removed the year this picture was taken. The Porcella boathouse, seen on the right, had its second floor enclosed by this time (see p. 16).

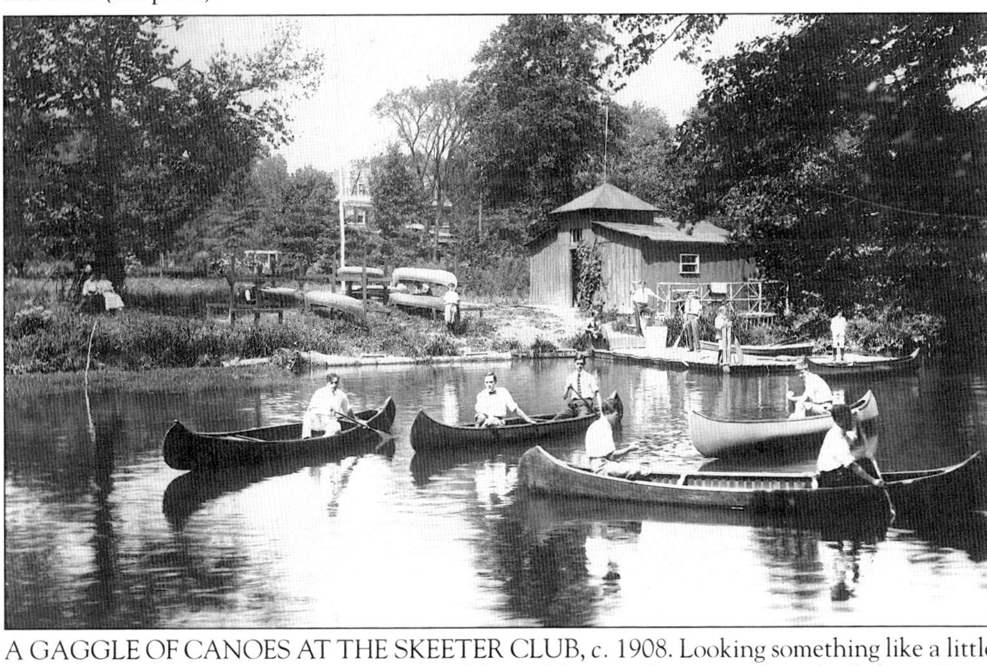

A GAGGLE OF CANOES AT THE SKEETER CLUB, *c.* 1908. Looking something like a little frontier fort, this was one of several canoe clubs and liveries that existed on the Rahway River in Cranford over the years. The Skeeter Club was located behind Central Avenue, southwest of Springfield Avenue. The first two canoeists from the left have been identified as Juan Bargos and William Drysdale.

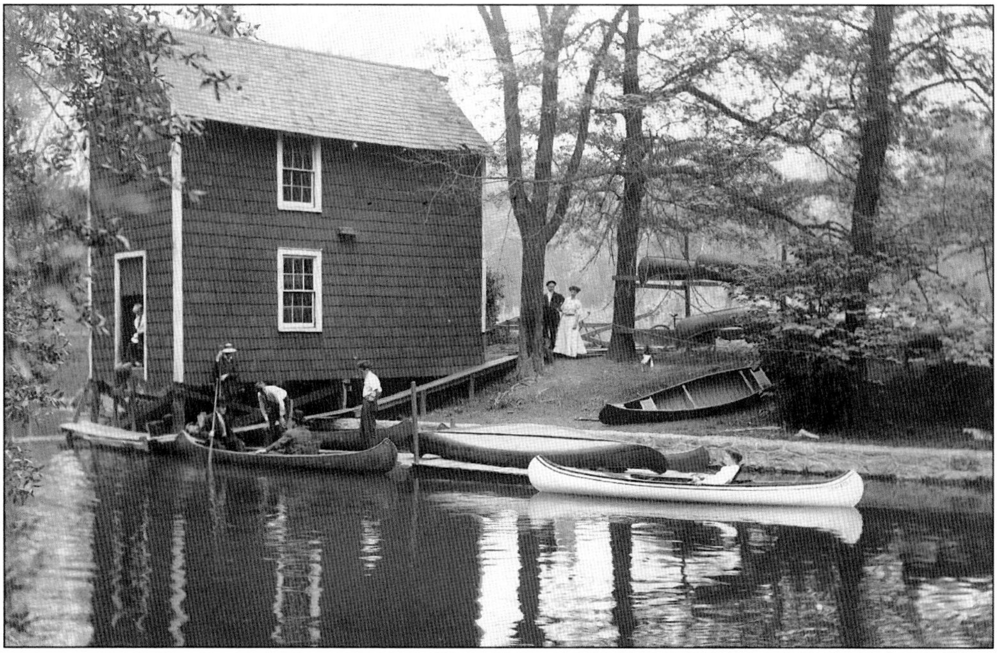

"LOBSTER SHANTY," RIVERSIDE DRIVE, 1890. Al Clark's "Lobster Shanty" canoe livery stood on the west bank of the Rahway, upstream from Crane's Ford, near what is now the intersection of Riverside Drive and Normandie Place.

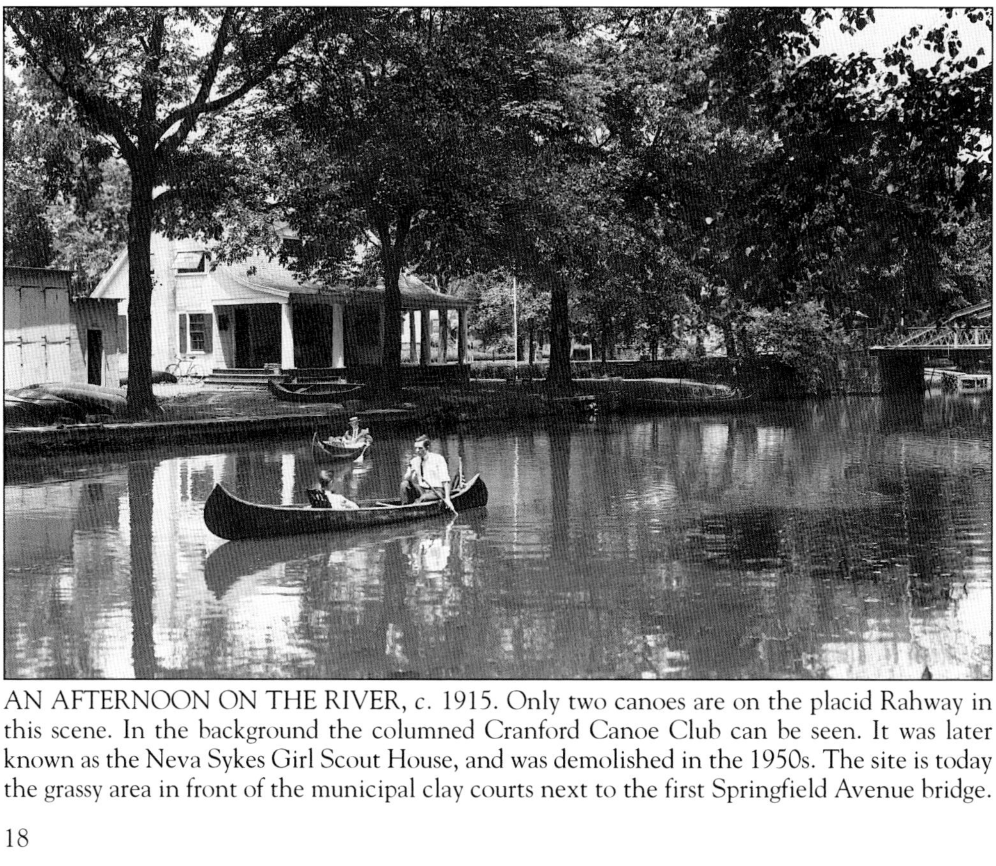

AN AFTERNOON ON THE RIVER, *c.* 1915. Only two canoes are on the placid Rahway in this scene. In the background the columned Cranford Canoe Club can be seen. It was later known as the Neva Sykes Girl Scout House, and was demolished in the 1950s. The site is today the grassy area in front of the municipal clay courts next to the first Springfield Avenue bridge.

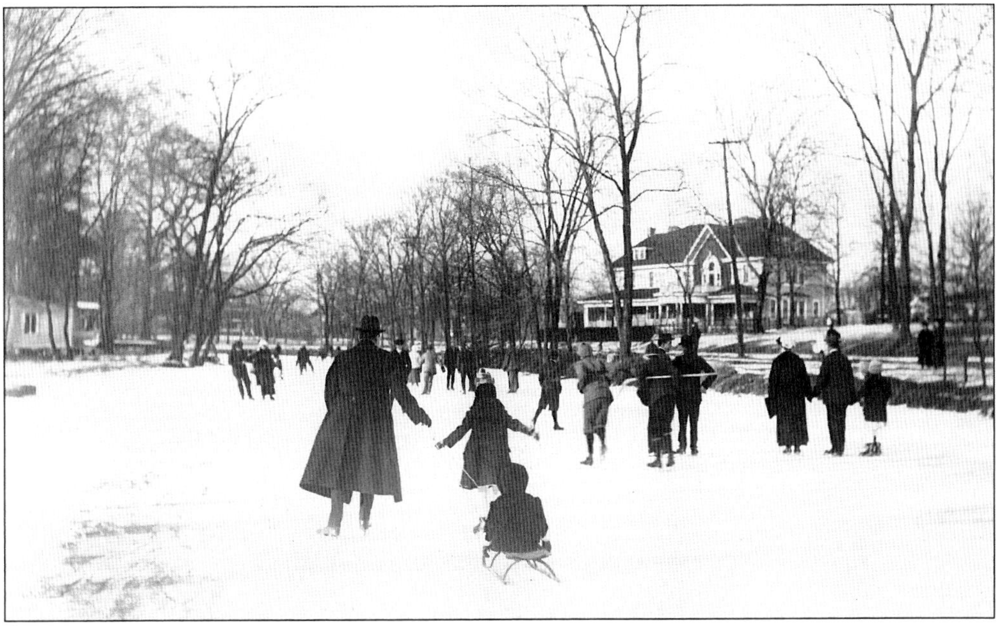

THE RIVER IN WINTER, *c*. 1900. The Rahway River provided recreation in winter as well as summer. On a Sunday afternoon, in front of the landmark Cranford Casino, entire families skated along the Rahway's frozen surface. But why was everyone skating away from the camera?

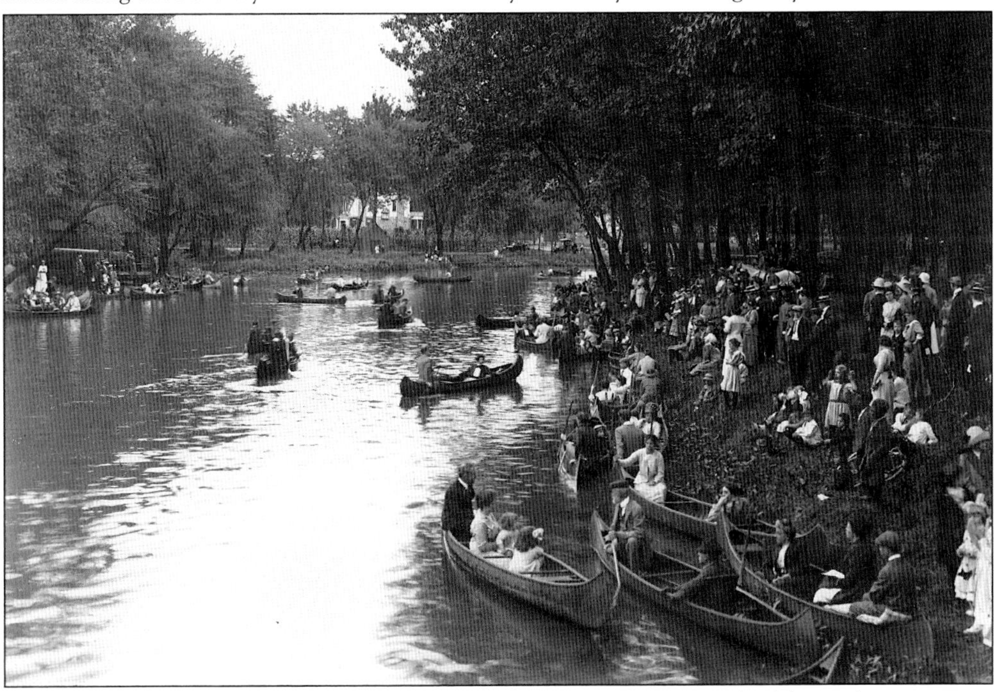

THE CARNIVAL IS ABOUT TO BEGIN, *c*. 1910. Since 1886 it had been the custom to hold an annual River Carnival on the Rahway River, with scores of imaginatively designed and beautifully decorated canoe-floats gliding through the water, their paths lighted by thousands of Japanese lanterns. Spectators crowded the banks and the water waiting for dark, when the "fairyland parade" would begin.

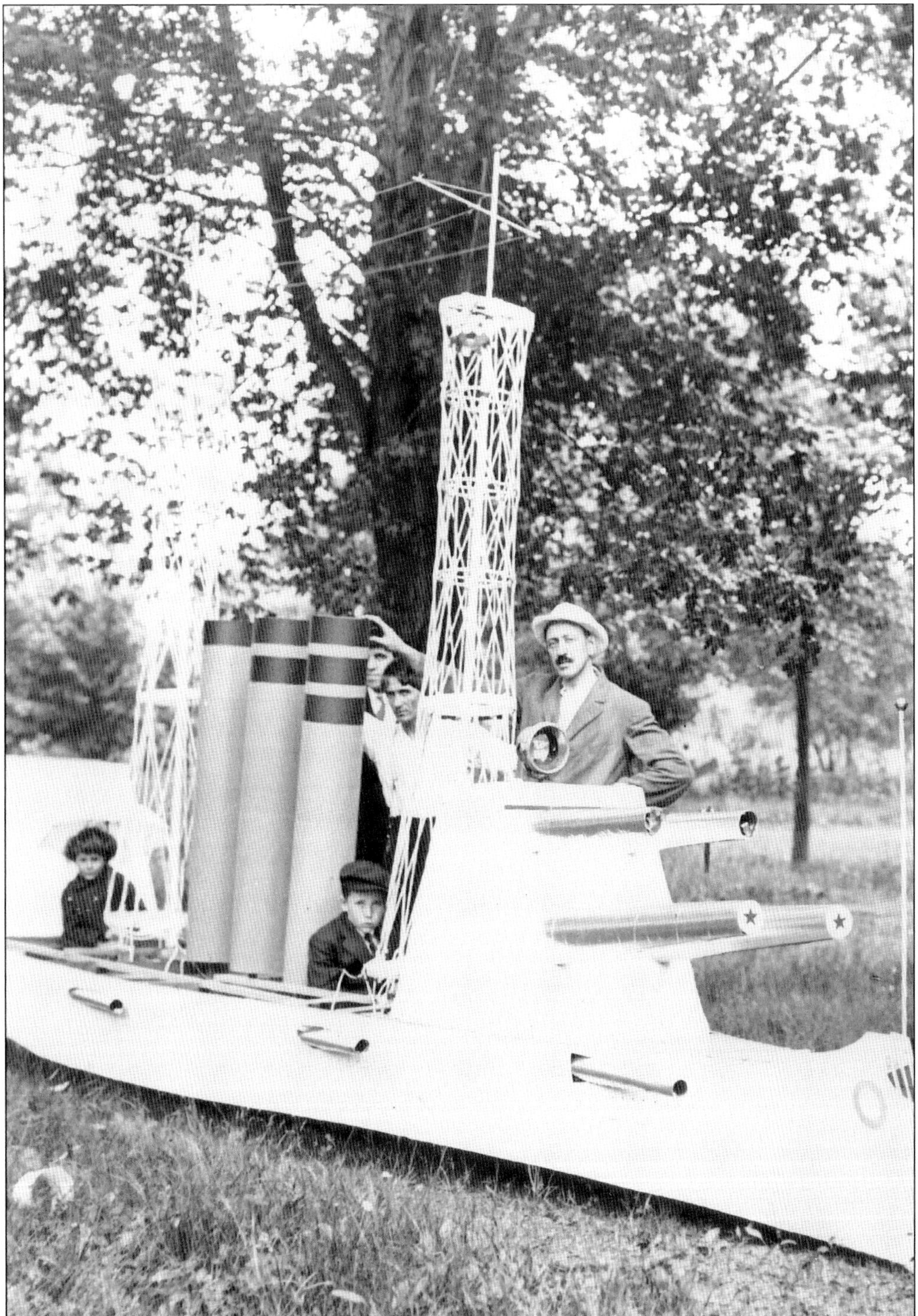

A GUNBOAT COMES TO CRANFORD. Albert B. Lewis (in hat) poses with his prize-winning "Gun Boat" that was entered in the 1914 River Carnival. The float was such a crowd pleaser that the Cranford Canoe Club exhibited the craft at a carnival in Asbury Park.

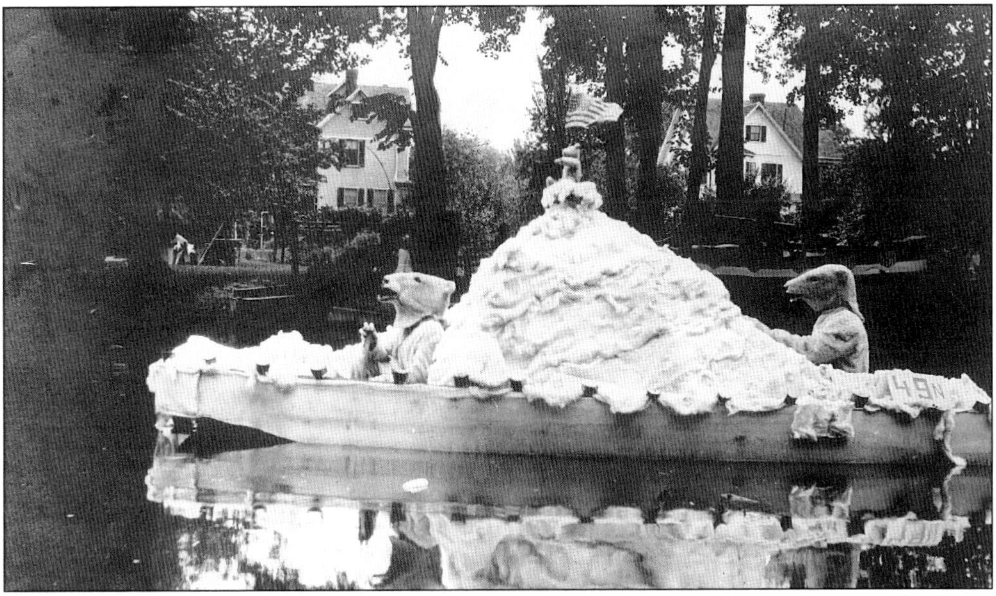

HONORING AN EXPLORER. A topical entry in the 1911 Carnival was two polar bears applauding Admiral Robert Peary's discovery of the North Pole. A tiny bear can be seen with an American flag at the top of the world. This was the year that the U.S. Congress officially recognized Peary's achievement.

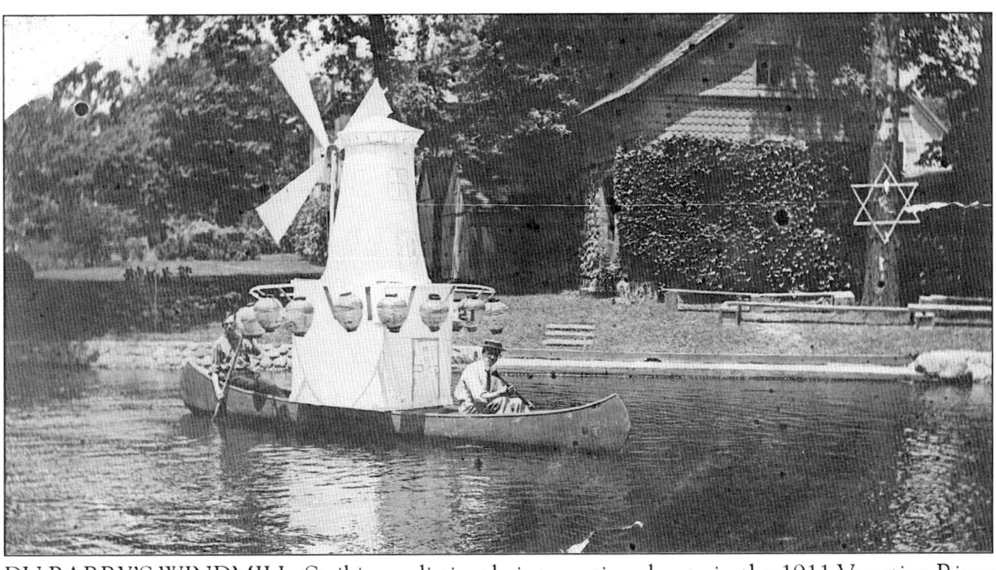

DU BARRY'S WINDMILL. Striking a distinctly international note in the 1911 Venetian River Carnival, Jules Du Barry navigated a Dutch windmill gaily decorated with Japanese lanterns.

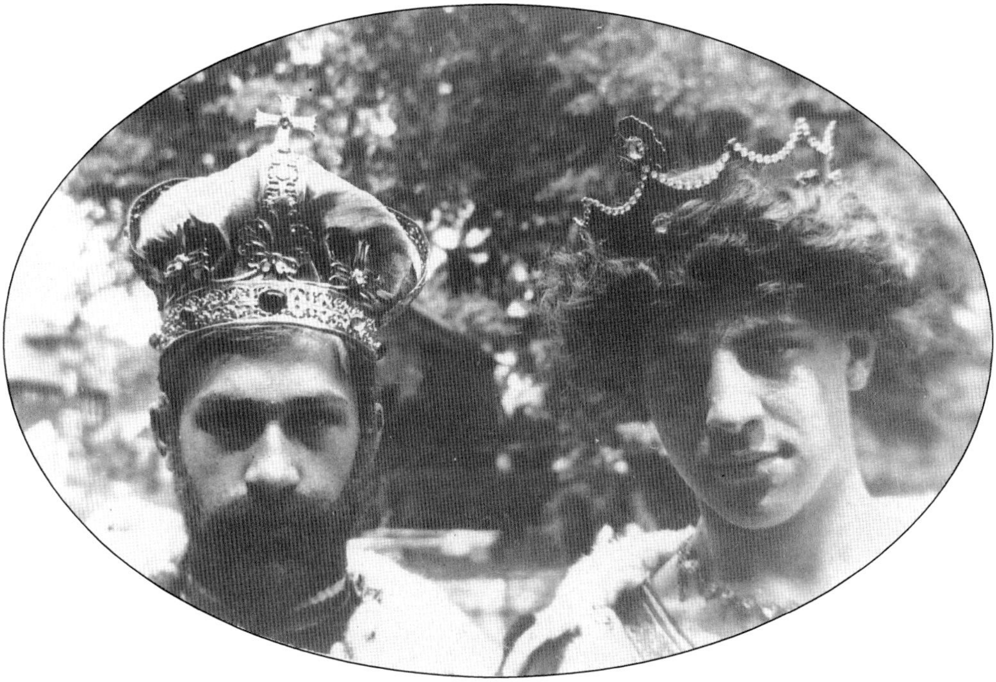

A KING AND HIS QUEEN. Another topical entry in the 1911 River Carnival was a representation of the recent coronation of England's George V, with the King and Queen riding a royal barge decorated with a huge crown and a Union Jack. The bearded George V looks genuine; Queen Mary is definitely suspect.

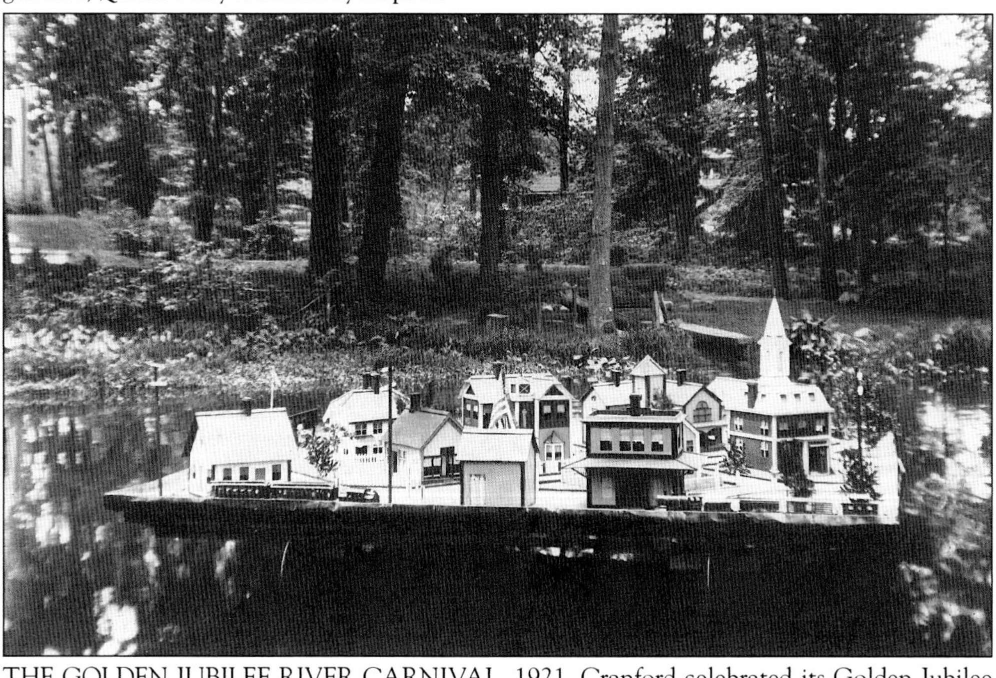

THE GOLDEN JUBILEE RIVER CARNIVAL, 1921. Cranford celebrated its Golden Jubilee (1871–1921) with a spectacular River Carnival that drew 20,000 spectators. A model of the town entitled "Cranford in 1871," entered by the Firemen's Club of Cranford, took first prize.

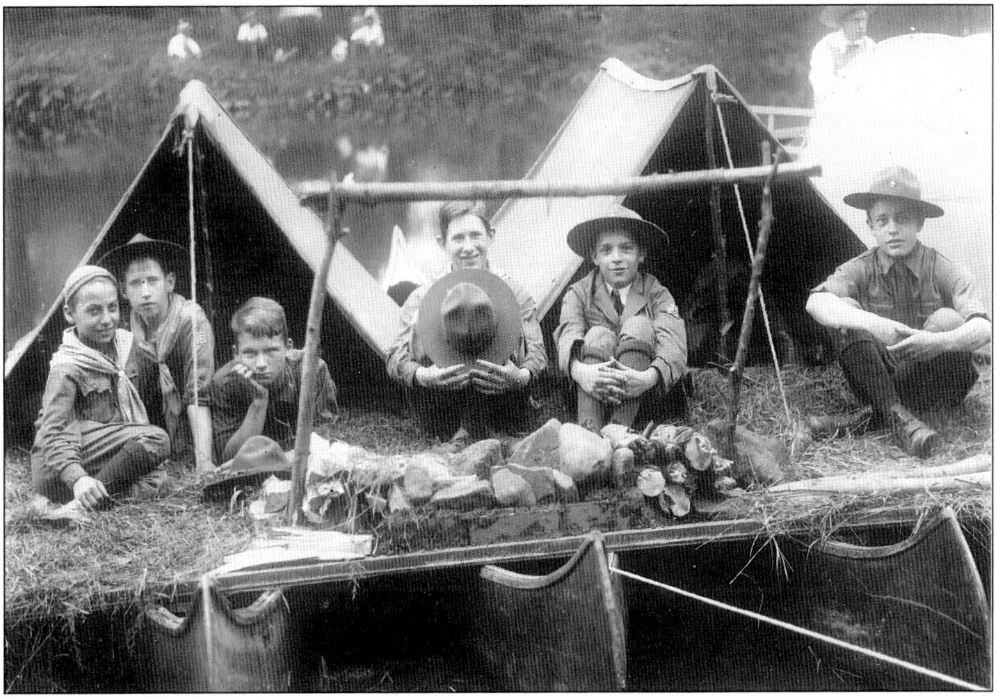

CAMPING ON THE RIVER, 1921. With tents pitched, six Boy Scouts from Troops 3 and 4 lounge in front of the fire. This "Camp Life" float, an entry in the Golden Jubilee River Carnival, sat atop three canoes.

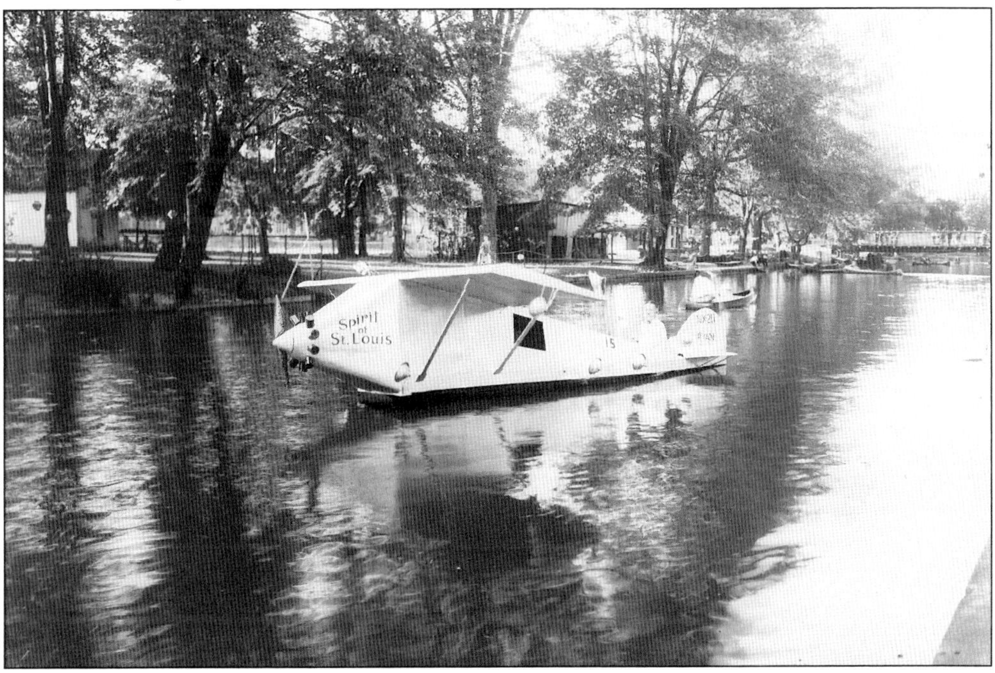

THE SPIRIT OF ST. LOUIS. Less than seven weeks after Charles Lindbergh's solo flight across the Atlantic, Harry R. Heins "flew" his replica Spirit of St. Louis in the 1927 River Carnival. His trip was not solo, however: an unseen Buster Weir operated the propeller.

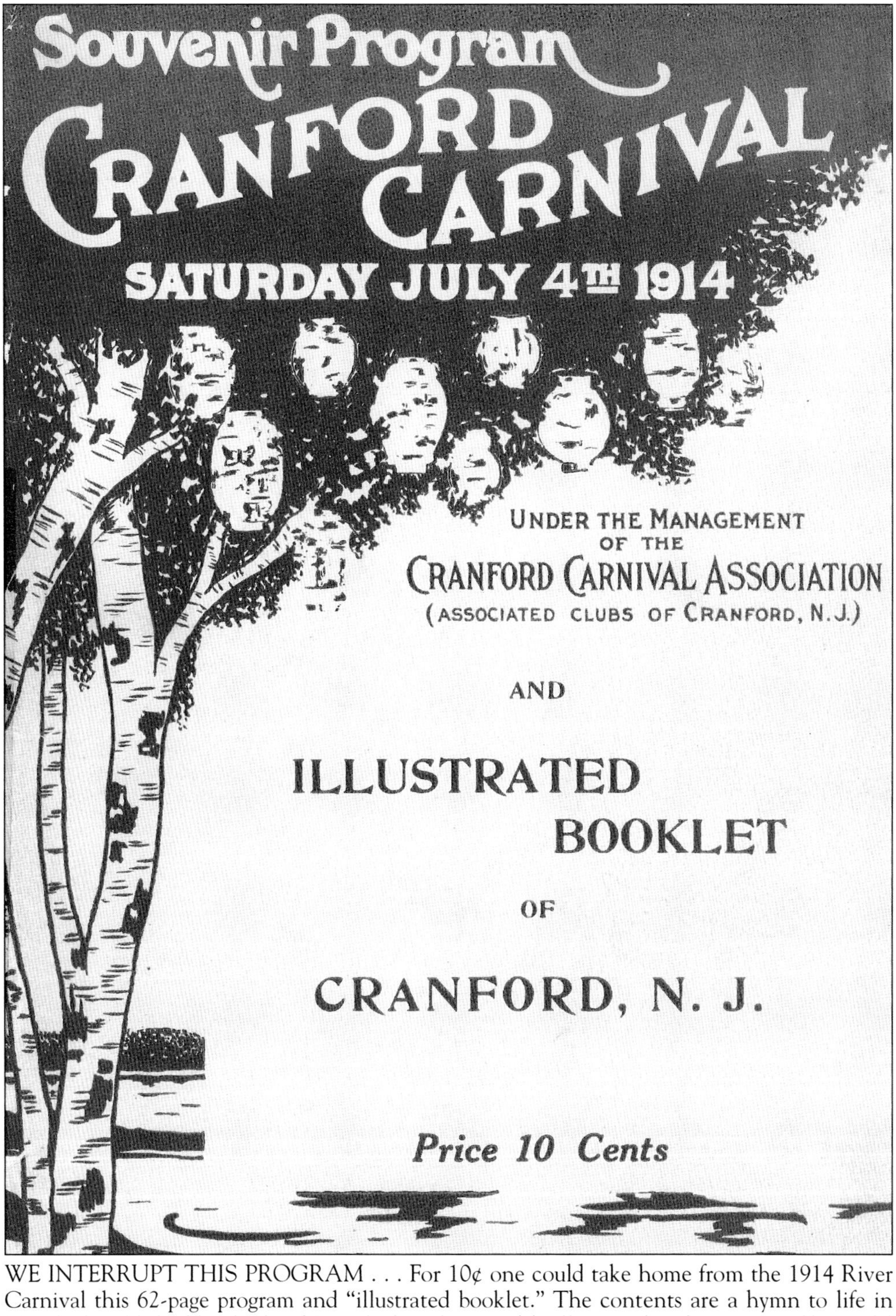

WE INTERRUPT THIS PROGRAM . . . For 10¢ one could take home from the 1914 River Carnival this 62-page program and "illustrated booklet." The contents are a hymn to life in Cranford, published by the local Board of Trade. Lavishly illustrated with pictures of beautiful homes, businesses, schools, churches, river scenes, and even Carnival floats, it not surprisingly contains advertisements for realtors and developers.

Two

Faces from the Past

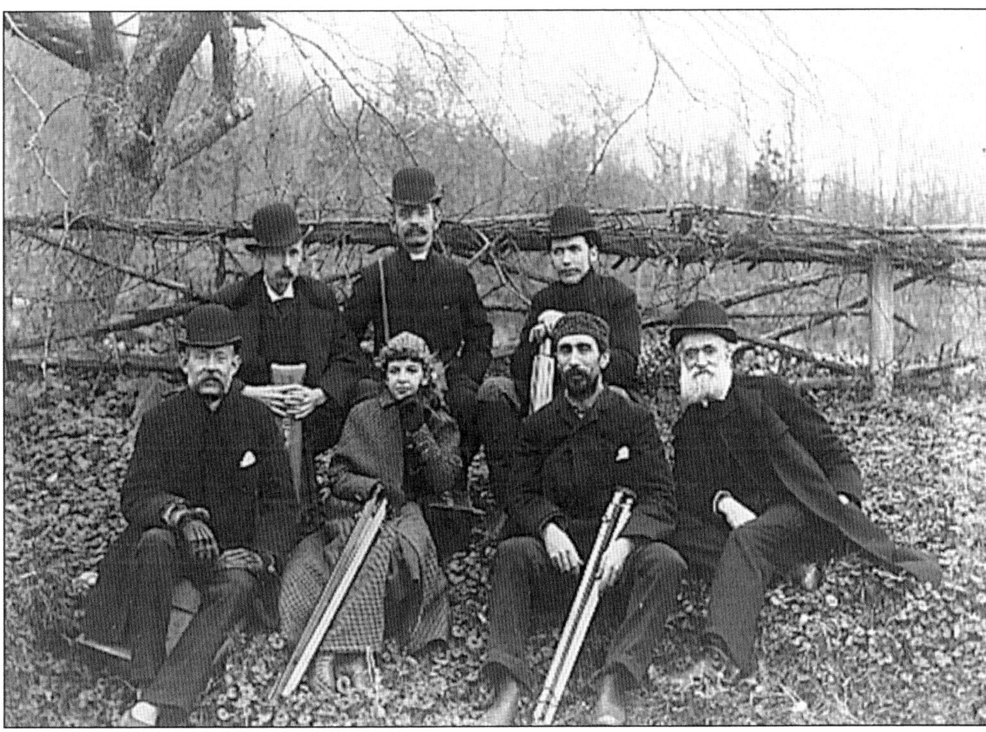

THE CRANFORD CAMERA CLUB, 1895. These tripod-toting members of the Camera Club seemed to enjoy posing for pictures as much as taking them. On a chilly day they strike a relaxed pose by a rustic fence on the outskirts of Cranford. One can only speculate as to whether any of their photographs are represented in this volume.

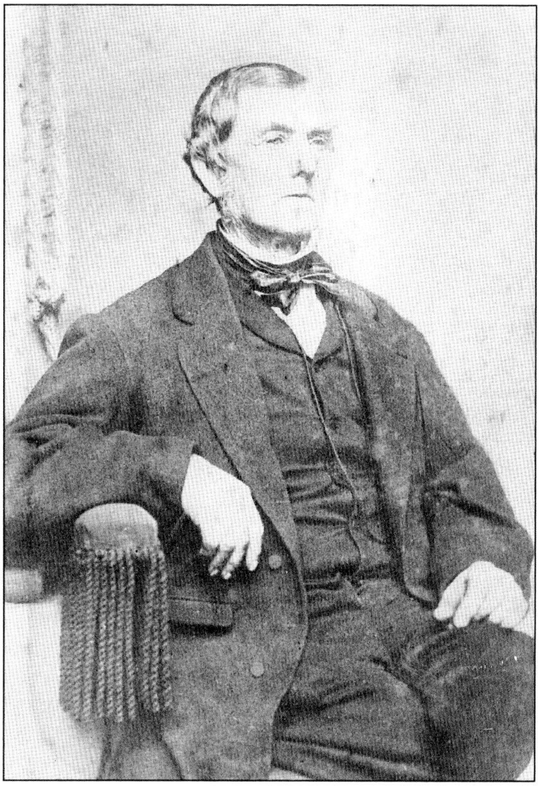

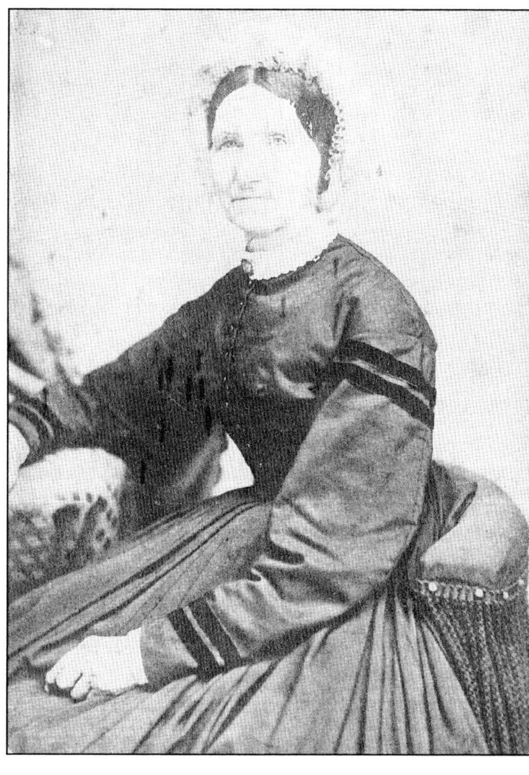

JOSIAH (1791–1873) AND ELECTA ROSS CRANE (d. 1879). Mr. and Mrs. Josiah Crane can properly be called the First Citizens of Cranford. Josiah, the "Father of Cranford," was born on his family's farm at Crane's Mills. In 1812 he married Electa Ross. The village that grew up near the Crane farm was called Craneville, and after Josiah sold most of his farm for real estate development, the village became Cranford. Active in the affairs of the community throughout his life, Crane was also a founder of and liberal contributor to the Presbyterian church in Cranford.

SYLVESTER M. CAHILL SR. (1805–1895). Cahill was a member of the committee appointed to secure passage of the act creating the Township of Cranford. The act was passed by the New Jersey Legislature on March 16, 1871, and at the first meeting of the Township Committee, on April 15, 1871, Cahill was elected "President," becoming Cranford's first mayor, in fact if not in name. A man of considerable wealth, Cahill was one of the largest property owners in nineteenth-century Cranford.

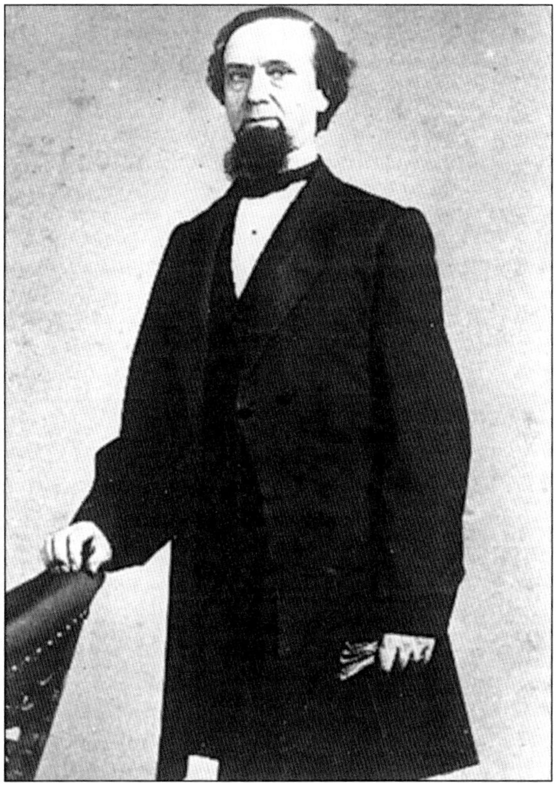

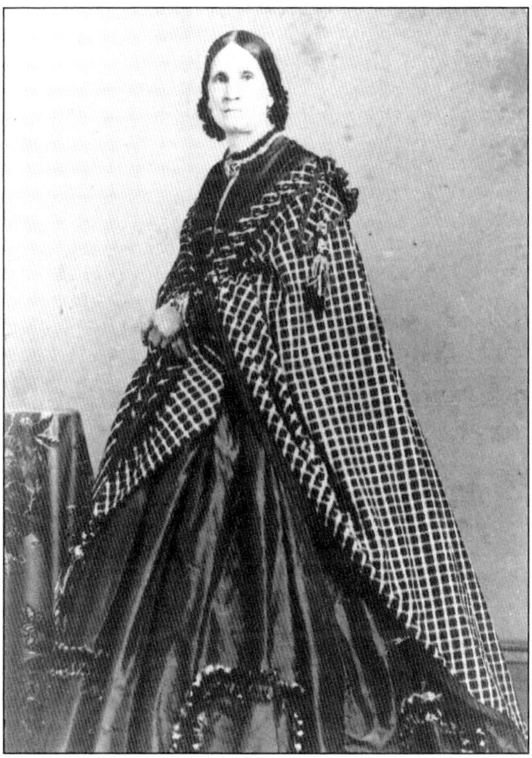

MARY BIGELOW CAHILL (d. 1881). Mary Cahill, the wife of Sylvester Cahill Sr., was the sister of Alden and William Bigelow, both prominent figures in Cranford's early history. She served for a time as matron of the Union County Jail in Elizabeth. This photograph was almost certainly taken in the 1860s. The dark silk taffeta dress with a floor-length mantle was typical of women's fashion in the years immediately after the Civil War.

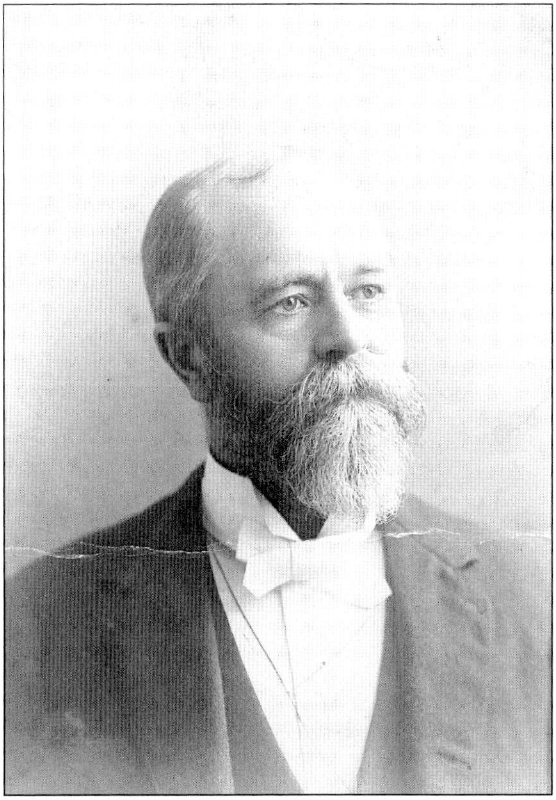

DR. JOSEPH KERR MacCONNELL (1836–1917). Dr. MacConnell moved to Cranford in 1869, where he practiced medicine for more than forty years. Although he was the town's first physician and was active in many community and civic affairs, MacConnell is perhaps best remembered for building his own suspension bridge on Eastman Street. He was succeeded in his medical practice by his son, Dr. C.W. MacConnell.

MRS. FANNIE E. BATES (1842–1918). A businesswoman and civic activist, Fannie Bates was known as "the Mother of Cranford." In 1892, after her husband's death, Mrs. Bates built Hampton Hall, Cranford's first fashionable residence hotel. Later, she also owned and operated the Riverside. In 1896 she founded and was elected the first president of the Cranford Village Improvement Association.

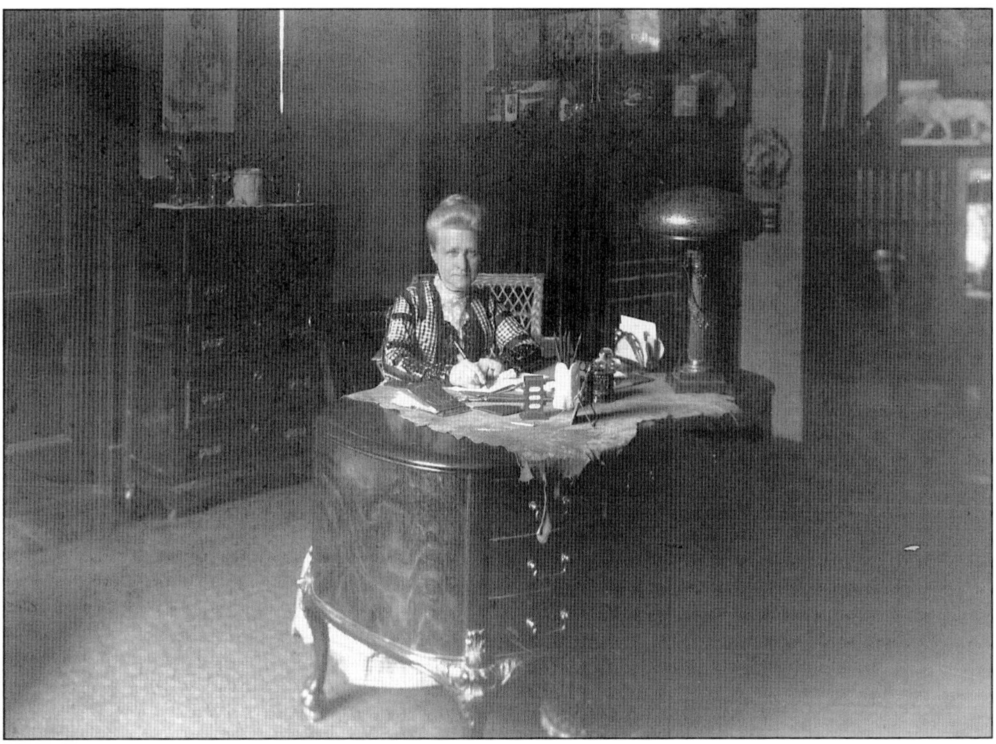

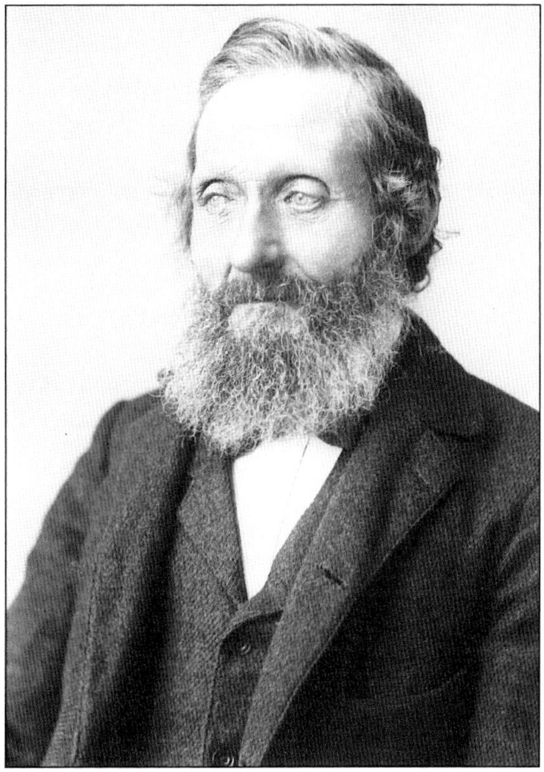

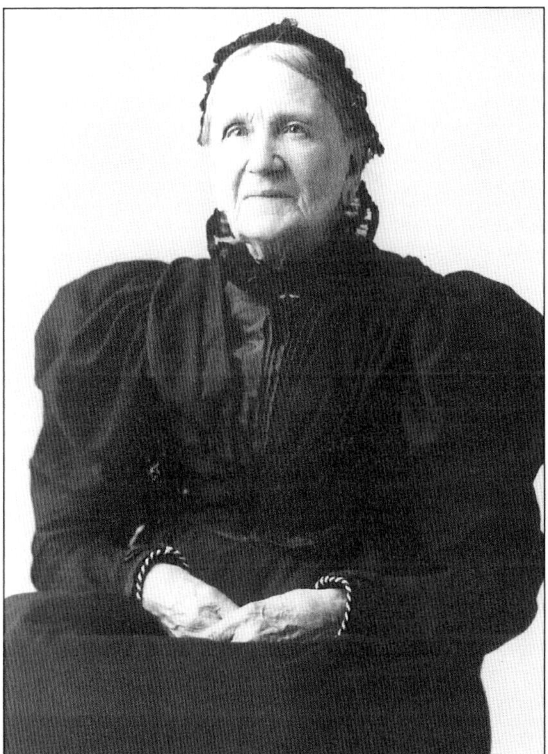

DAVID (1815–1904) AND JANE RANKIN (1816–1899). David Rankin was a native of Scotland. He and his wife arrived in Cranford in 1839 and established themselves on a large farm in what is now the southwestern part of the township bordering Garwood (the farm acreage was bisected by Burnside Avenue; Rankin Avenue marks its western boundary). The Rankins arrived just a short time after the railroad passed through Cranford, and this connection with the outside world signalled dramatic changes ahead. As the years passed, the hard-working farm couple were transformed into large-scale property owners in a rapidly growing community. The change in fortune had little effect on the Rankins, however. The farm remained a farm until after their deaths.

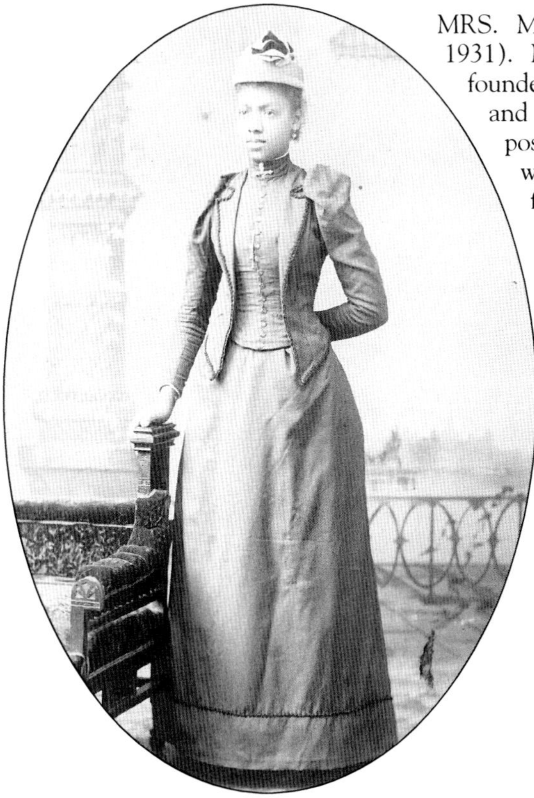

MRS. MARTHA EASON GOODMAN (1870–1931). Mrs. Martha Goodman was one of the founders of St. Mark's AME Church in Cranford and served the church as a deaconess. She posed for this portrait photograph about 1890, wearing a two-piece dress and jacket of silk faille, the latest in women's fashion.

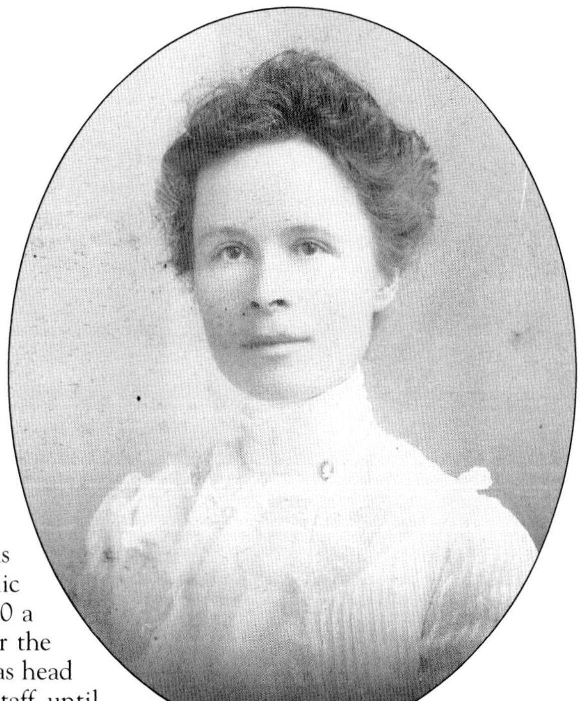

MAY D. BRADLEY. May Bradley was appointed librarian of the new public library in June 1910, at a salary of $350 a year. She continued in this position for the next thirty years. After stepping down as head of the library, she remained on the staff until 1947. Miss Bradley died in 1960.

THOMAS A. SPERRY (1864–1913). One of the founders of Sperry and Hutchinson, the S & H Green Stamp Company, Thomas Sperry was a prominent figure in Cranford banking activities and one of the largest property owners in the township. His handsome home stood at Prospect Street and Claremont Place, now the site of English Village. He also owned the 312-acre Osceola Farms on the banks of the Rahway in South Cranford. Osceola Farms became Winfield Park.

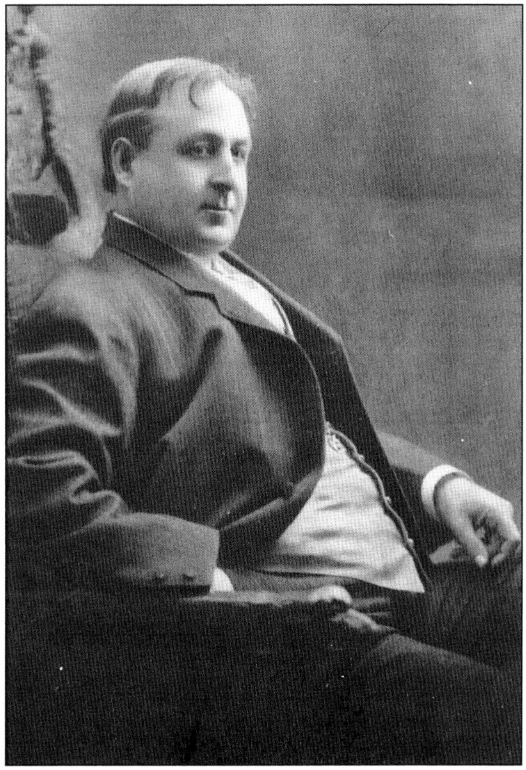

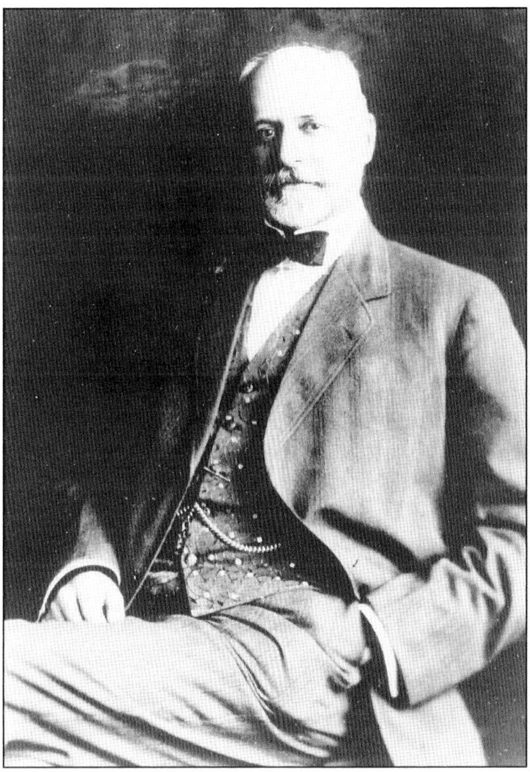

WILLIAM MILLER SPERRY (1858–1927). A businessman, banker, and civic leader, William M. Sperry was associated with his brother in the S & H Green Stamp Company. He was a founder of the Cranford National Bank and a director of the Cranford Mutual Building and Loan Association. After the disastrous fire of 1912, he helped rebuild the old Opera House Block, and he erected the Sperry Building, which still stands on the corner of Alden Street and North Avenue. He also donated the land for Sperry Park.

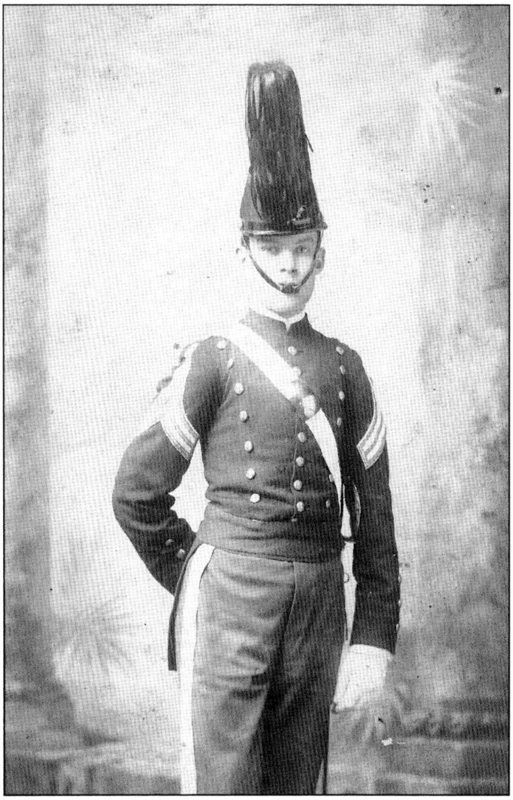

HERBERT FERGUSON. Attired in his dress uniform, sword by his side, young Herbie Ferguson of Cranford looks every bit the soldier. In 1898 he graduated third in his class from the New York Military Academy.

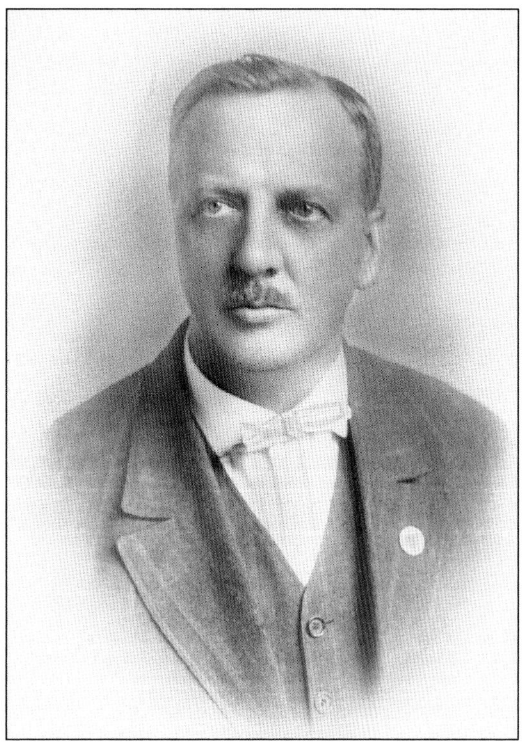

JAMES E. WARNER (1866–1933). James E. Warner founded the *Cranford Citizen* in 1908. He bought the rival *Cranford Chronicle* in 1921 and merged the two papers. Appalled by the growing pollution of the Rahway River, he campaigned for years for a county park along the river. Following World War I, Warner's dream was expanded into a demand for a county-wide system of parks. It became a reality in 1921 with the creation of the Union County Park Commission.

TWO HAMS. Investor and financier Benjamin Franklin Ham (1836–1910), on the right, was one of Cranford's wealthiest citizens, and he was one of the founders of the Cranford Thief Detecting Society. In 1900 Ham sold his seat on the New York Stock Exchange for the then record price of $50,000. Ham is shown here with his brother James Madison Ham, treasurer of the Union Pacific Railroad and a frequent visitor to Cranford.

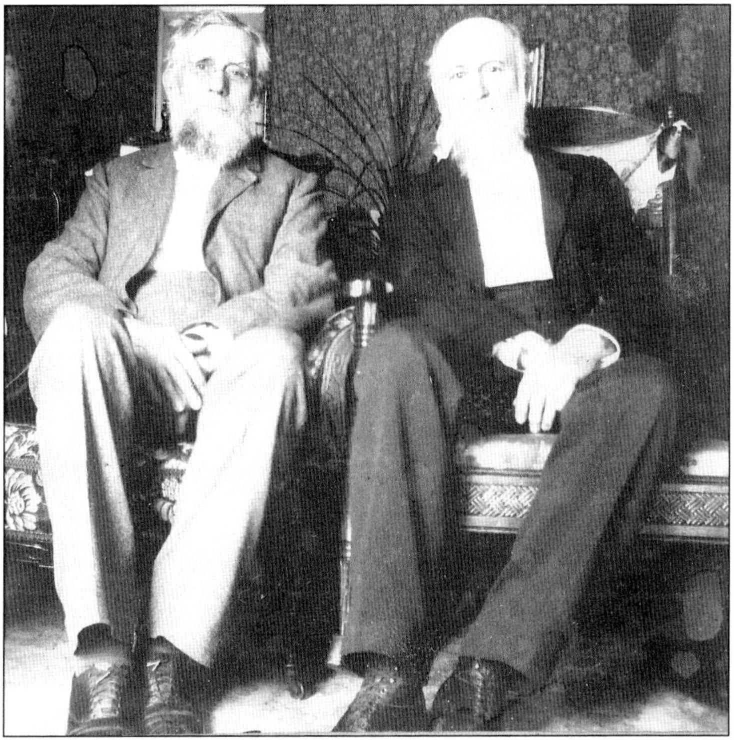

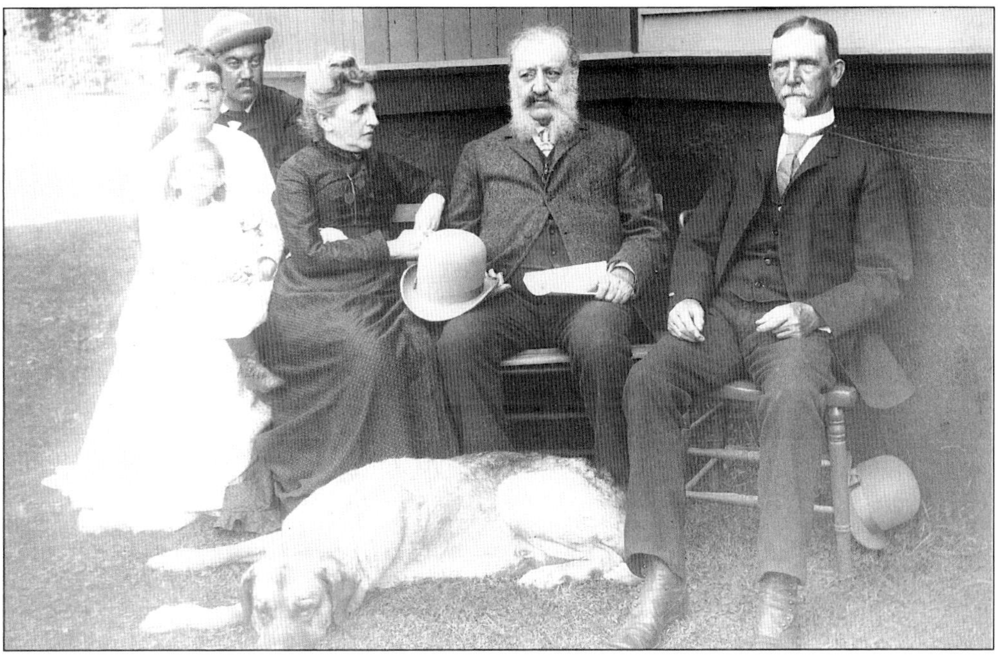

WILLIAM DRYSDALE (1852–1901) AND FAMILY. William Drysdale, a well-known *New York Times* reporter and the author of a series of popular stories for boys, sits in the back of this family photograph, looking singularly unhappy. The others are, from left to right: Mrs. William (Adelaide Bigelow) Drysdale, holding young Billy Drysdale (1886–1916); a couple, probably William Drysdale's parents; and Mrs. Drysdale's father, Alden B. Bigelow (1827–1906).

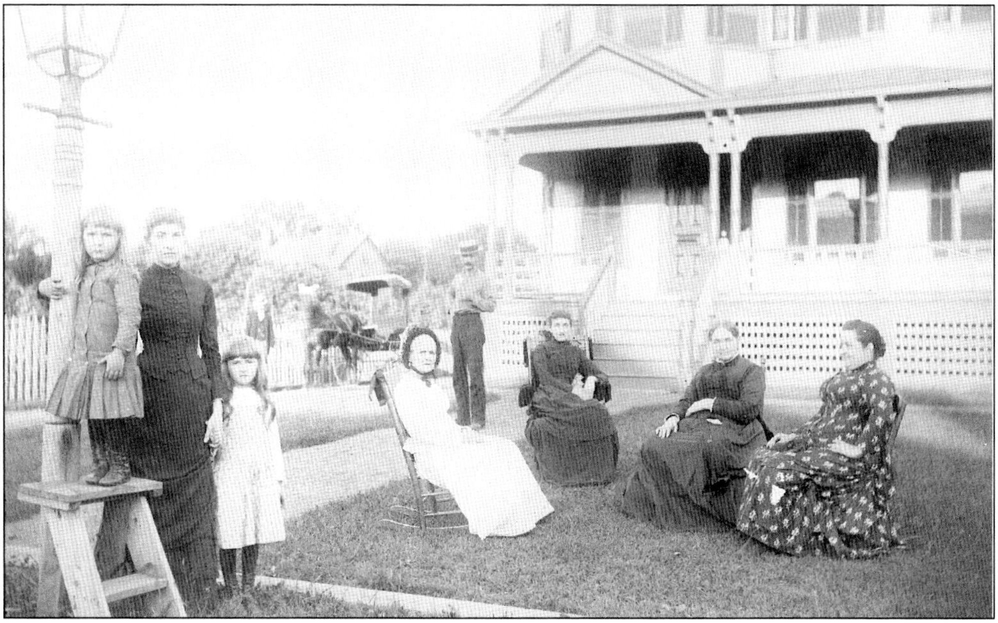

THE PARMENTIER FAMILY, *c.* 1890. Four generations of Parmentier women assembled on the front lawn for this photograph. The gentlemen stayed in the background. On the left, the youngest member of the group stands on steps that are affixed to the street lamp.

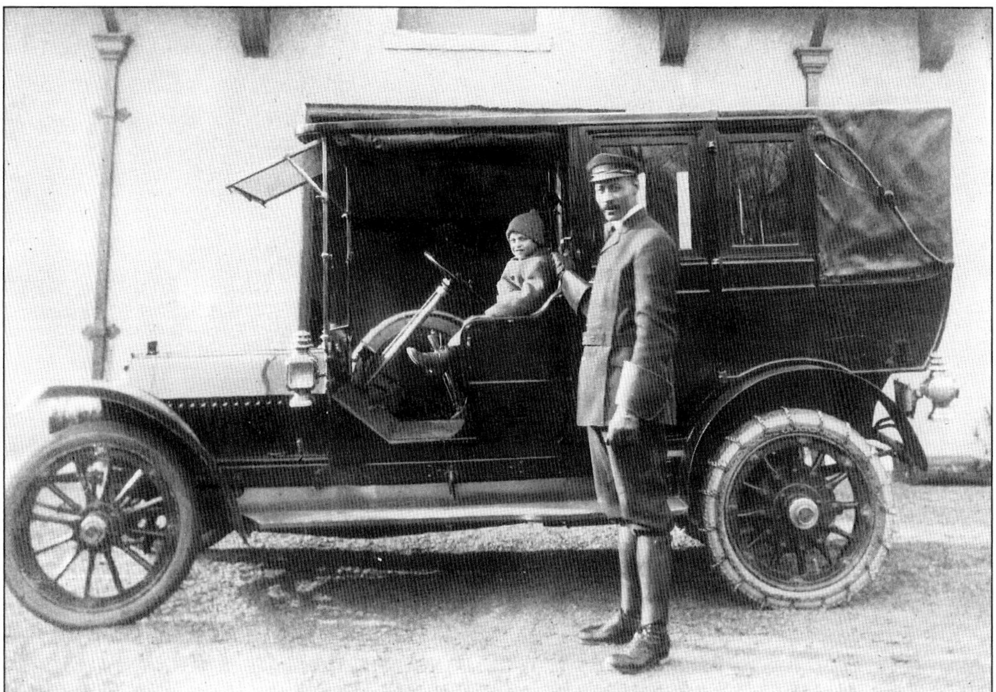

LEON JONES (1881–1943). Wearing leather gaiters and driving gauntlets, Leon Jones poses beside an elegant new limousine. The young child could not be identified. Note the open driver's seat and the tire chains on the car's rear wheels. The chains were not the complete answer to ice and snow, however, and Jones drove a sleigh during the winter months.

LEMUEL (1867–1955) AND IRENE FOWLKES EVANS. A native of Virginia, Lemuel Evans settled in Cranford in 1891, and eight years later married Miss Irene Fowlkes. Evans was the steward at the Cranford Casino from its beginning (as the Cranford Country Club) in 1892 until the building was taken over by the American Legion in 1934. Mr. and Mrs. Evans are shown here seated on the steps of the Casino about 1910.

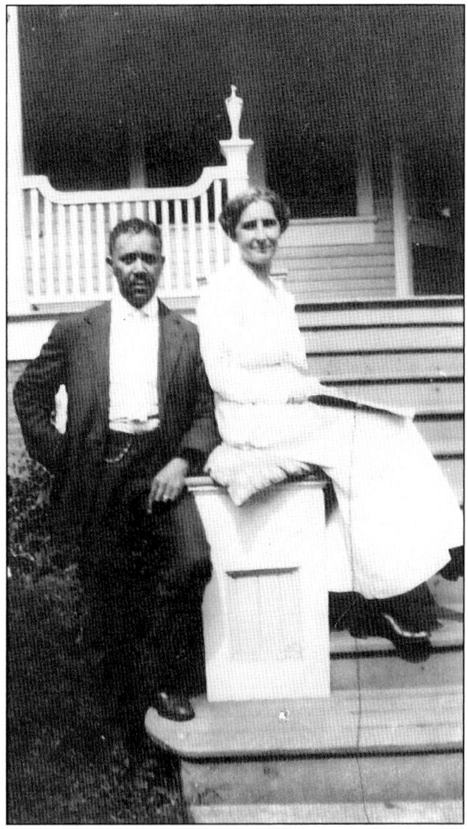

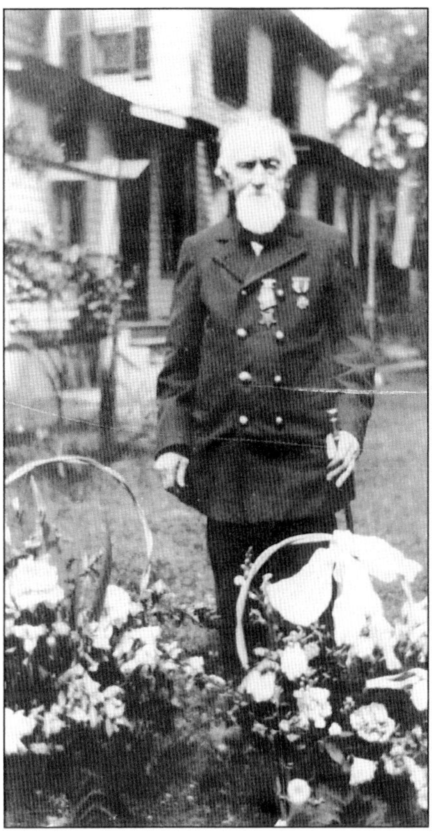

WILLIAM W. MENDELL (1836–1930). Because of his many years as Justice of the Peace in Cranford, W.W. Mendell was known as "Judge." A veteran of the Civil War, he entertained generations of schoolchildren with stories of the war, and he became famous locally for marching in every parade and appearing at public functions dressed in his old army uniform. His home and office were at 110 Walnut Avenue, now occupied by The Jumble Store.

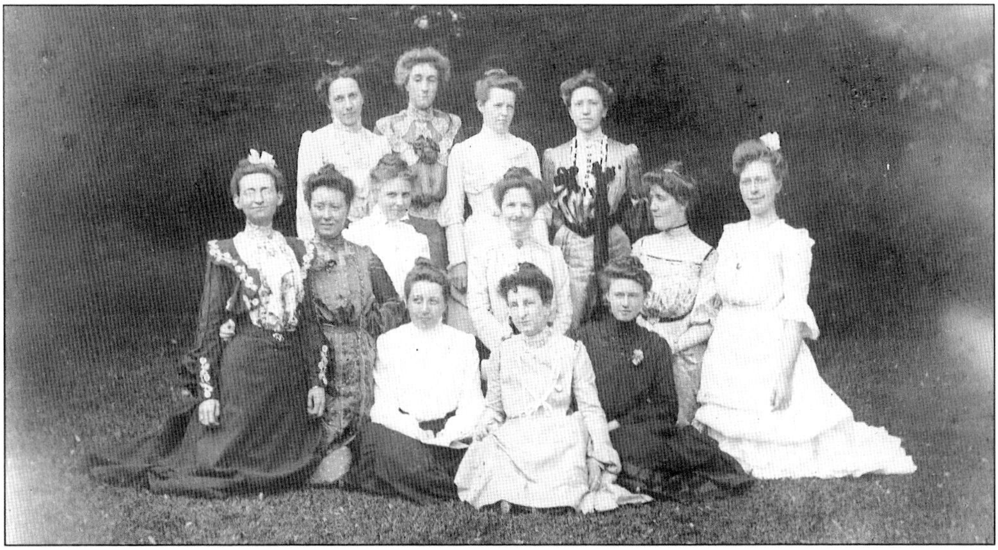

THE ROSE VILLA MUSIC CLUB, *c.* 1900. The foremost music society in Cranford, the Rose Villa Music Club was founded by Ethel V. (Mrs. John H.) Thompson (1870–1944), shortly after she came to Cranford as a bride in 1890. Membership was limited to twenty-five women, all skilled musicians, who met every two weeks and presented musical programs. Mrs. Thompson (front row center) was the first president of the group and remained president until her death in 1944.

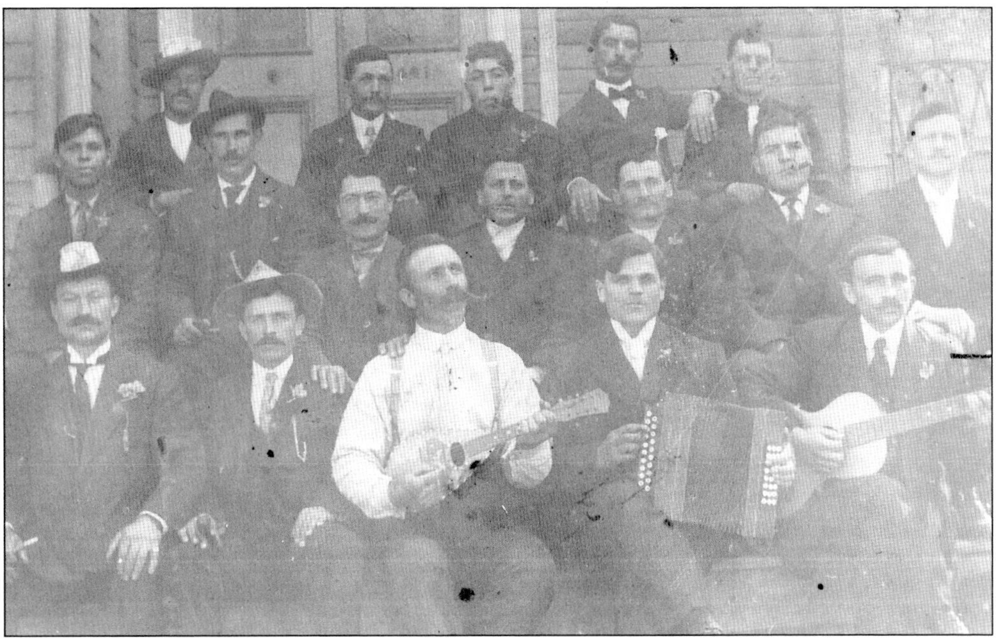

NEWCOMERS. After 1880, immigrants from the village of Monteferrante, Italy, began to settle in Cranford. Seventeen of the newcomers gathered at the Orchard Street home of Louis Colonari (front row center) in 1904. The group included, from left to right: (front row) F. Massa, J. Della Serra, Colonari, F. DiFabio, and C. DiFabio; (middle row) J. Della Serra, J. Labate, F. DiTullio, J. Massa, N. DiCrace, G. Giannobile, and N. Polidoro; (back row) J. DiFabio, C. Della Serra, P. Massa, J. Del Nero, and J. Iaione.

ALBERT HARRIS (1896–1973). Harris is remembered primarily as a long-time employee of Seager's Drug Store in downtown Cranford. Only a handful of old-timers remember Harris as a pitcher/first baseman for the Cranford Dixie Giants. Harris served in the navy during World War I, and he is wearing the New Jersey Service Medal awarded for his two years of military service.

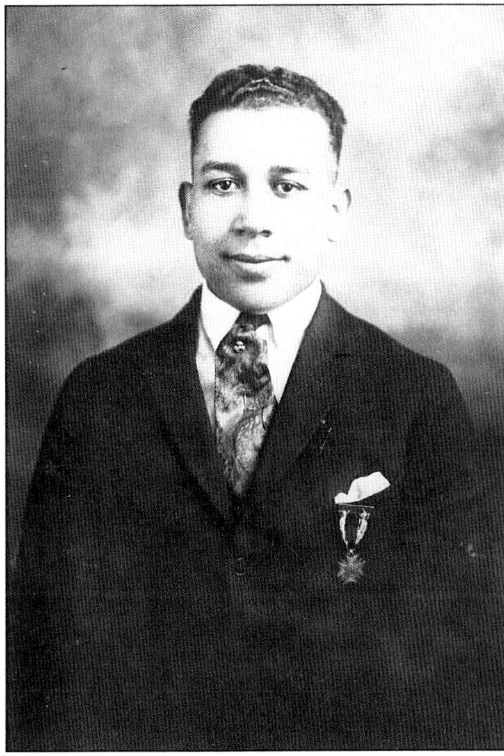

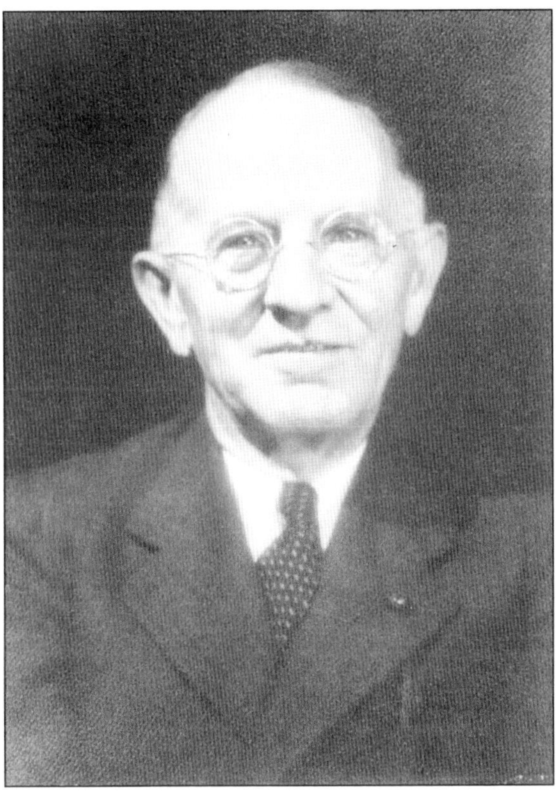

WILLIAM BRAGDON (1879–1969). An architect, William Bragdon was a founder and long-time trustee of the Cranford Historical Society, and was an important figure in the Society's development. In the early 1930s, under the pen name I.B. Herodotus, he wrote a series of delightful articles on Cranford's history for the *Citizen and Chronicle*. In 1937 he published the equally delightful *Cranford: An Outline History*.

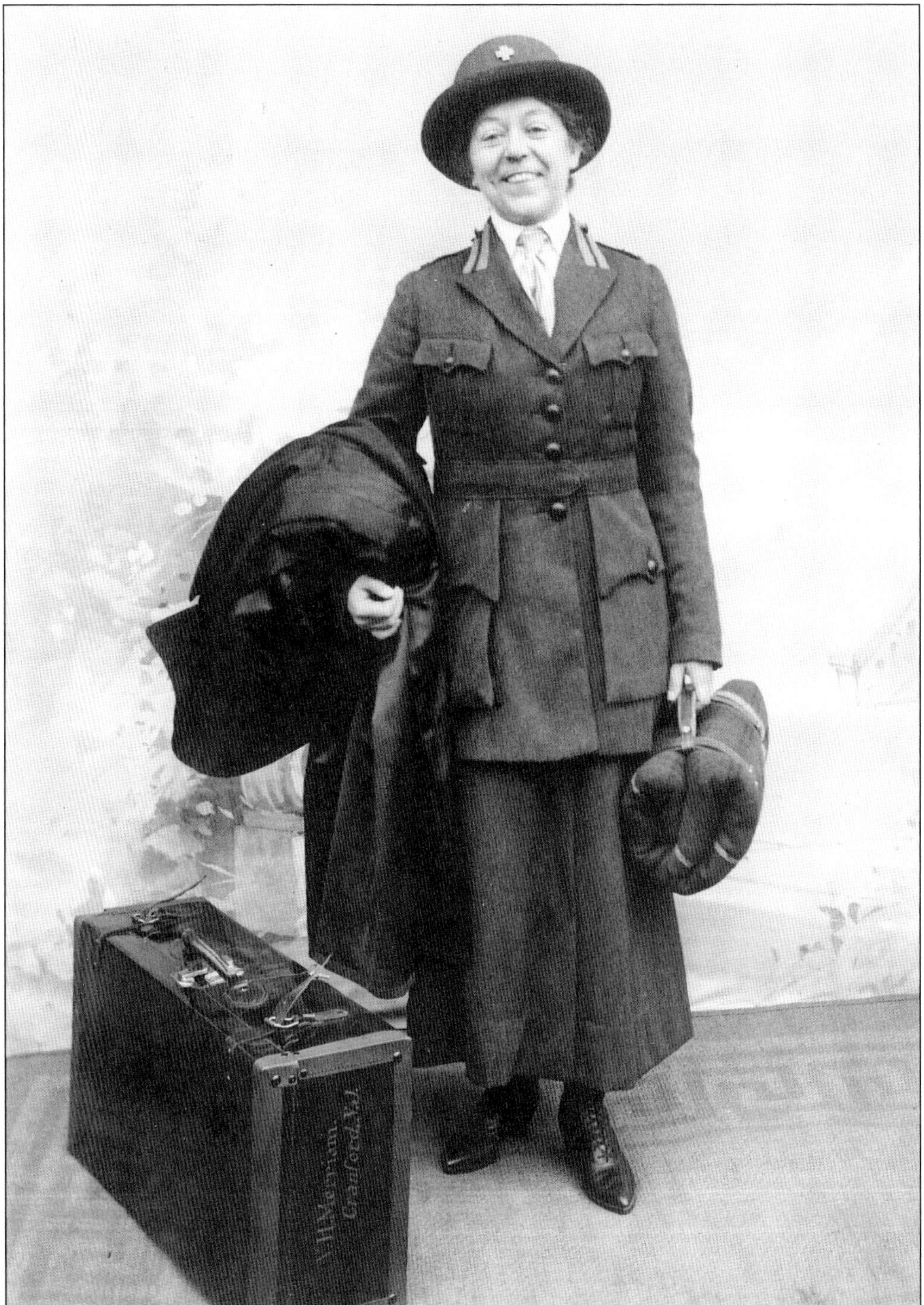

VERA HEATON MERRIAM, 1917. With bags packed and wearing her American Red Cross uniform, a smiling Vera Merriam is ready to embark for France to join the AEF after America's entry into World War I. Miss Merriam was an aunt of Curtis Culin III, a World War II hero from Cranford.

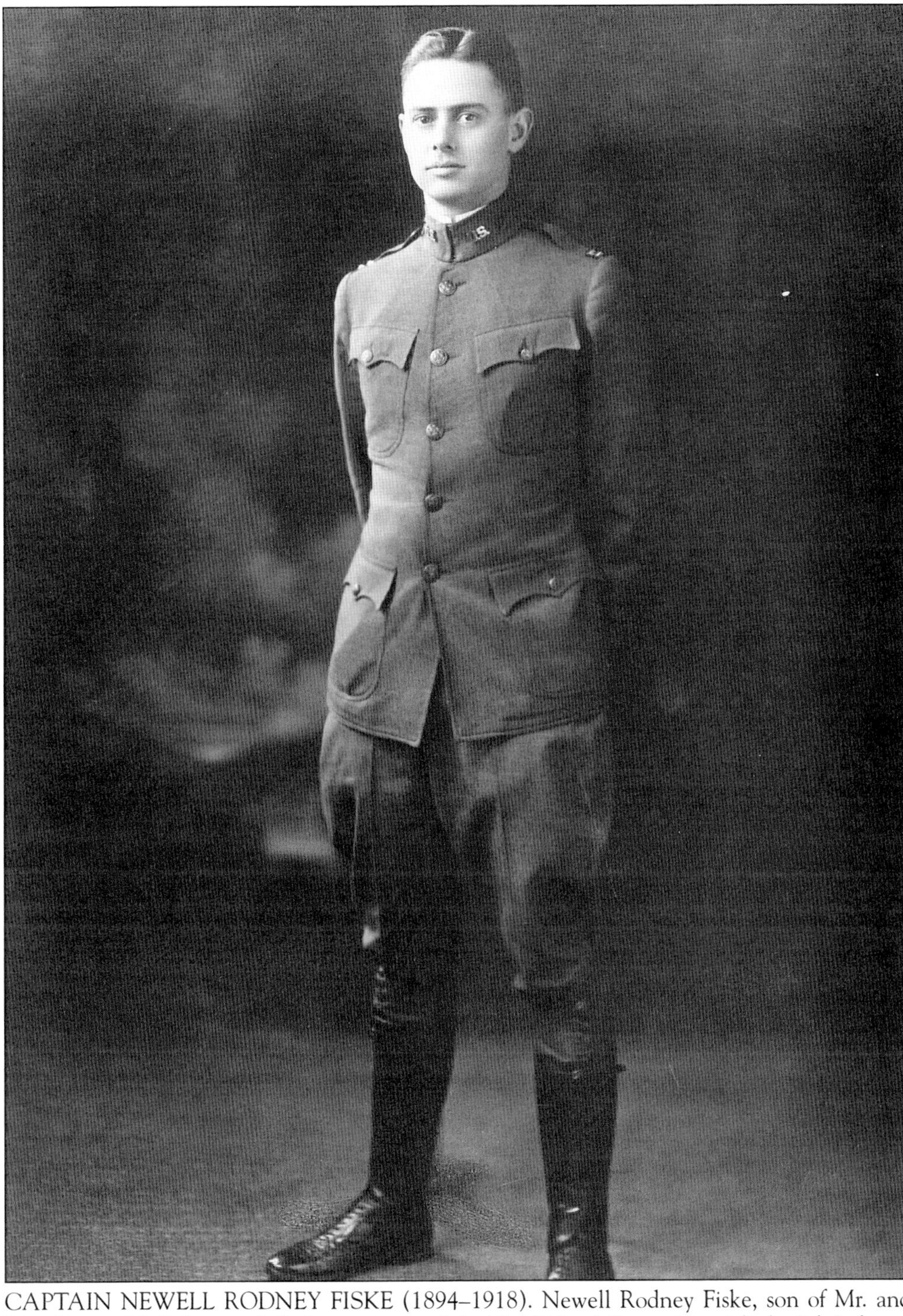

CAPTAIN NEWELL RODNEY FISKE (1894–1918). Newell Rodney Fiske, son of Mr. and Mrs. Harvey N. Fiske, was killed in action on July 15, 1918, while serving with the 7th Infantry Regiment, 3rd Division, in France. He was the second Cranford serviceman to be killed in action in World War I. In 1920 the Cranford Veterans of Foreign Wars Post No. 335 was named in his honor.

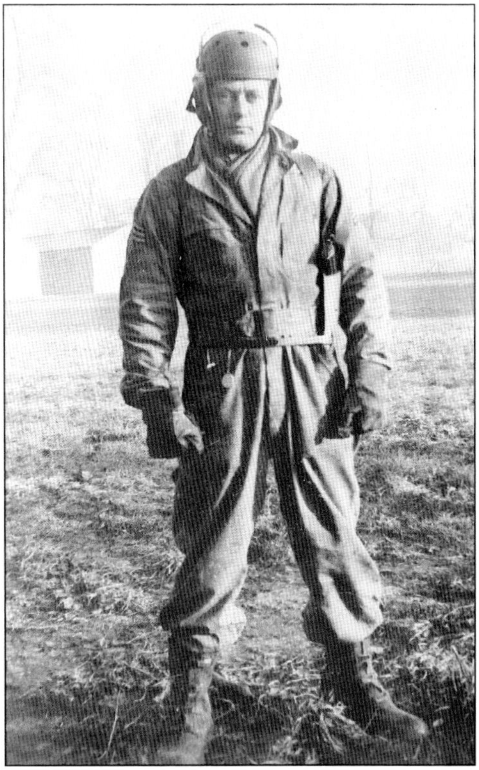

SERGEANT CURTIS G. CULIN III (1915–1963). During the Allied invasion of Europe in 1944, the dense hedgerows separating French fields proved to be impenetrable barriers to American tanks. Sergeant Curtis Culin devised a four-pronged "Rhino" attachment for tanks that allowed them to drive directly through the hedgerows. Awarded the Legion of Merit for his invention, Culin was later wounded and lost a leg. A plaque dedicated to Sergeant Culin is affixed to a boulder on the North Union Avenue lawn of the Cranford Municipal Building.

THE SHAHEENS. A portrait of S.A. Shaheen (d. 1946) appears to look down on his son Victor Shaheen (1916–1978). S.A. Shaheen originally was in business with his father at the A. Shaheen & Sons silk mills on Centennial Avenue, and he later founded Builders General Supply Co., where he was succeeded by Victor. Major real estate developers, the Shaheens built more than two hundred homes in Cranford during the early decades of this century.

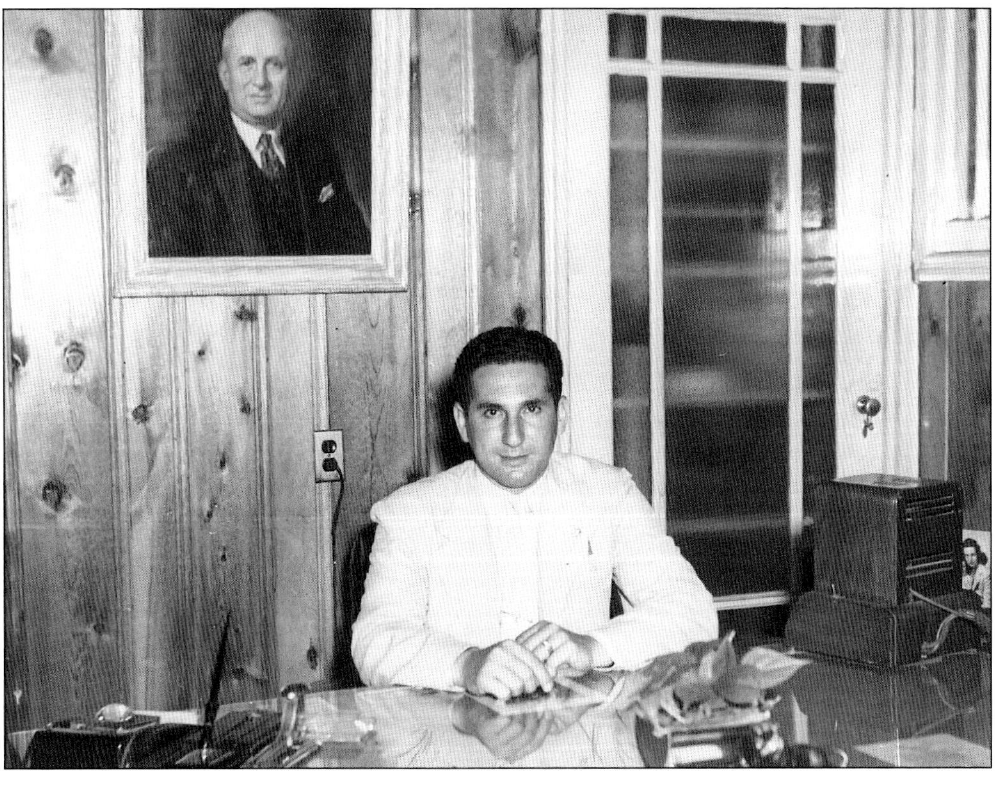

Three

Special Events

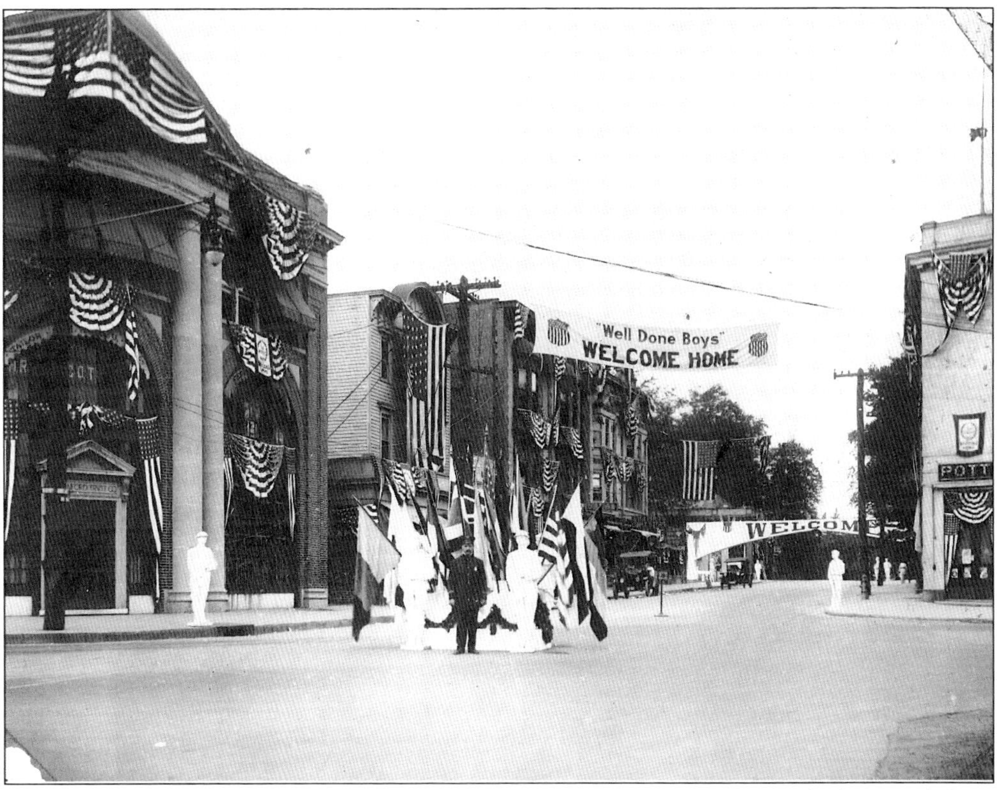

"WELCOME HOME" DECORATIONS, SEPTEMBER 13, 1919. Cranford extended an enthusiastic official welcome to the men and women who returned from World War I service "over there." Providing an unusual touch were the life-size effigies of soldiers and sailors that lined the parade route at North and North Union Avenues.

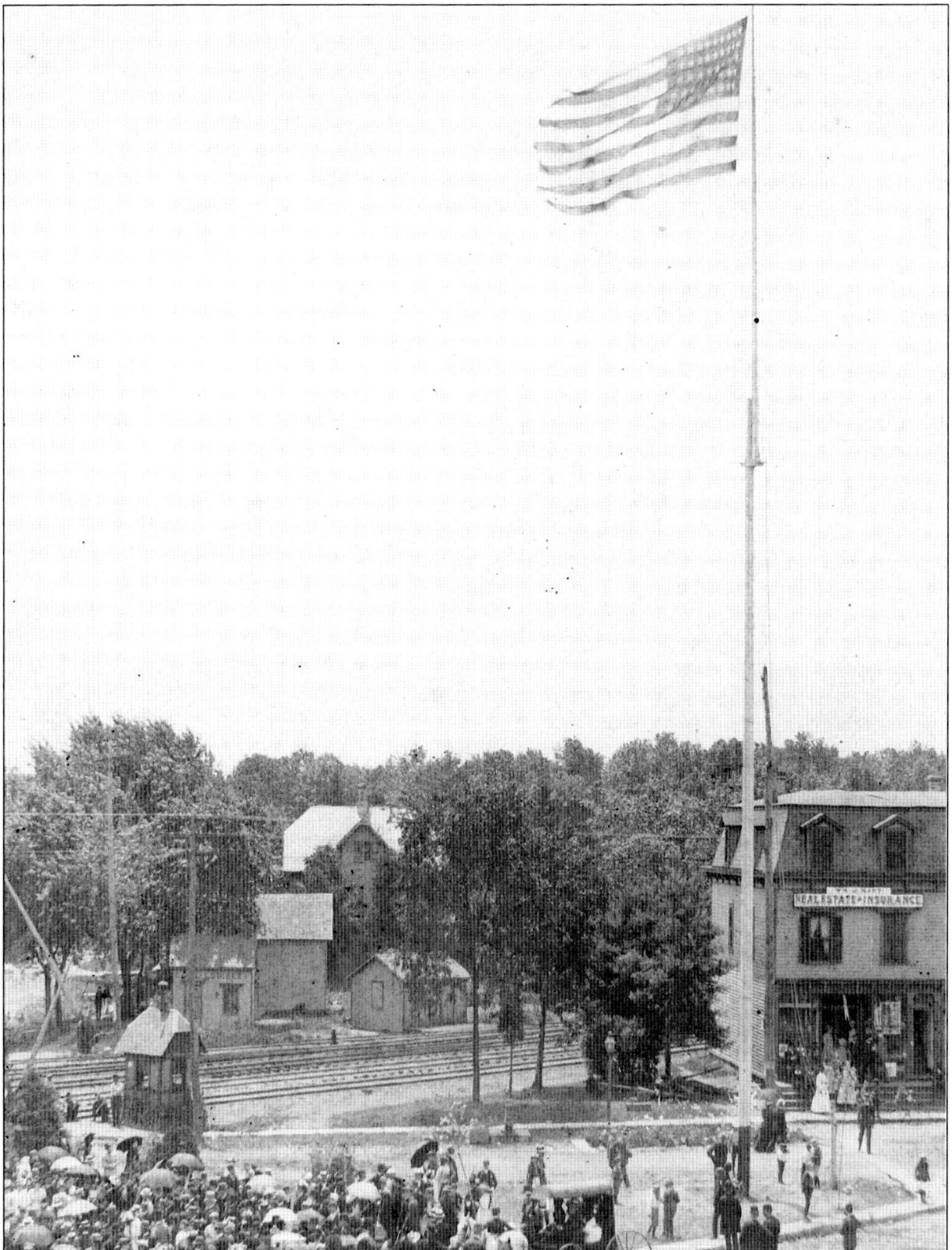

A FOURTH OF JULY FLAG RAISING, 1891. An enormous forty-four-star flag was raised on the township flag mast to mark the admission of Wyoming as a new state. The site is the triangle formed by the intersection of Eastman Street with North and North Union Avenues, today's Eastman Plaza. This was the heart of downtown Cranford then as it is now. A railroad watchman's shanty is on the left and behind it and across the tracks are the offices of a coal and lumber yard. On the right is William J. Hart's Real Estate and Insurance Office in the Miller Building.

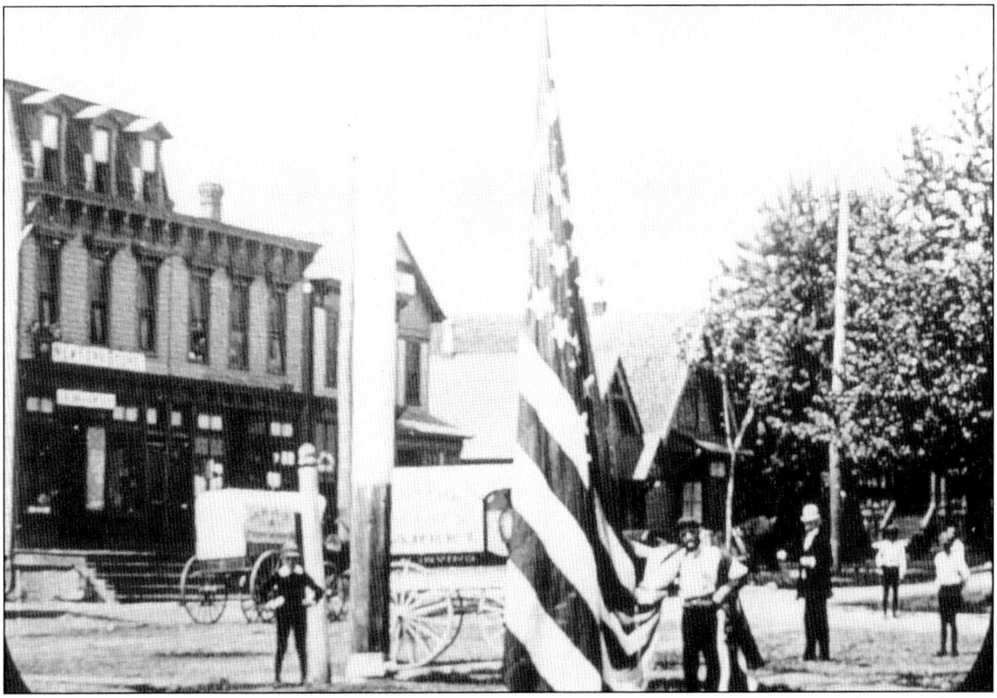

LOWERING THE FLAG, JULY 4, 1891. In this view, taken from an old glass slide, Cranford's great forty-four-star flag has been lowered at the end of the day (see opposite page). Judge W.W. Mendell, a Civil War veteran, served as Grand Marshal of the parade that day, and music was supplied by the Roselle Band. In the left background can be seen Miller's New York Store.

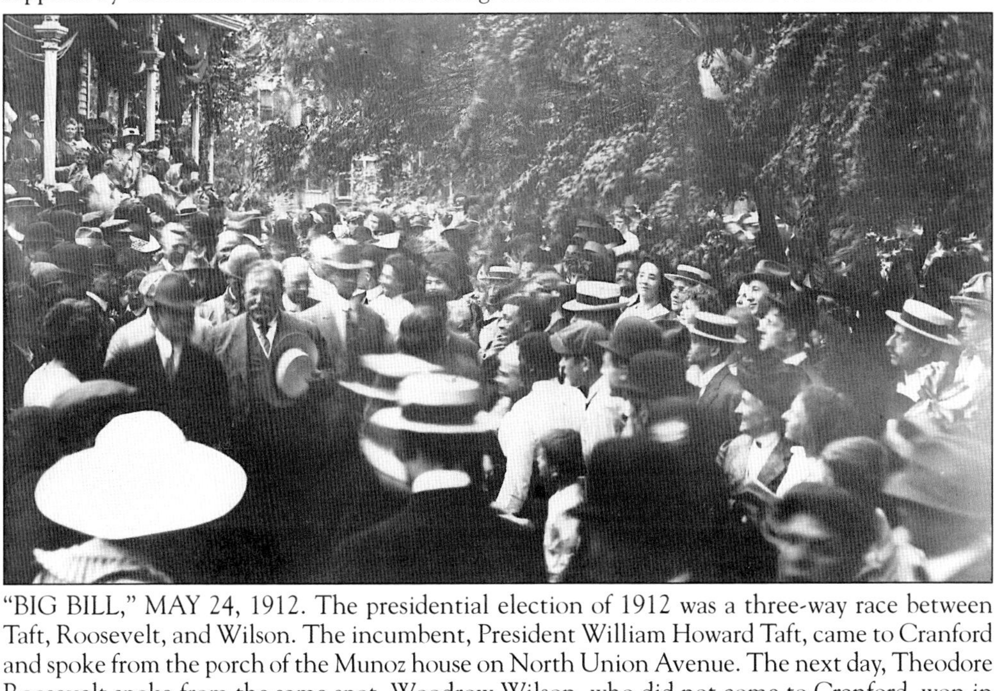

"BIG BILL," MAY 24, 1912. The presidential election of 1912 was a three-way race between Taft, Roosevelt, and Wilson. The incumbent, President William Howard Taft, came to Cranford and spoke from the porch of the Munoz house on North Union Avenue. The next day, Theodore Roosevelt spoke from the same spot. Woodrow Wilson, who did not come to Cranford, won in November. Taft is the smiling gentleman holding his hat in his hand at the left of the picture.

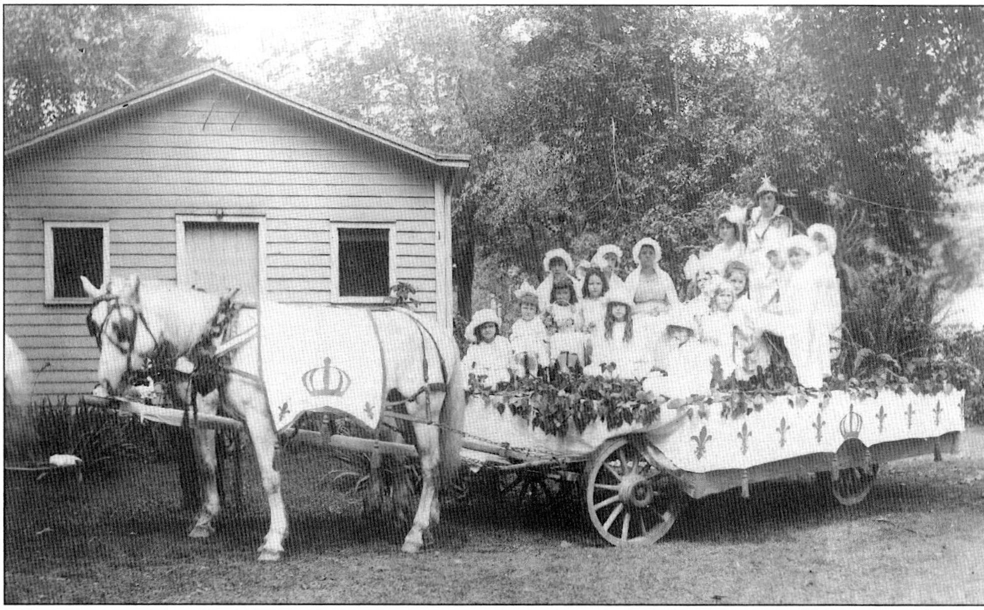

THE CHILDREN'S PARADE, 1915. In place of the traditional River Carnival, Cranford held a Children's Carnival in 1915, and it was a rousing success. The high point of the festivities was the Children's Parade. This float carried the Carnival Queen, Miss Gertrude Loveland, surrounded by a bevy of white-gowned ladies-in-waiting. The noble steeds drawing the royal throng appear totally disinterested.

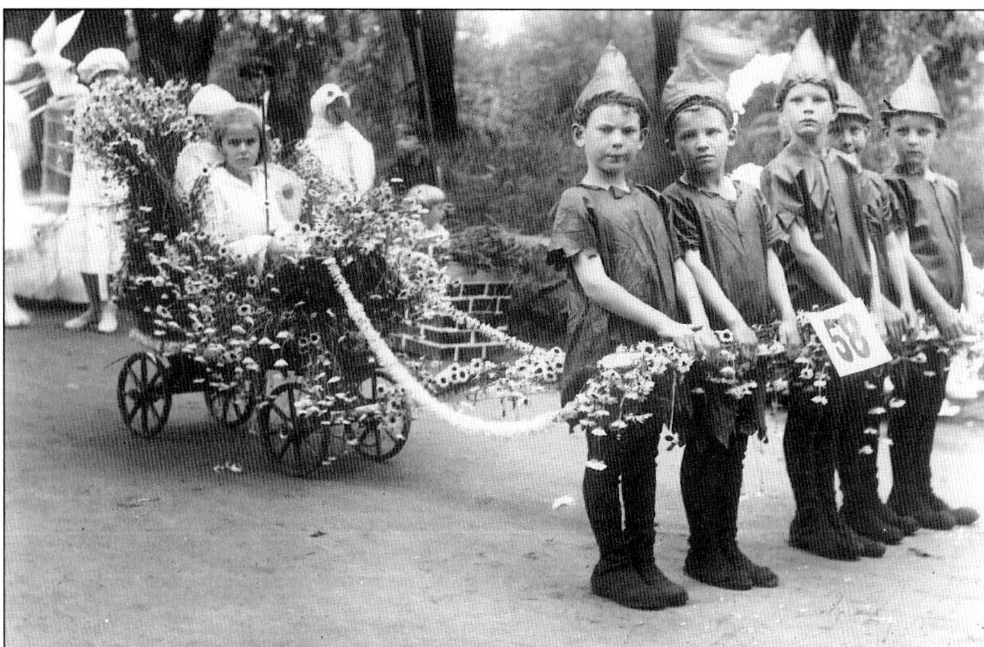

THE ELVES AND THE PRINCESS. Looking at the camera with expressions ranging from curiosity to exasperation, five sturdy elves prepare to pull the carriage of the little princess, Marie Stanke, in the 1915 Children's Parade. The elves are, from left to right: Clifton Cox, Bradley Rosencrantz, Stuart McFadden, Milton Stanke, and Richard McFadden.

THE STRONGMAN, CHILDREN'S PARADE, 1915. The most entertaining parade participants were the younger children, who competed in a variety of categories. Three-year-old strongman Charrick V. Rosencrantz, a "Heavy Weight Lifter," won third prize in the Express Wagon Class.

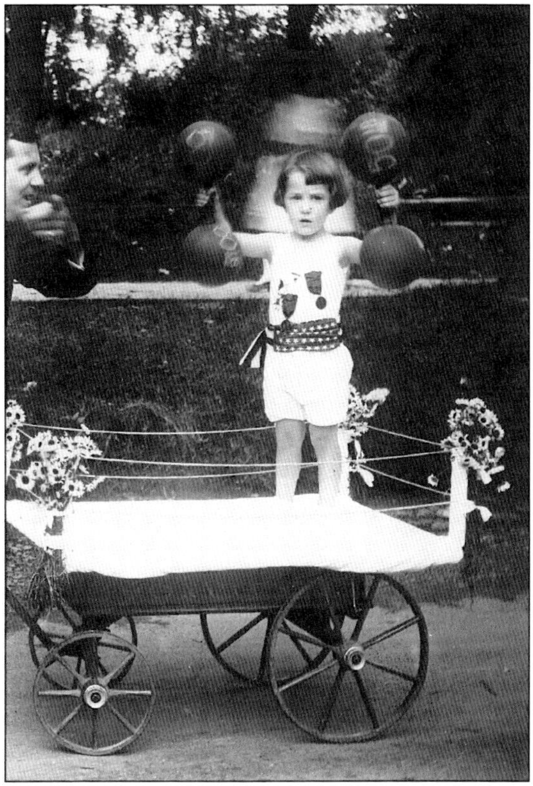

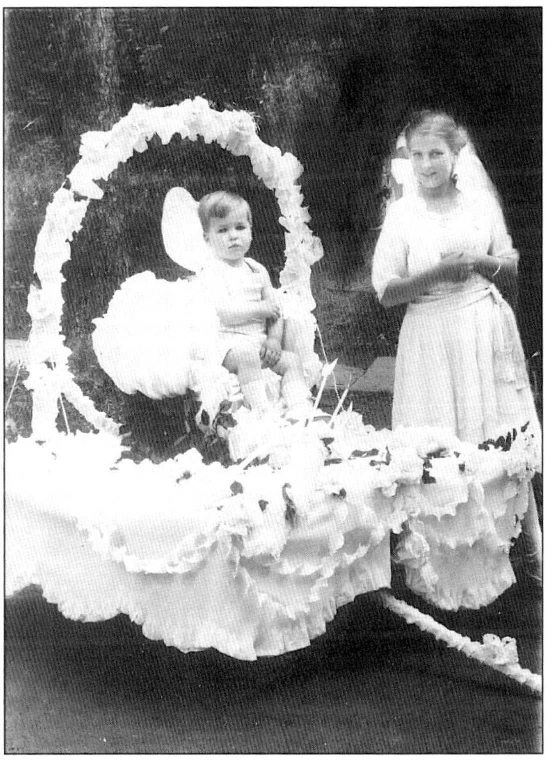

THE HANDSOMEST BABY. Twenty-month-old Richard Rohr Zundel, as "Cupid," accepts quite calmly his celebrity as a photographer's model and winner of the Businessmen's Association Cup as the handsomest baby in the 1915 parade.

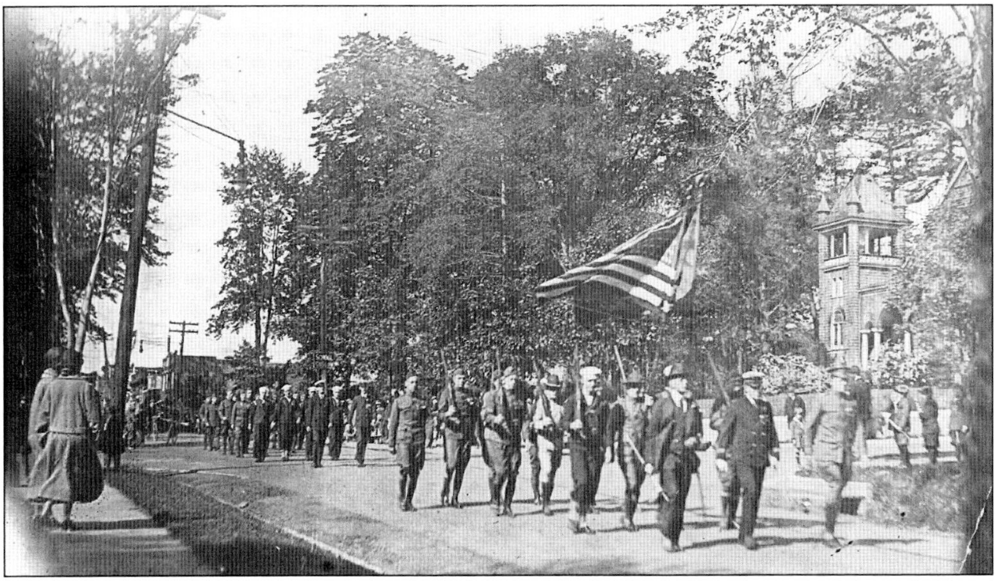

MEMORIAL DAY, 1924. Soldiers and sailors, some of whom were veterans of World War I, marched in the parade up North Union Avenue. Led by Harvey Fiske (left front, in suit), father of the first Cranford man killed in the war, and Captain J.B. Dryden (in naval uniform), the procession is seen crossing Springfield Avenue. The picture was taken from in front of the Crane-Phillips House, later the museum of the Cranford Historical Society.

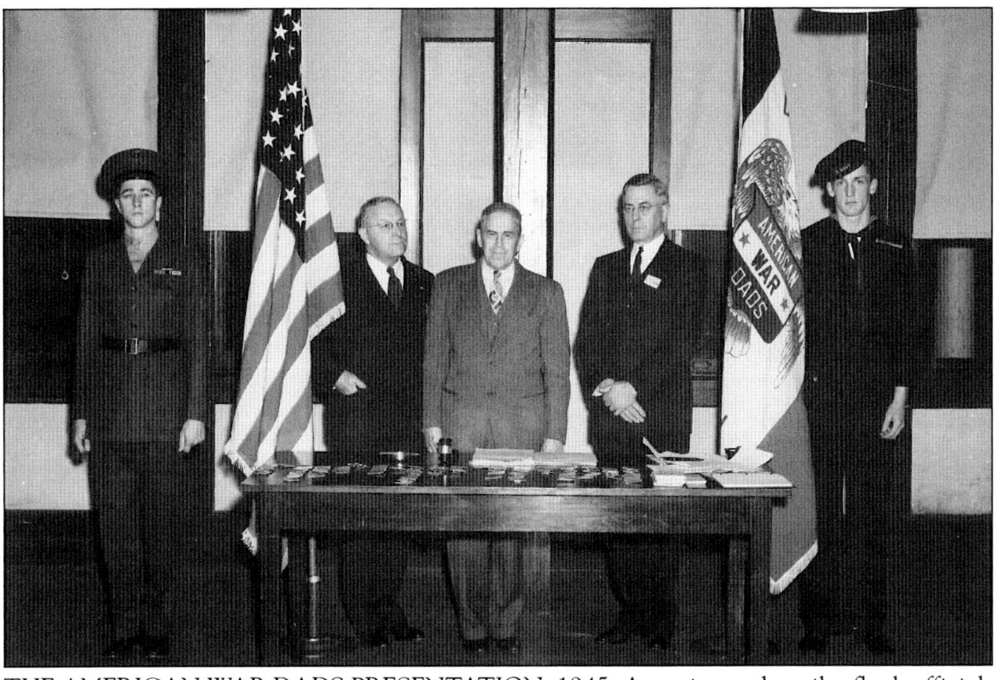

THE AMERICAN WAR DADS PRESENTATION, 1945. A marine and a sailor flank officials at a presentation for Cranford's "War Dads." Between the flags, from left to right, are: Nelson King, manager of English Village; Winchester Britton, president of Packing Engineering; and Cranford Mayor George Osterheldt. The War Dads aided disabled veterans in their adjustment back to civilian life.

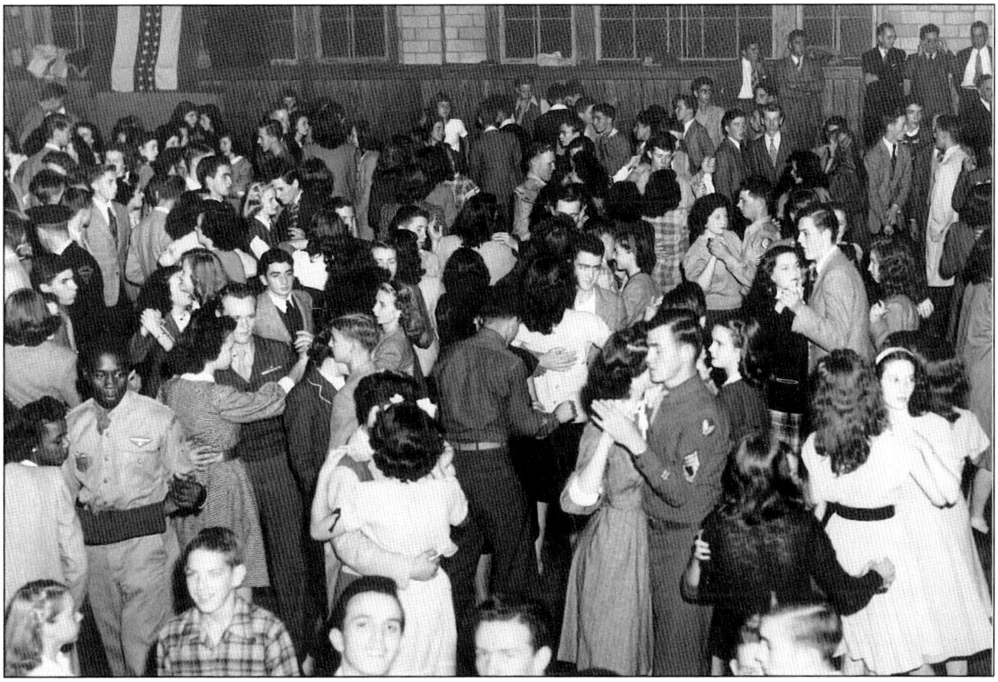

THE USO DANCE AT CRANFORD HIGH, 1946. Young servicemen and civilians flocked to the Cranford High School gymnasium for a dance sponsored by the United Services Organization (USO). See if you can spot the Cranford police officer, lost in the crowd.

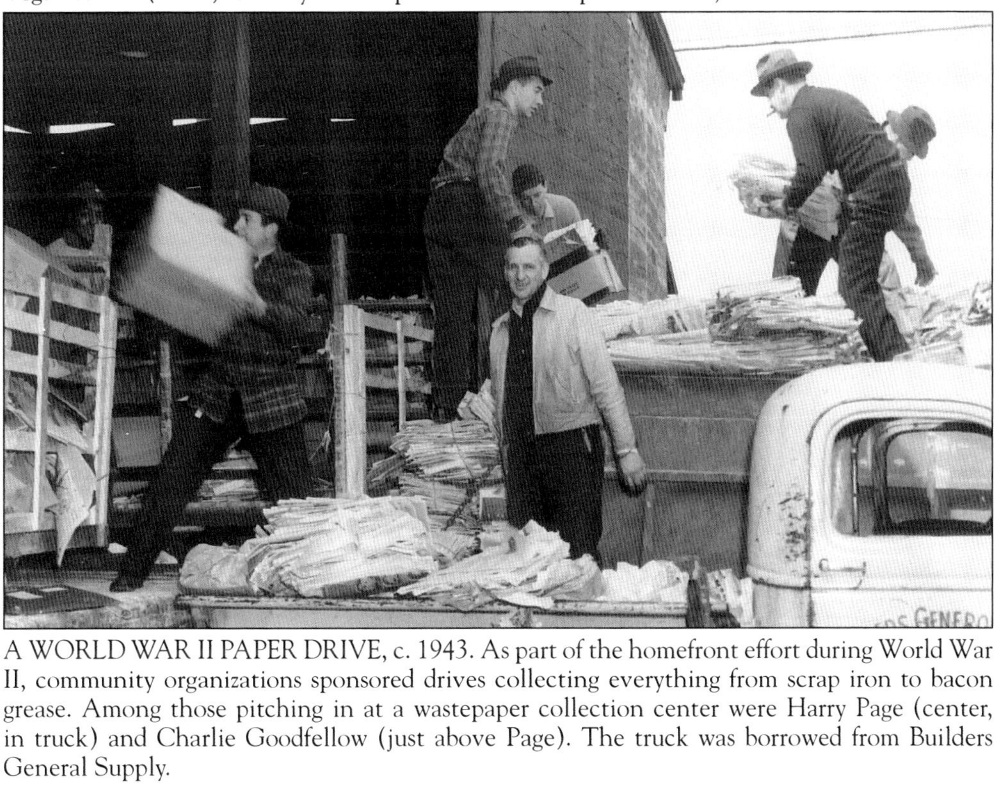

A WORLD WAR II PAPER DRIVE, c. 1943. As part of the homefront effort during World War II, community organizations sponsored drives collecting everything from scrap iron to bacon grease. Among those pitching in at a wastepaper collection center were Harry Page (center, in truck) and Charlie Goodfellow (just above Page). The truck was borrowed from Builders General Supply.

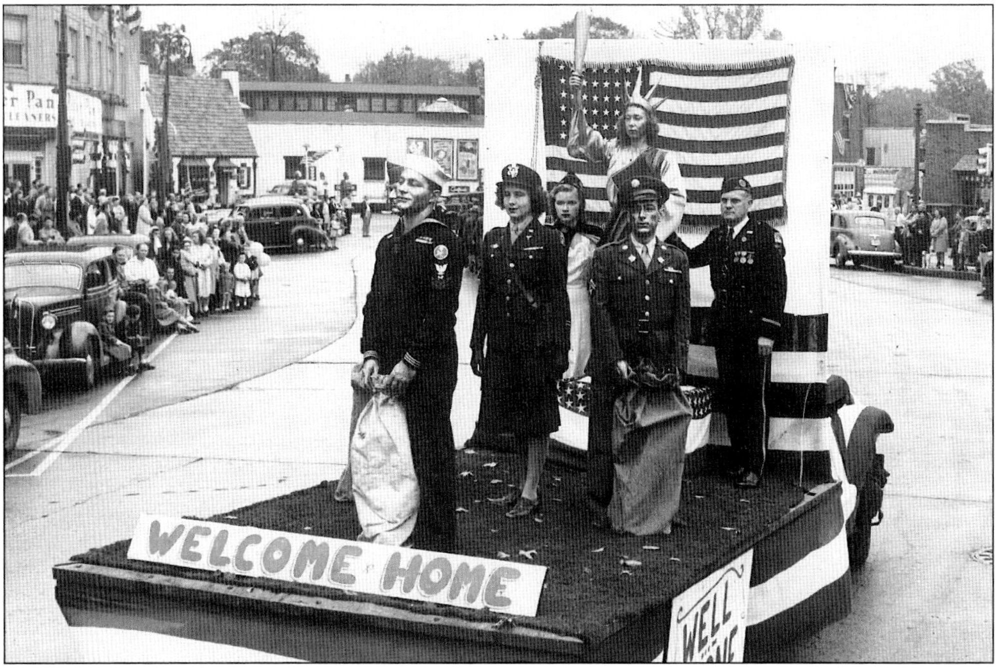

WELCOME HOME AND WELL DONE, 1946. At the close of World War II, Cranford held a "Welcome Home" parade to honor the town's sons and daughters who had served their country. Slowly wending its way along the North Avenue parade route is the float of American Legion Post 212, extending a heartfelt "Well Done."

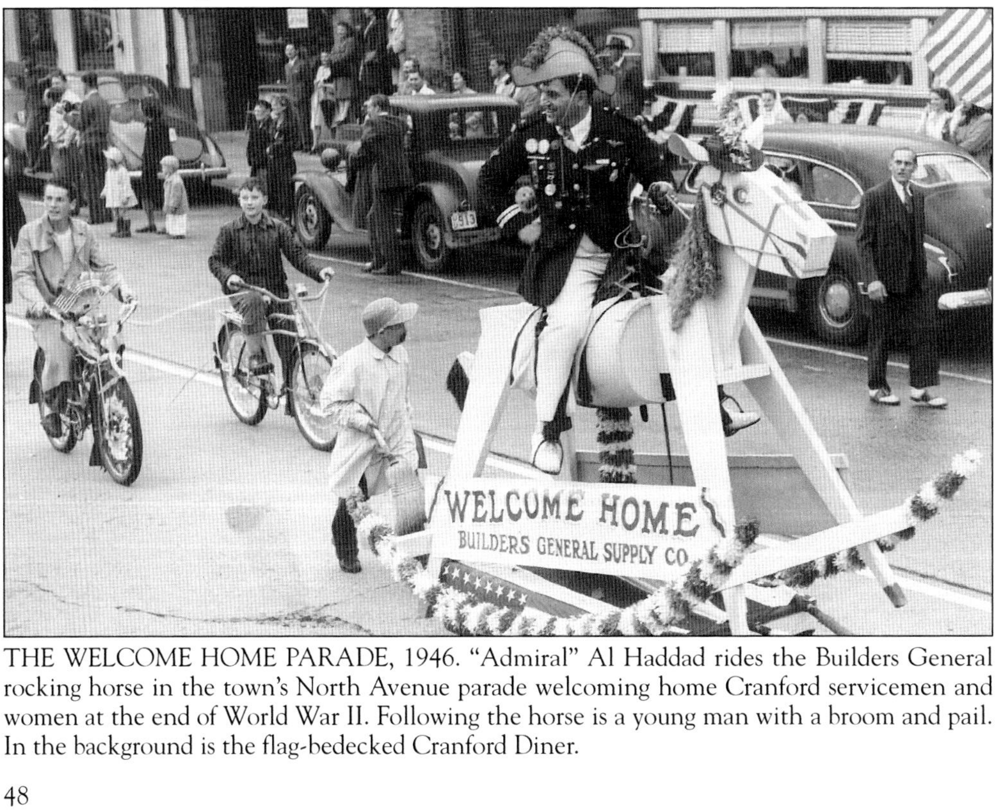

THE WELCOME HOME PARADE, 1946. "Admiral" Al Haddad rides the Builders General rocking horse in the town's North Avenue parade welcoming home Cranford servicemen and women at the end of World War II. Following the horse is a young man with a broom and pail. In the background is the flag-bedecked Cranford Diner.

Four

Downtown

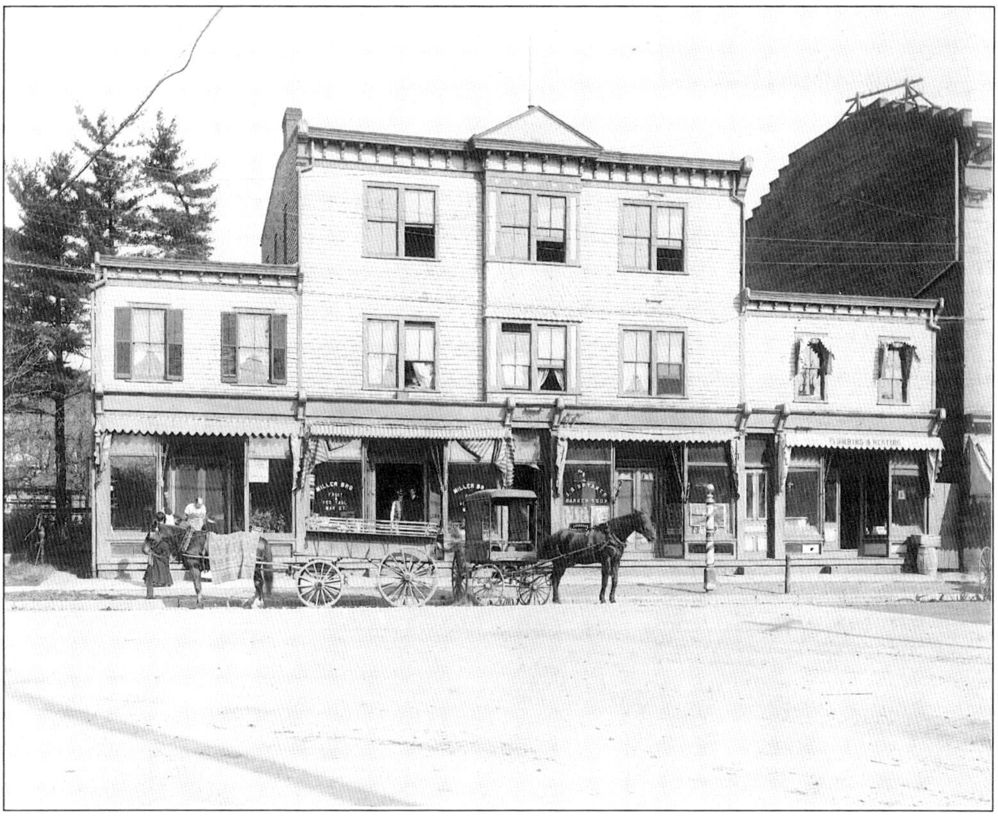

THE MILLER BUILDING IN 1895. Also known as the Miller Block, this building was built in 1894 to the west of and adjoining the Opera House Block. It stood on North Avenue between Eastman Street and North Union Avenue, about where the Cranford Bookstore and the Cortina Restaurant are today. The building housed Lang's Shoe Repair, Miller Brothers Market, J.H. Bryant's Barber Shop & Pool Parlor, and a plumbing and heating shop.

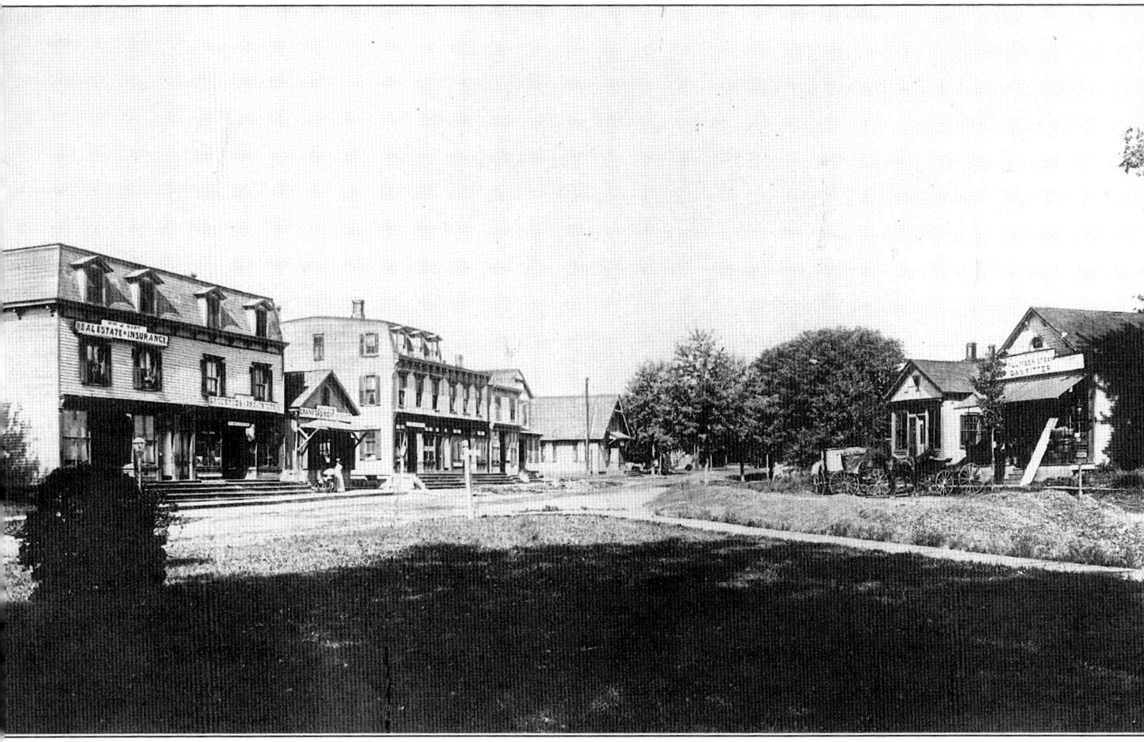

GRASS GREW IN THE STREETS OF CRANFORD, 1888. The intersection of North Avenue and Eastman Street was the business center of Cranford in 1888. Store signs that can be deciphered read, from left to right: Wm. J. Hart, Real Estate & Insurance; J.L. Derby, Groceries & Provisions (which also held the local post office); J.N. Irving, Cranford Meat Market; and at the extreme right, W.Y. Redfern, Plumber and Steam Gas Fitter, located on the site of today's Cranford Bookstore. The building with the peaked roof in the center of the picture is Cranford Hall, the local Republican "wigwam" and home of the township offices. Today's post office would be located behind the trees that are to the right of Cranford Hall. Note the woman pushing a parasol-covered baby carriage along the board walk in front of the Cranford Meat Market, and the horse-drawn vehicles parked in front of the plumber's shop.

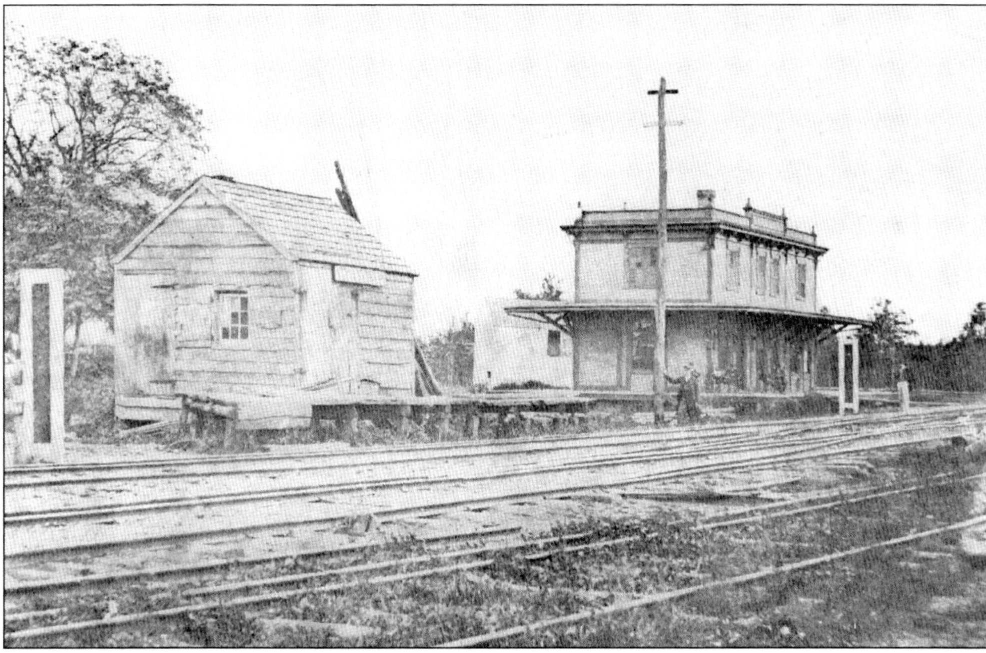

CRANFORD'S FIRST TWO RAILROAD STATIONS. The forlorn-looking shed on the left, built in 1844, served as the town's first railroad station. It was moved in 1865 to make way for the new station on the right. Local tradition has it that schoolchildren chalked "Craneville" on the shed in the 1840s and the name stuck, only to be changed to "Cranford" by a town vote in the late 1860s.

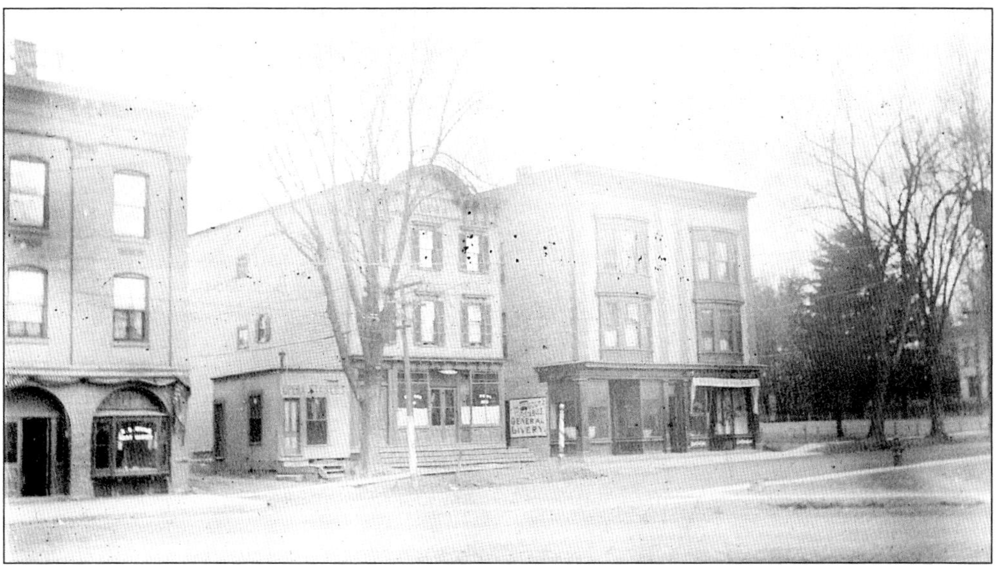

NORTH UNION AVENUE NEAR THE CORNER OF NORTH AVENUE, *c.* 1890. The building in the center and the one to its right are still standing today. Note the open lot from that point on to Alden Street. The central building with the curved facade was built in 1888 and housed a pool hall, barber shop, and apartments. Today it is occupied by Gentlemen's Corner. To the left of the center building can be seen a shack housing the office of the "Opera Stables."

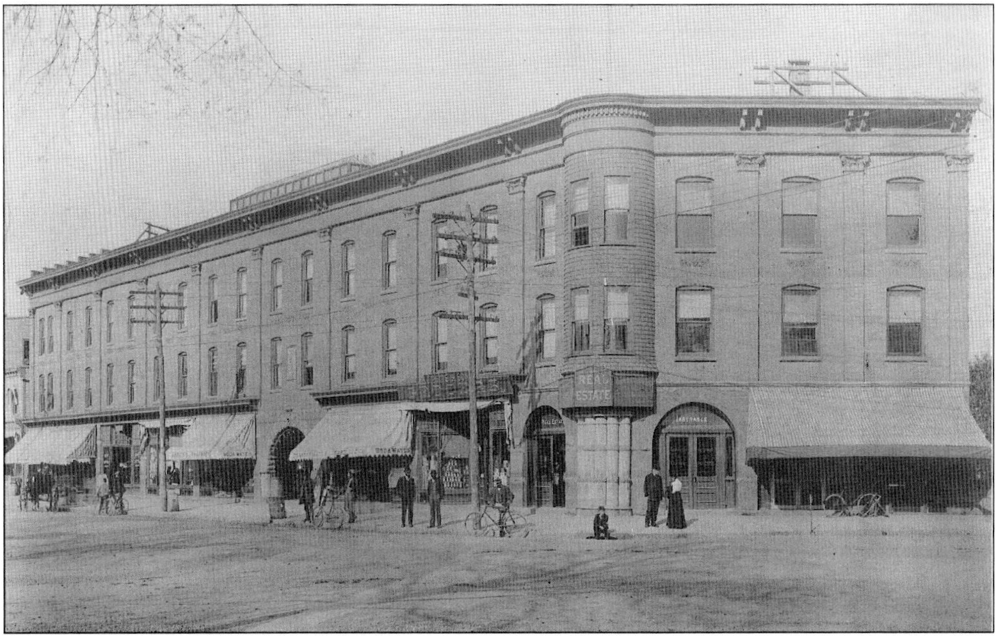

THE CRANFORD OPERA HOUSE BLOCK IN 1898. Erected in 1892 by J. Walter Thompson, this building was on the north side of North Avenue. The post office and the public library were also located in the building. Along the avenue one can see the New York Haberdasher, Berry & Co. Clothing, Marien's Pharmacy, Lusardi's Ice Cream Parlor, J. Potts & Son Grocers, and Ferguson & Van Name Insurance and Real Estate.

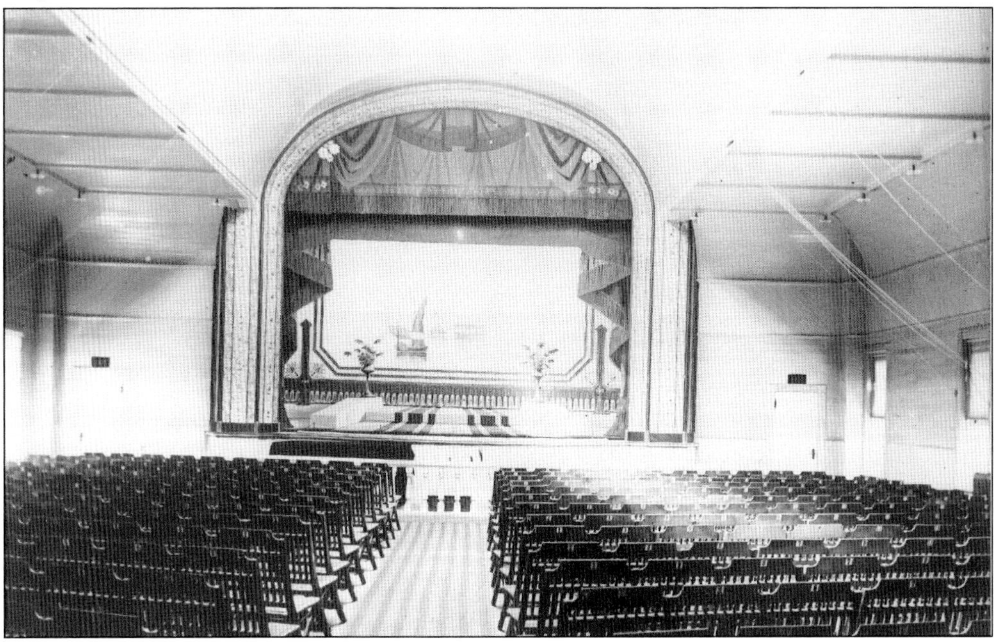

THE OPERA HOUSE THEATER. When the Opera House opened in 1892 it had a five-hundred-seat theater on the third floor. It was used for school commencements, public meetings, political rallies, and, of course, for the lectures, minstrel shows, operettas, and musical performances so popular in the 1890s.

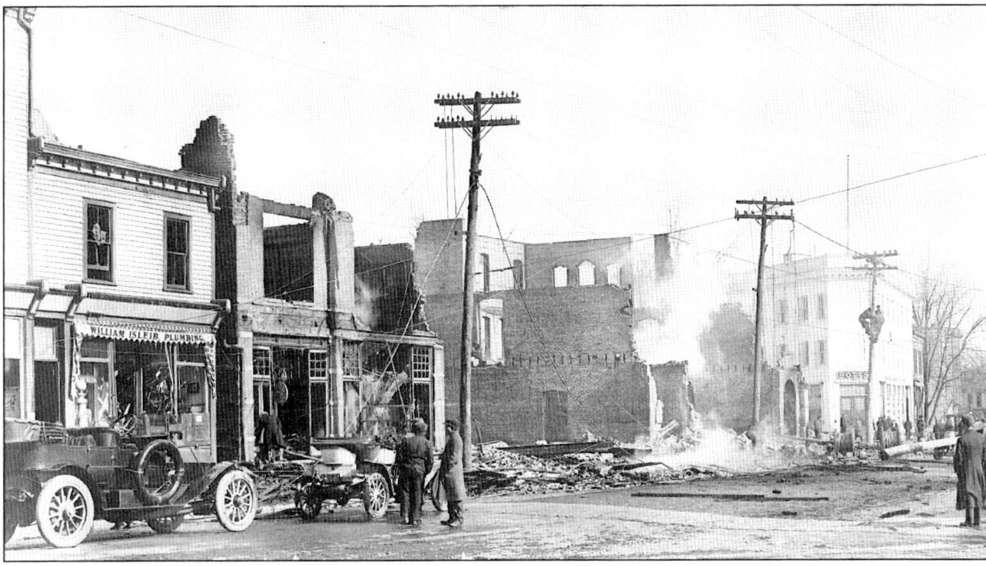

THE OPERA HOUSE BLOCK FIRE. Cranford's most destructive fire leveled the Opera House Block on the cold winter day of February 3, 1912. The ruins of the building were still smoldering when linemen began replacing melted telephone and electrical cables, as shown in this souvenir postcard view. Firemen saved the wooden Miller Building and William Isleib's plumbing shop, seen at left.

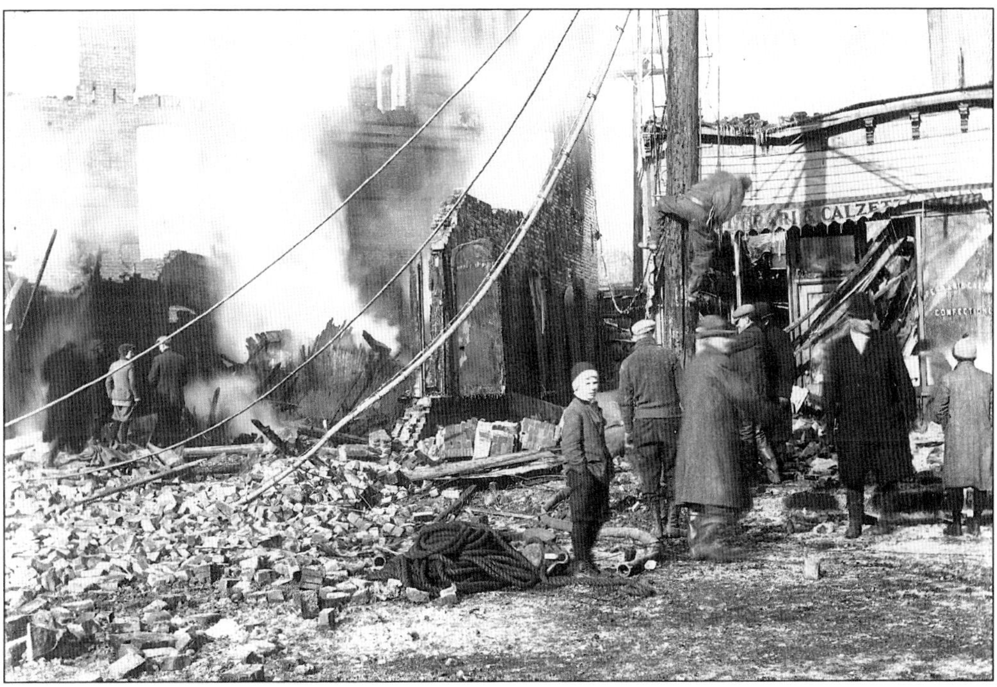

INSPECTING THE RUBBLE, 1912. Onlookers watch linemen at work and walk through the smoking ruins of the Opera House Block in February 1912. The heavily damaged Ferrari & Calzetta Confectioner shop is on the right, the first store on the west side of North Union Avenue. The Opera House Block was replaced by the Cranford Trust Company Block, which dominates downtown Cranford today.

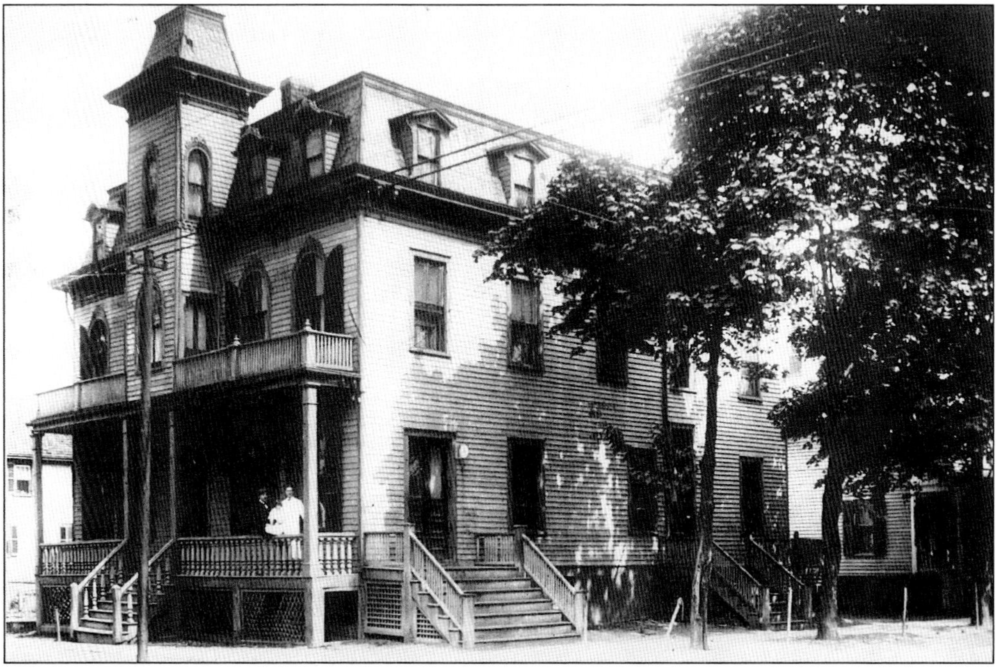

THE CENTRAL HOTEL IN 1880. Built about 1875, the hotel stood on the southeast corner of Walnut and South Avenues, where United Counties Trust Company now stands. The Central was famed for its large and convivial barroom. In the early 1900s manager Joseph Ehrhardt offered electric fans, a piano, and a ladies' parlor. The hotel was torn down in 1929.

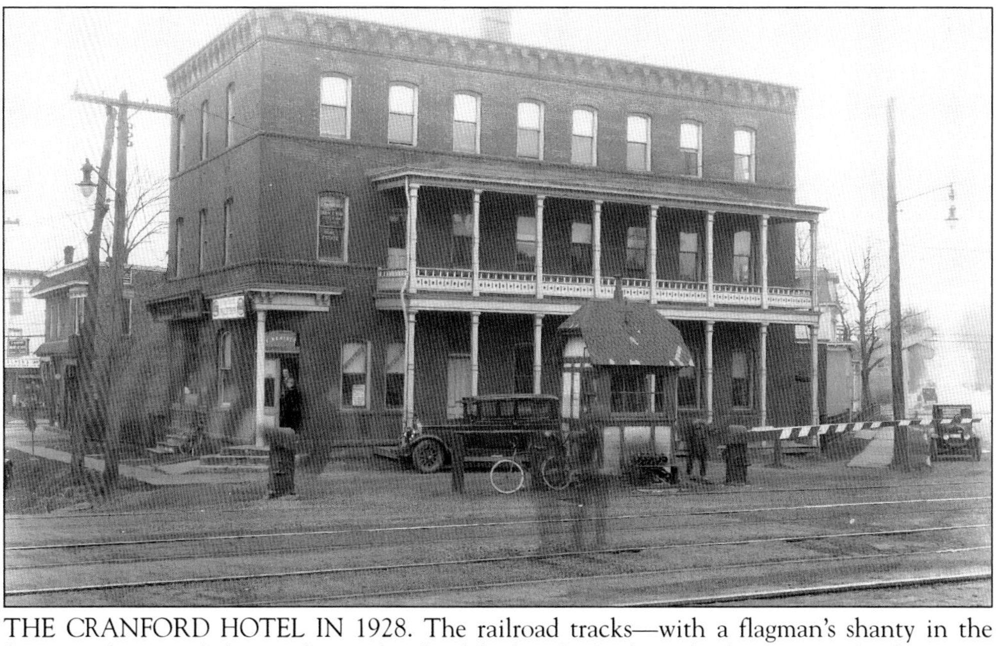

THE CRANFORD HOTEL IN 1928. The railroad tracks—with a flagman's shanty in the foreground—passed close to the north side of the hotel, which was built in 1892–93. The corner entrance leads to the shop of F. Kantner, Upholsterer, and the doorway on the Walnut Avenue side is for Peninsular Paints and Varnish. The left corner of the second floor houses the real estate office of Frank B. Ham.

CRANFORD'S POST OFFICE STAFF, *c.* 1895. The post office was located in the Opera House Block on North Avenue, between Eastman Street and North Union Avenue. From left to right are: Letter Carrier Harry Crane, Postmaster John L. Derby, Asst. Postmaster John C. Crane, Letter Carrier Walter Reinhart, and Township Tax Collector T.A. Crane.

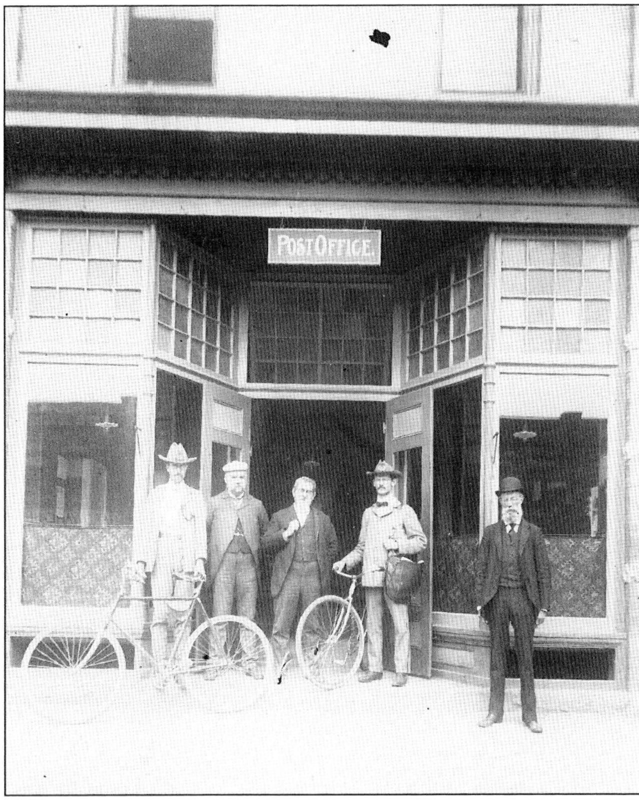

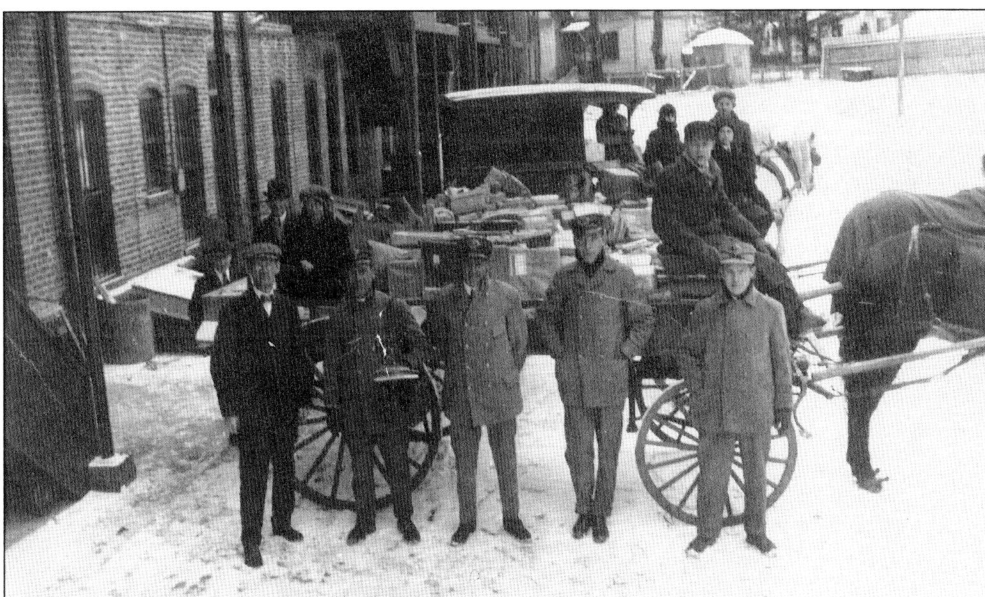

POSTAL WORKERS, DECEMBER 1917. Uniformed mail carriers and their junior helpers stand in the snow at the rear entrance to the post office before starting out to deliver the Christmas mail. There were no trucks or jeeps. Each carrier had to hire his own horse and wagon for delivery.

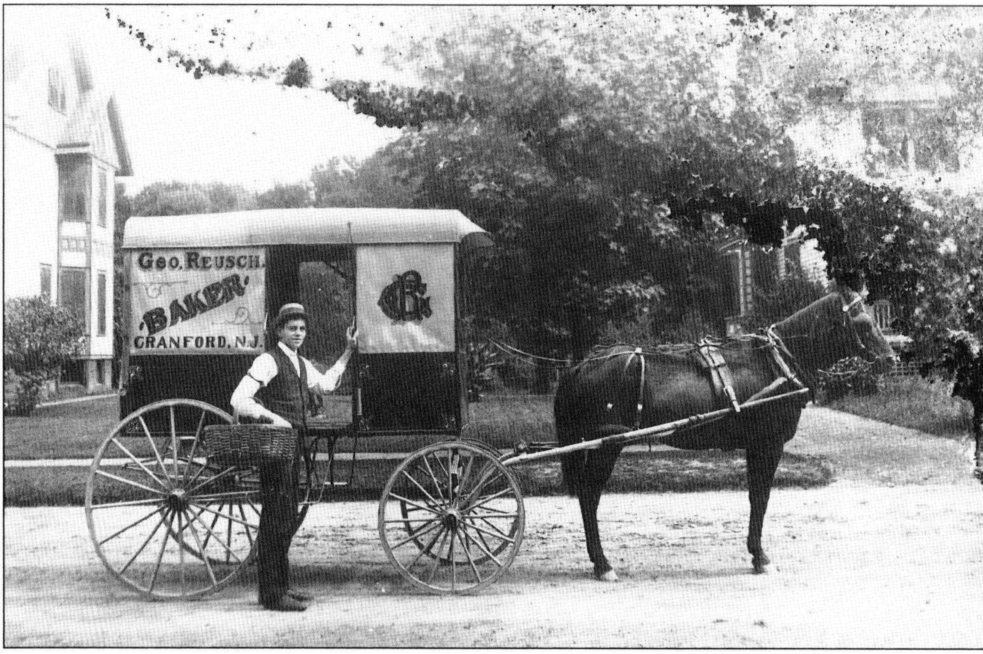

THE "PIEMAN" VISITS CENTRAL AVENUE, *c.* 1910. Edward Reusch stands next to his father's bakery wagon while delivering goodies to the Montenecourt house on Central Avenue. The Reusch Bakery was located at 17 Eastman Street.

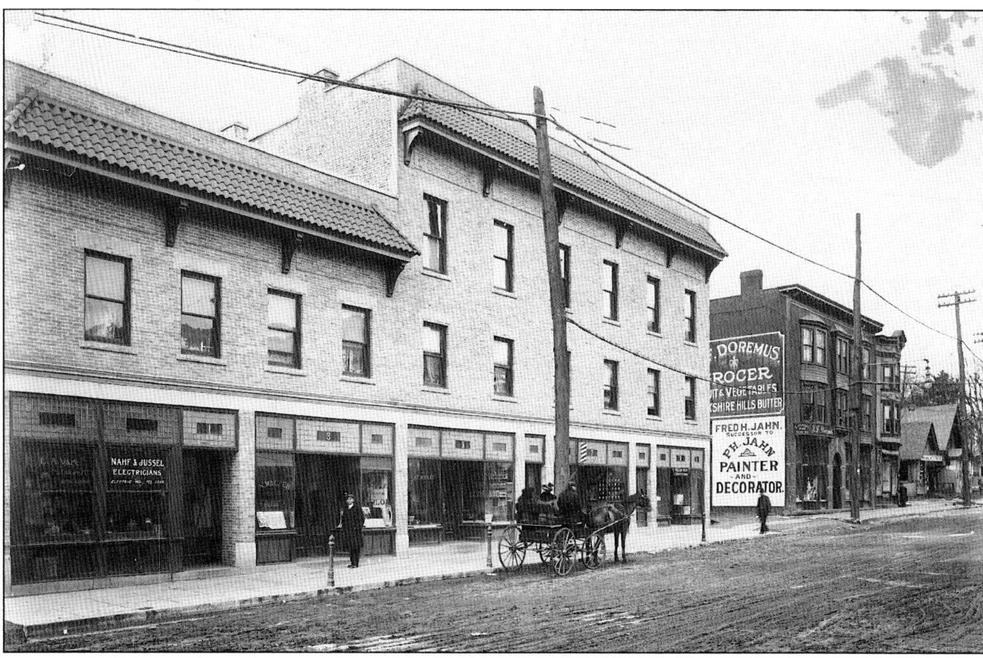

EASTMAN STREET, *c.* 1910. Hitching posts line the dirt street named for a Cranford developer. Businesses along the block included L.A. Vare Paintcraft, Nahf & Jussel Electricians, N. Magzen Tailor, J.E. Miller Fruit & Vegetables, a barber shop, William Islieb Plumbing, J.F. Doremus Groceries, and Philip Jahn, painter and decorator. The peaked-roof building at the far right served as the township offices.

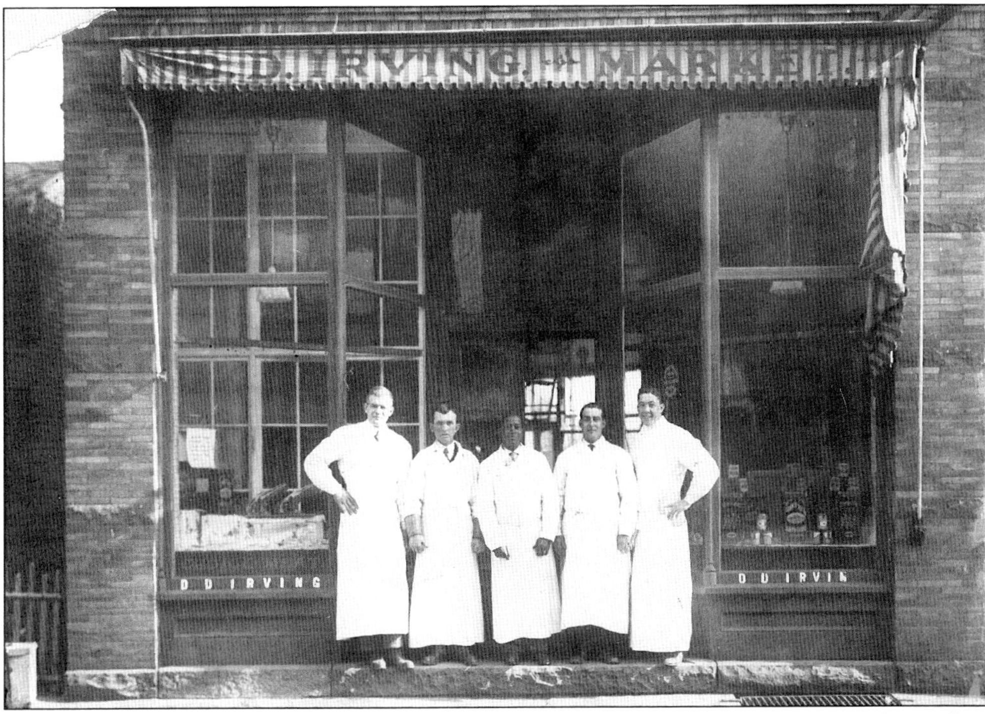

THE D.D. IRVING MARKET IN 1910. The five-man staff poses in front of their shop selling "Choice Meats and Provisions" at No. 1 Opera House Block, near the corner of North Union and North Avenues. J.N. Irving opened the market in 1872, and it was carried on by his son David.

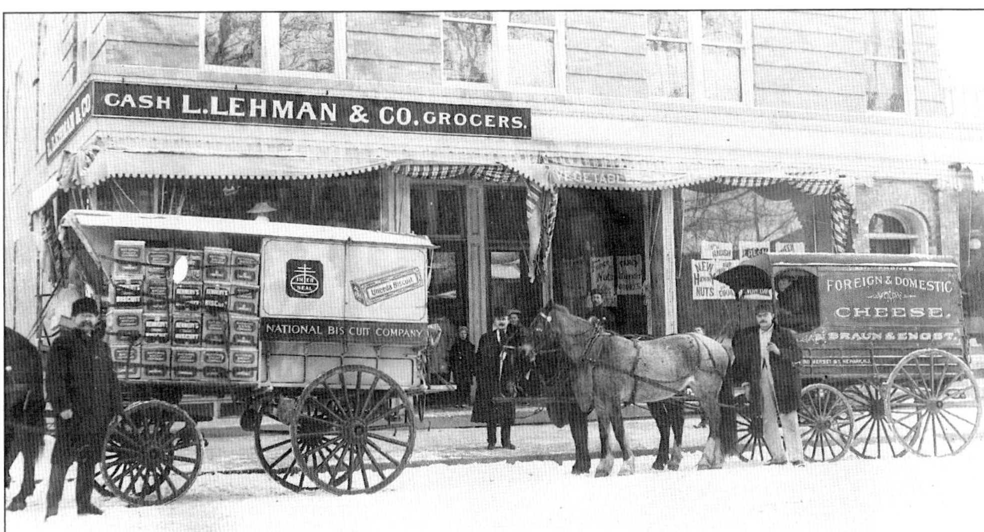

DELIVERIES ON A COLD WINTER MORNING, 1910. The Nabisco wagon and the Braun & Engst cheese wagon from Newark have arrived at L. Lehman & Co., "cash grocers," in the Masonic Building on the corner of North Union Avenue and Alden Street. Specials advertised in Lehman's windows included horseradish and new hickory nuts. Today, the old Masonic Building houses a fitness center, an ice cream parlor, and a beauty salon.

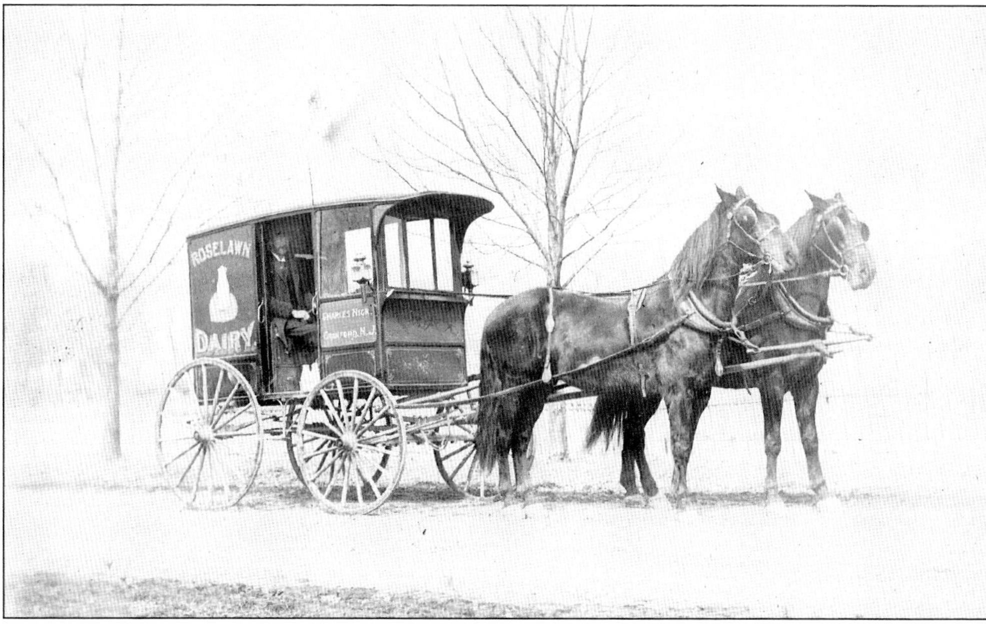

CHARLES NICK IN HIS DAIRY WAGON, *c.* 1895. Nick operated the Roselawn Dairy out of his house on North Avenue East from 1891 until 1898. The house was razed years later to make way for the Garden State Parkway exit ramp.

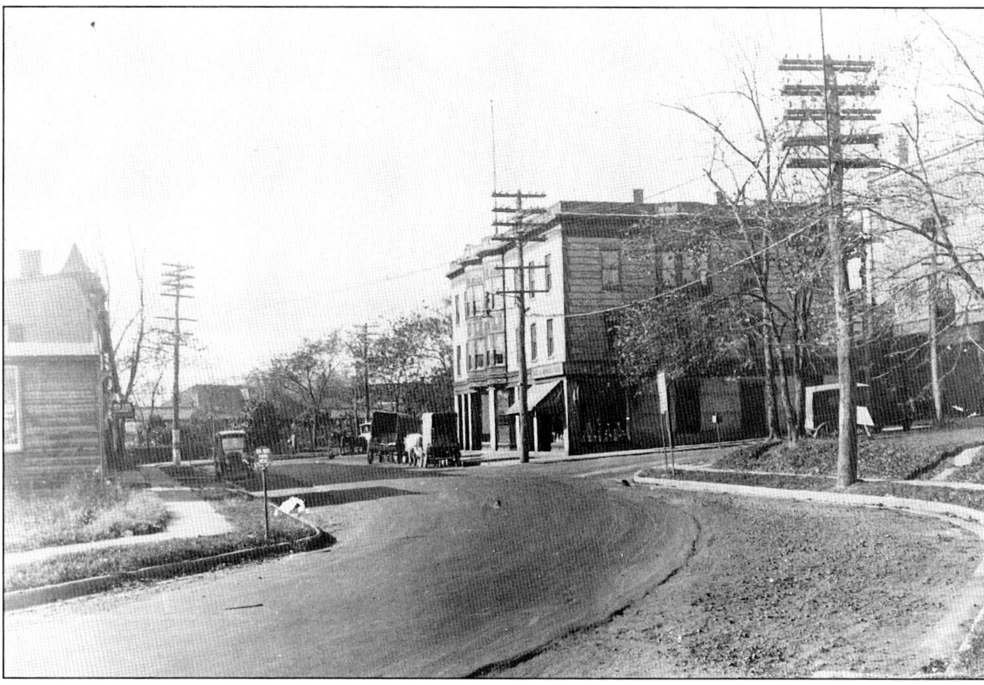

NORTH AVENUE EAST AT ALDEN STREET, 1922. A "tin lizzie" and several horse-drawn delivery wagons are parked along North Avenue in this view looking west. At the far bend in the road on the left is the Wo Lee Laundry, long a fixture in downtown Cranford at different locations. Street signs were quite specific at this time. The one on the corner to the left-center of the picture reads "Do Not Park Here."

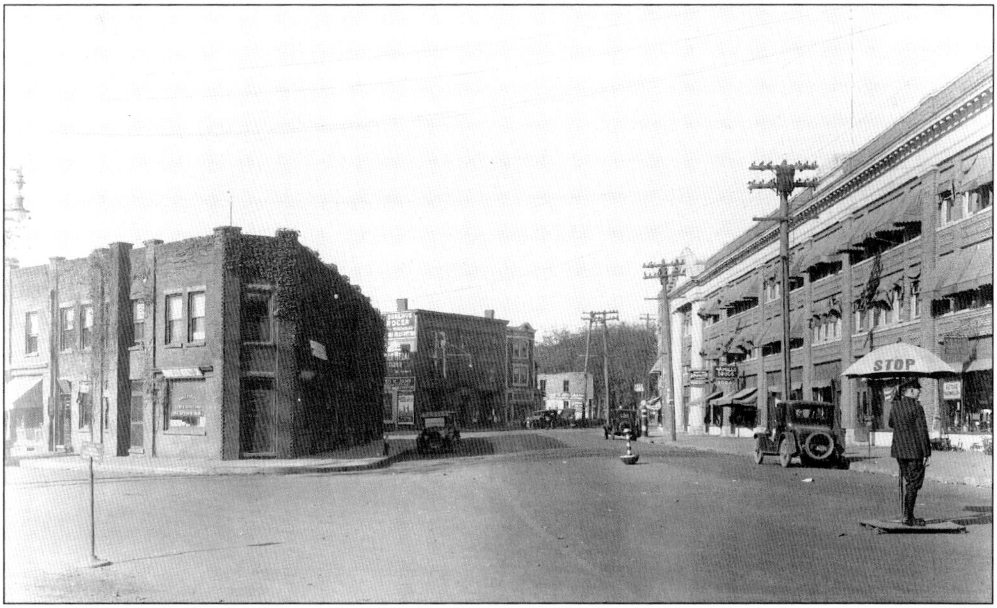

THE INTERSECTION OF NORTH AND NORTH UNION AVENUES, OCTOBER 21, 1922. Officer James Galvin rotated his "Stop-Go" umbrella to control the heavy traffic. The Potter or Chronicle Building on the left (Eastman Plaza today) was torn down a month after this picture was taken. Some of the stores on the right included Reze Shoes, an automotive store, Apollo Drugs, and the A.C. Pike Hardware Company.

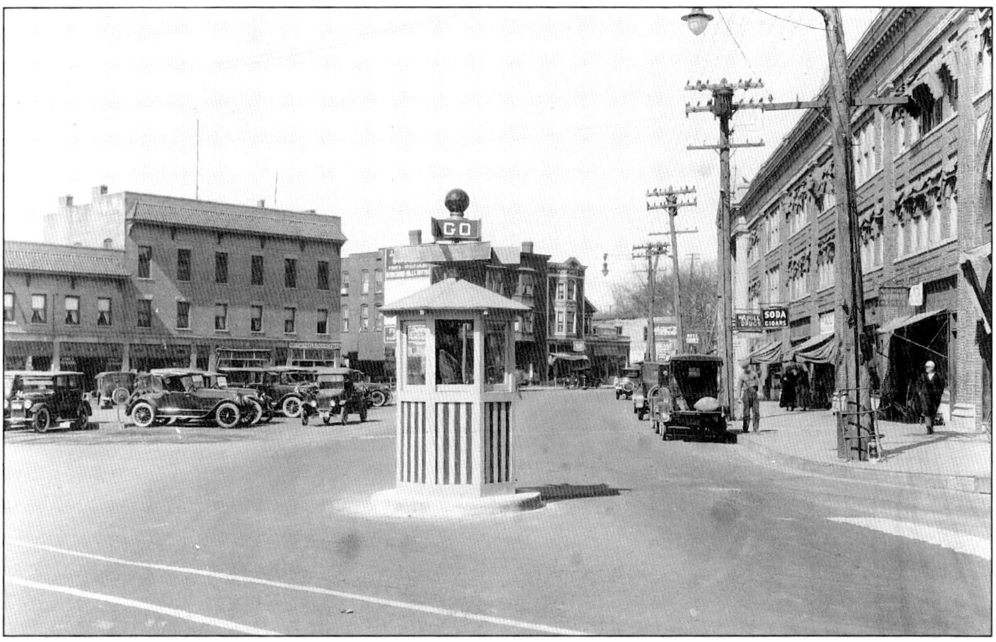

"THE GREEN LIGHT HOTEL," 1924. Officer John J. McNerney signals "go" from the brand new traffic box set squarely in the middle of the intersection of North and North Union Avenues. Today's Eastman Plaza is at the left. Because the shanty provided shelter for the police, it was immediately dubbed "The Green Light Hotel." It was quickly decided that the location of the "hotel" was unsafe, so it was moved toward the southwest corner.

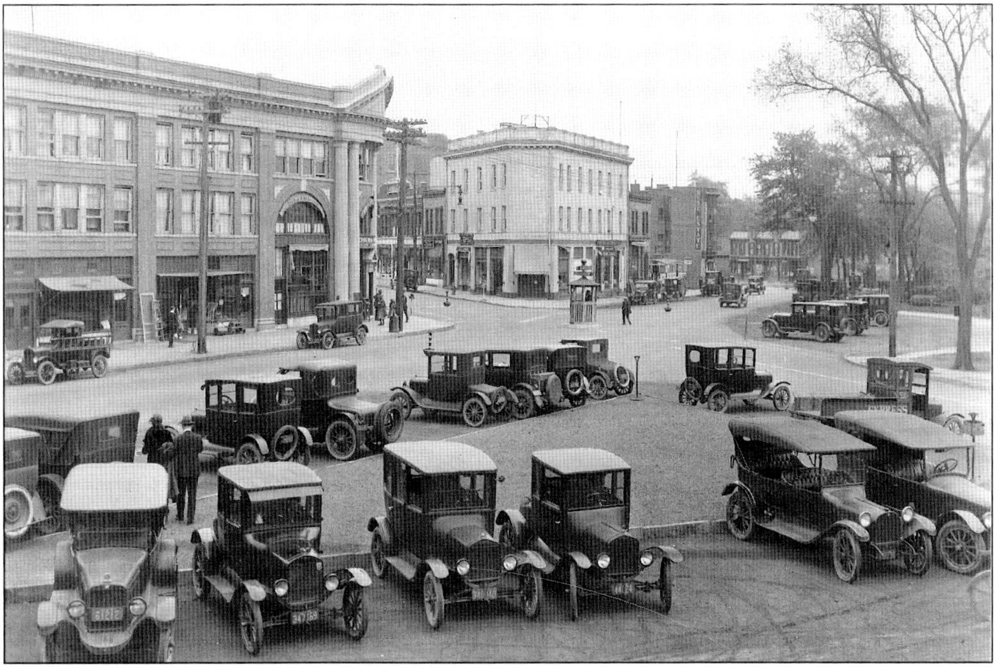

THE CENTRAL BUSINESS DISTRICT, 1924. "Flivers" and "tin lizzies" are parked at the triangle intersection of North Union and North Avenues with Eastman Street, site of Eastman Plaza today. The Cranford Trust Building in the background on the left replaced the Opera House Block after the great fire of 1912.

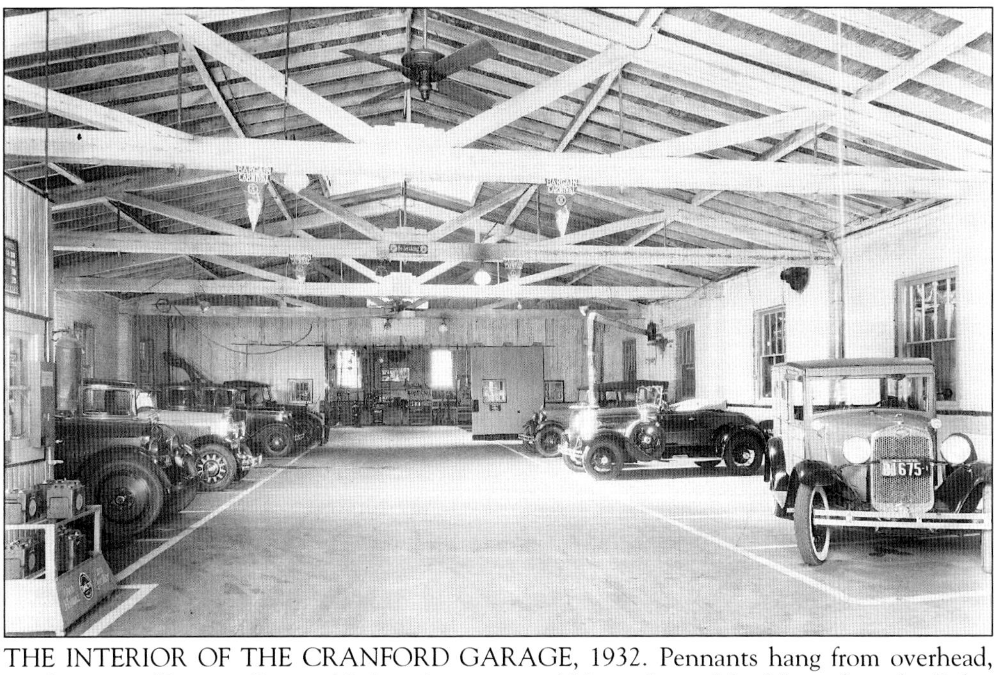

THE INTERIOR OF THE CRANFORD GARAGE, 1932. Pennants hang from overhead, proclaiming a "Bargain Carnival." Auto batteries could be recharged for 25¢ each at the Delco battery charger at the left of the picture. The vehicle in the right foreground is a "woody" station wagon with roll-up side-curtains. The garage was located at 31 North Avenue.

ONE OF CRANFORD'S LAST BLACKSMITHS, 1928. One of a vanishing breed of craftsmen, blacksmith Balthazar Joseph Eichinger, better known as "BJ," stands in front of his shop, which specialized in "Spring Service" for automobiles and wagons. BJ's shop stood on the northwest corner of Chestnut and High Streets.

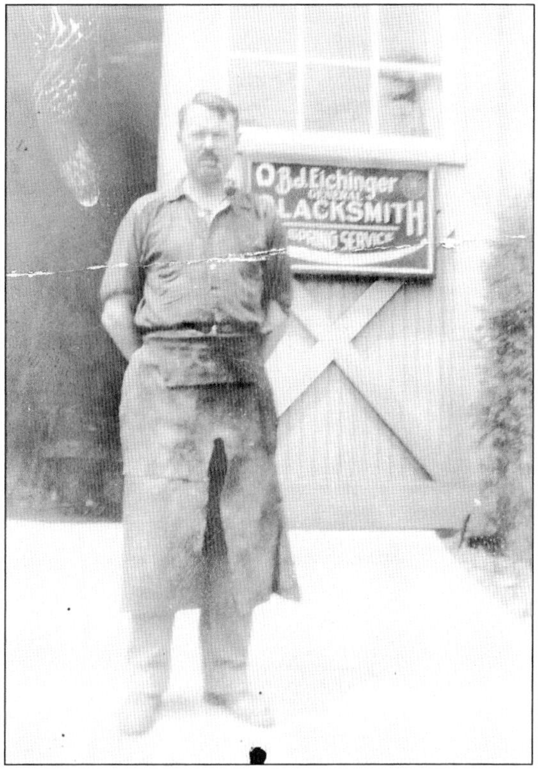

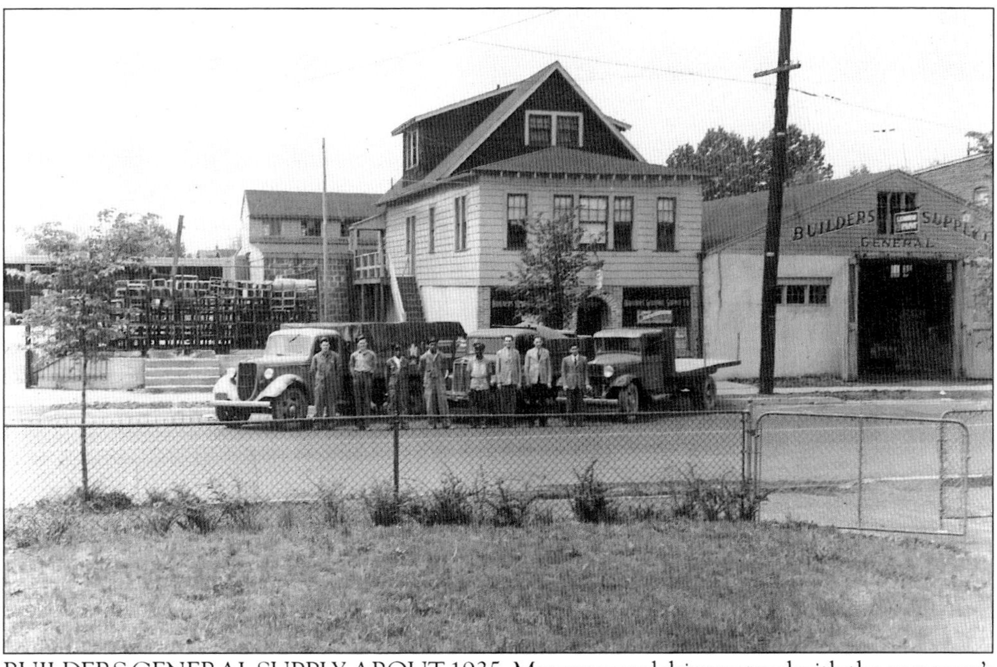

BUILDERS GENERAL SUPPLY ABOUT 1935. Managers and drivers stand with the company's three trucks in front of a much smaller Builders General Supply, a business started in 1932 by S.A. Shaheen. At the time this picture was taken the company had just added a home-planning service, an optimistic move in the midst of the Great Depression.

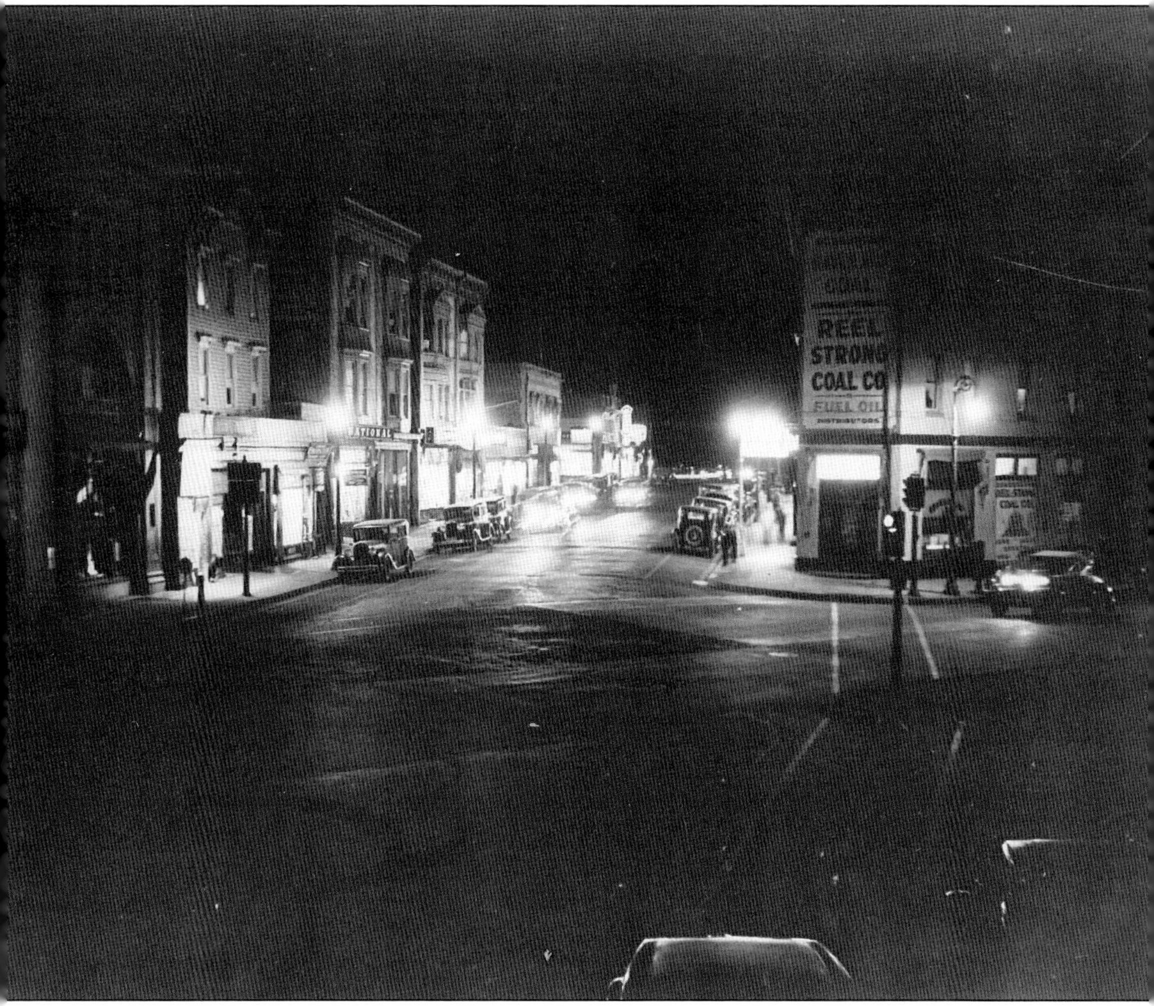

AN EVENING DOWNTOWN, 1935. This is the way the intersection of North Avenue and North Union Avenue, the heart of Cranford, looked on a night sixty years ago. Except for the automobiles, the scene is not much different from today. In addition to the offices of the Reel-Strong Coal Company (on the corner at right), other businesses along North Union Avenue at this time included the Cranford Cleaners, National Cigar & Stationery, Cranford Cut-Rate Drugs, Klein's Delicatessen, the Cranford Window Shade Co., the Cranford Flower Shoppe, Speeds Auto Store, and the Cut Rate Barber Shop. In 1986 Cranford became the first municipality in the state of New Jersey to create a Special Improvement District (SID) in order to improve, upgrade, and maintain its downtown area. A Downtown Management Corporation (DMC) oversees this work.

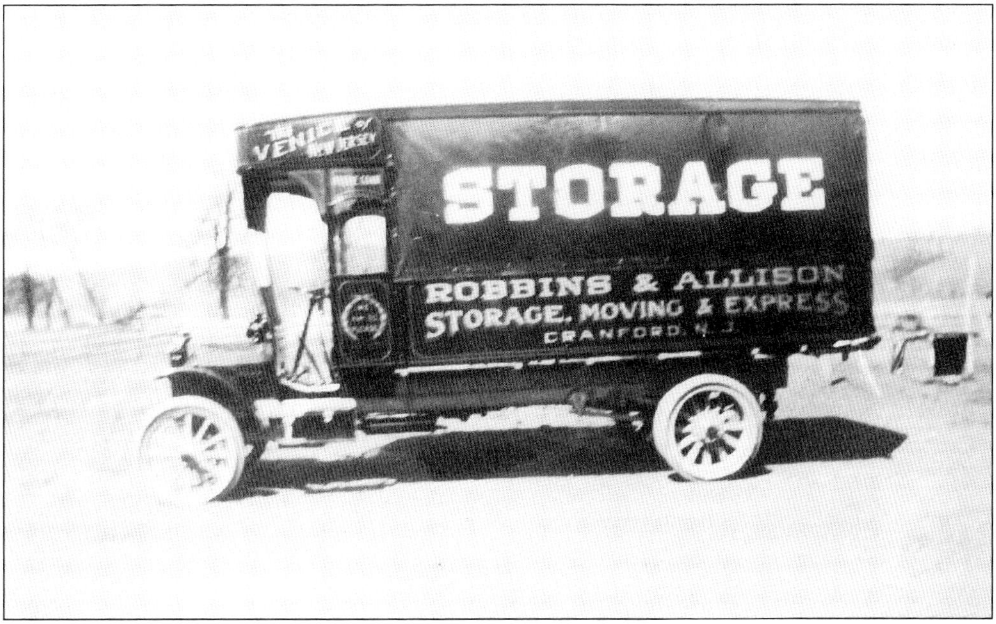

A ROBBINS & ALLISON MOVING VAN, 1924. A canvas and isinglass windscreen protected the driver in the open cab of this van. On the side of the cab is a wreath with the words "We Aim To Please." Cranford's famous motto, "The Venice of New Jersey," is also lettered on the truck.

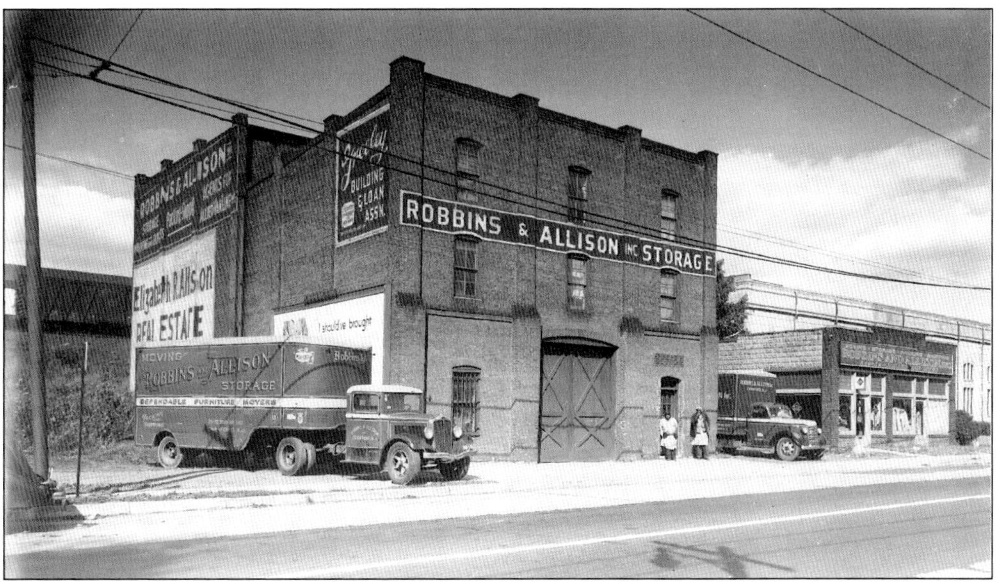

ROBBINS & ALLISON INC., 1945. This landmark business in Cranford is still located at 213 South Avenue East. Two of their distinctive orange moving vans can be seen. The company's office, to the right of the brick warehouse, has served in recent years as headquarters for the Chamber of Commerce and the Downtown Management Corporation. In the background on the right is the old South Avenue trolley power house.

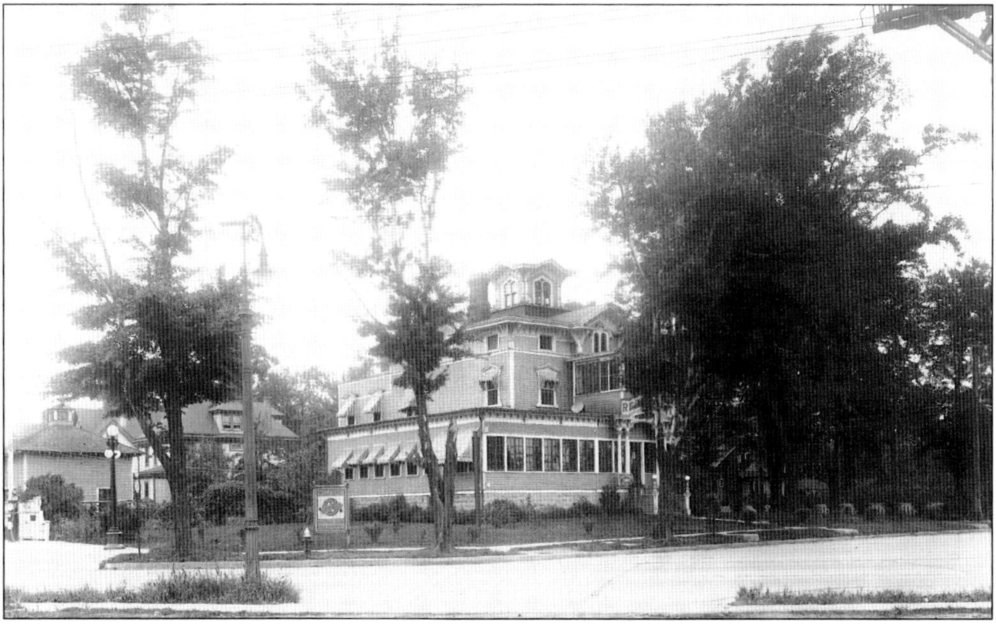

HAYASHI'S RESTAURANT, 1934. F.M. Hayashi operated Cranford's largest and most popular restaurant, at the intersection of Miln Street and North Avenue West, the site of today's post office. The restaurant was built by expanding the former home of Dr. J.K. MacConnell, the township physician in the late nineteenth century.

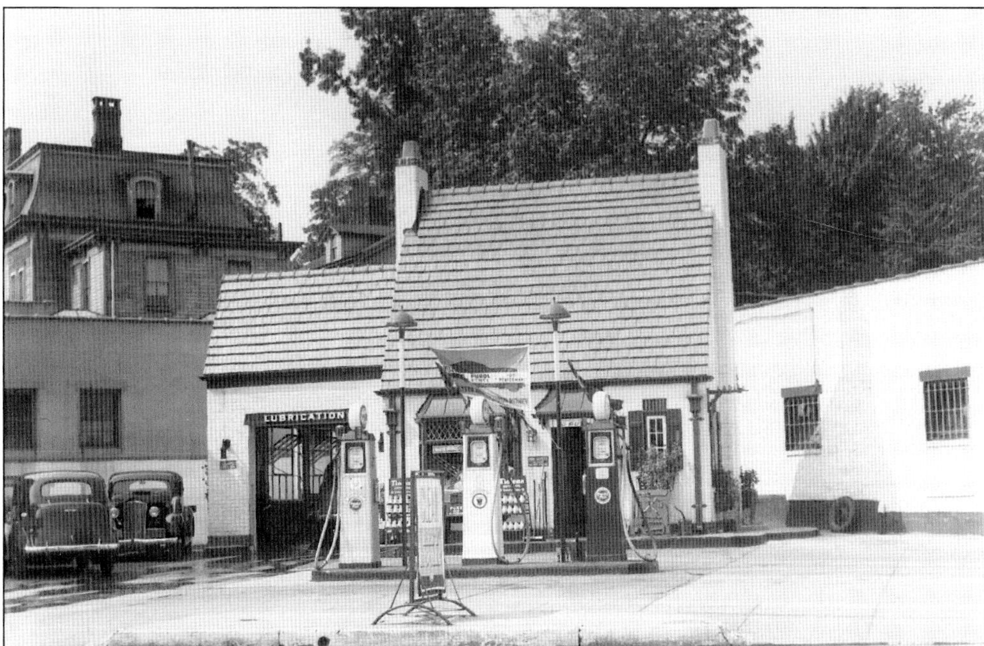

THE PUROL SERVICE STATION, *c.* 1940. This little brick cottage gas station had a tile roof, wood-shuttered windows, and a single repair bay. Three grades of "Super-Solvenized" Purol Pep gasoline were offered, as well as Tiolene Motor Oil and "Clean Rest Rooms." Still at 24 North Avenue, the cottage is today a hairdresser's salon.

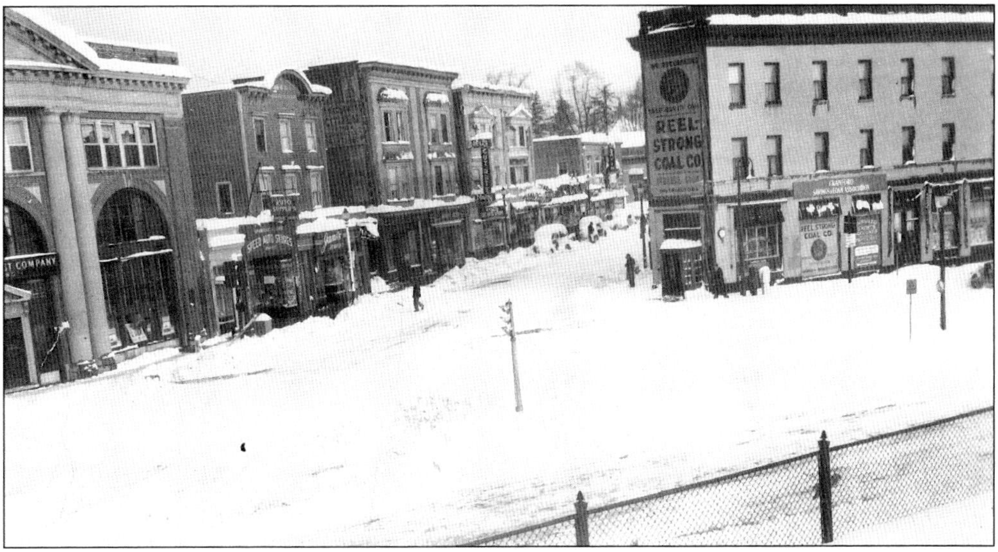

DOWNTOWN INTERSECTION, DECEMBER 27, 1947. The intersection of North Avenue and North Union Avenue at 11:00 am, two days after Christmas. The snow reached 26 inches on the level that morning. The Blizzard of '47 dumped more snow than the famed Blizzard of 1888. The Reel-Strong Coal Company and the Cranford Savings and Loan Association occupied the corner offices on the right.

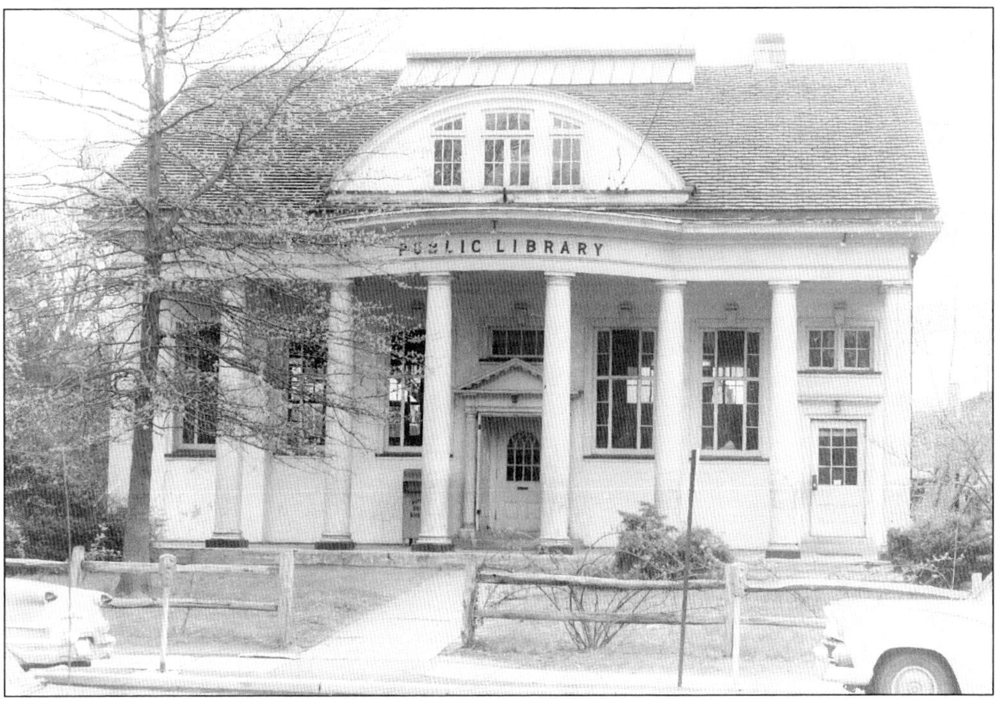

THE CRANFORD PUBLIC LIBRARY IN 1961. Located on the south side of Miln Street, midway between Alden and Eastman, the public library presented a striking appearance with its eight Doric columns. Built with a Carnegie grant in 1910, it did not follow the usual architectural pattern of Carnegie libraries. The building was razed in 1962, and the site is now a parking lot. The new public library is located at 224 Walnut Avenue.

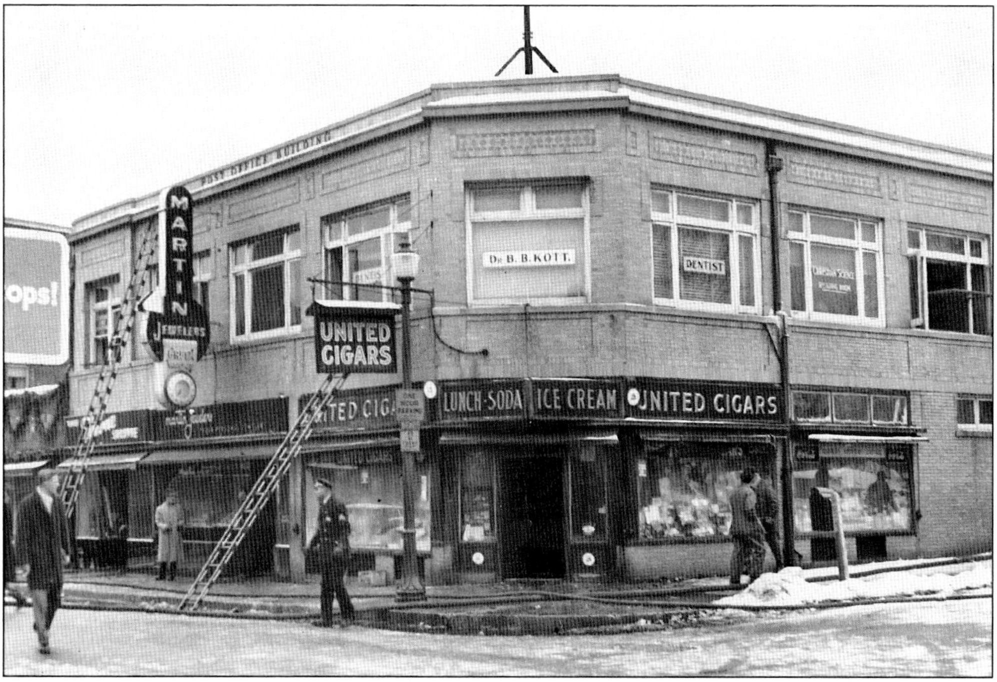

A FIRE IN THE OLD POST OFFICE BUILDING, JANUARY 23, 1948. The fire in this building on the southwest corner of North Union Avenue and Alden Street caused $100,000 in damage. The police officer in the scene is Sergeant Lester Powell. Businesses in the building at this time included Martin Jewelers, the United Cigar store, Dr. B.B. Kott (dentist), and the Christian Science Reading Room.

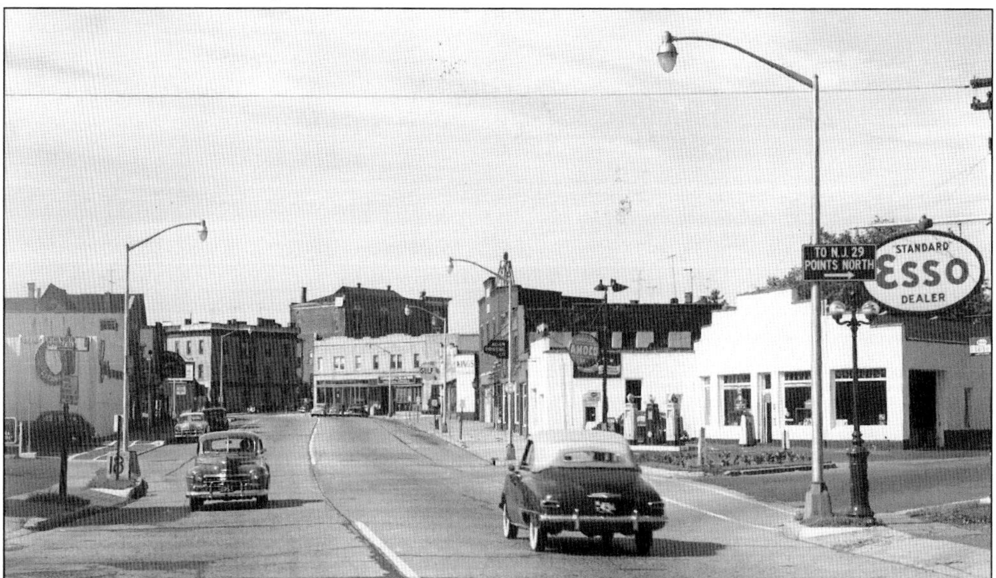

NORTH AVENUE EAST AT SPRINGFIELD AVENUE, 1950. Several of these businesses are in the same location today, including Swan Cleaners and Marino's Sea Food Market. Gasoline at this time was selling for 18.9¢ a gallon. The two-story building in the center background of the picture housed the township offices. Notice the absence of traffic.

Five

School Daze

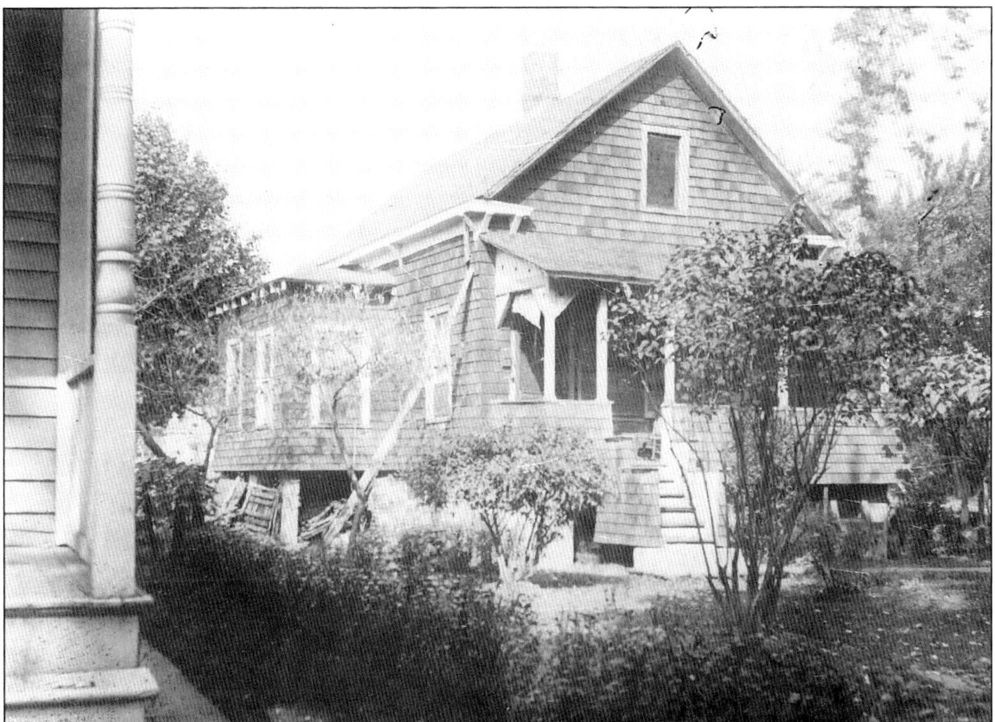

THE OLD RED SCHOOLHOUSE ABOUT 1910. This nondescript building was formerly Cranford's schoolhouse, built in 1805. According to tradition, it was the third school to stand at what is now the corner of Lincoln and South Union Avenues. It was a model schoolhouse for its day, measuring 16-by-24 feet, with four windows on each side. The students sat on slab benches. The school continued in use until 1867, and the building was also used for the occasional religious service. The schoolhouse was then moved to Grove Street, where it became a home. It was razed in 1945.

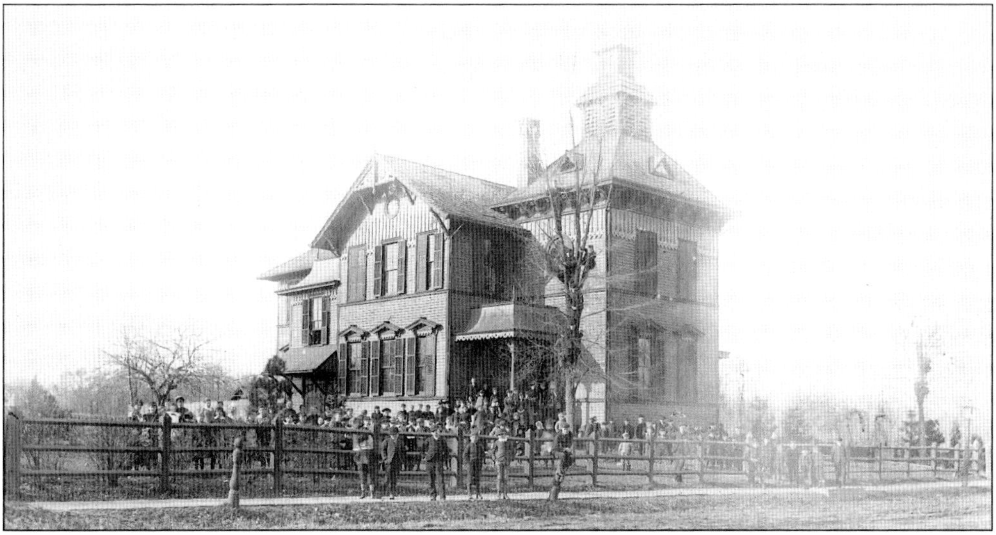

GRANT SCHOOL IN 1884. School's out and the kids are even in the trees in this view of the first of two Grant schools, built 1869–70. Listed as Public School No. 1, this was Cranford's first official district school. The ornate, wooden eight-room building was razed in 1898. It stood on the corner of Holly Street and Springfield Avenue, which was also the site of the second, brick Grant School.

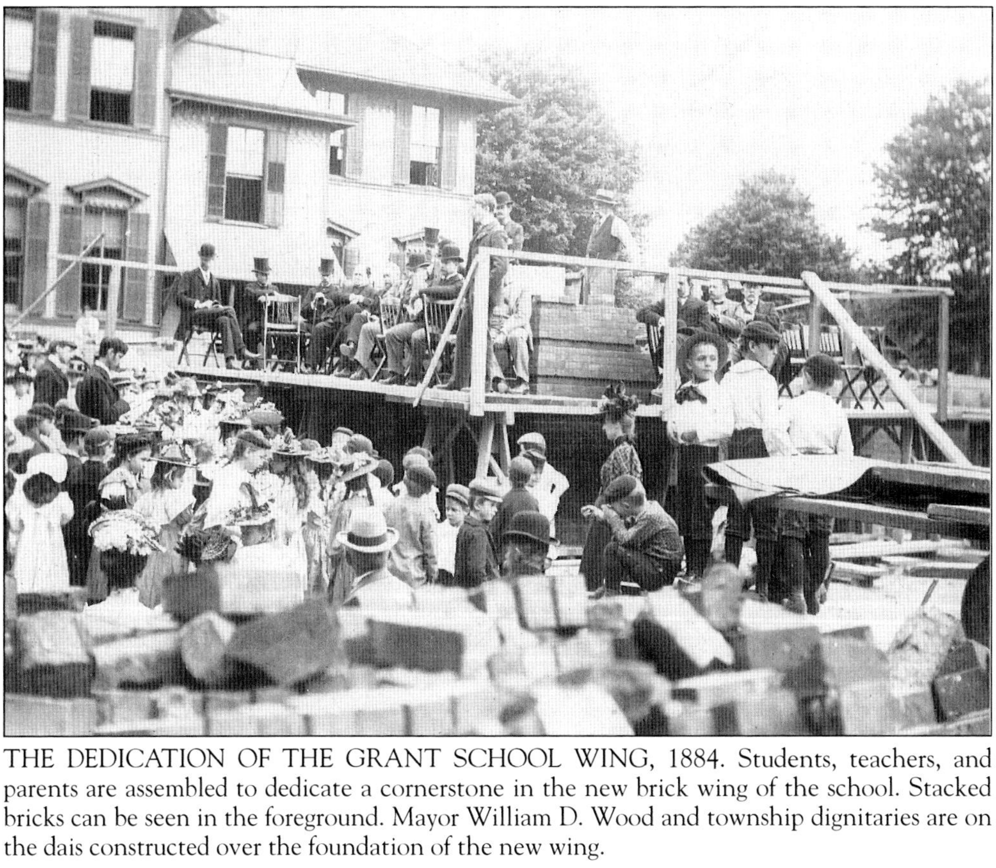

THE DEDICATION OF THE GRANT SCHOOL WING, 1884. Students, teachers, and parents are assembled to dedicate a cornerstone in the new brick wing of the school. Stacked bricks can be seen in the foreground. Mayor William D. Wood and township dignitaries are on the dais constructed over the foundation of the new wing.

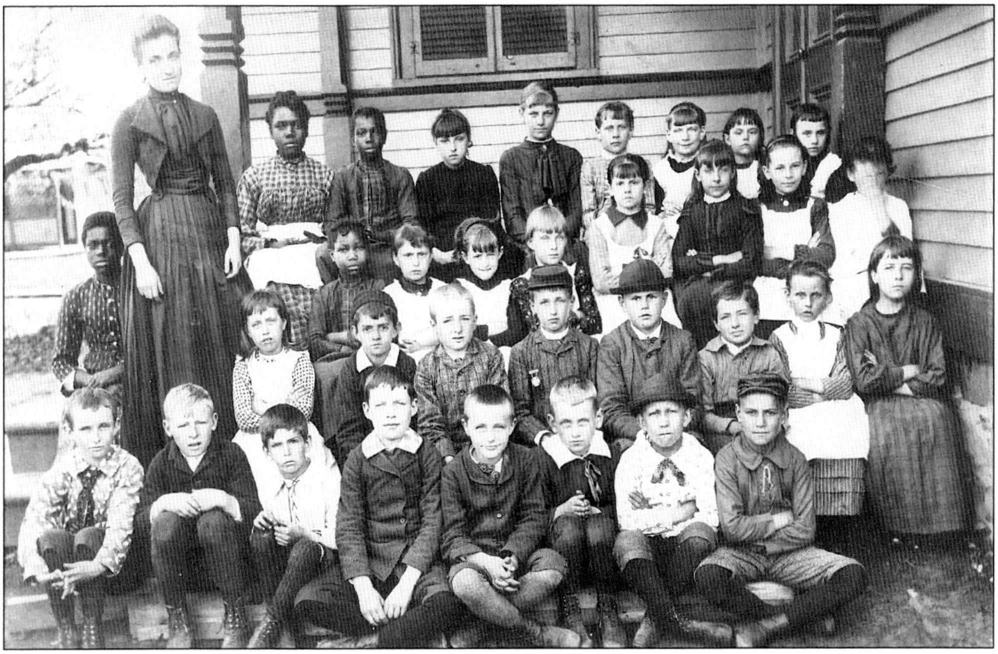

MRS. McFARLAND'S CLASS, 1890. Thirty-three scholars in this mixed-age class are gathered on the front porch of Grant School. Mrs. McFarland is standing on the left. A boy in the center of the second row from the bottom is wearing a Civil War-style kepi and what is probably a marksmanship badge (his father's?). This group is somewhat less formally dressed than the group in the photograph below.

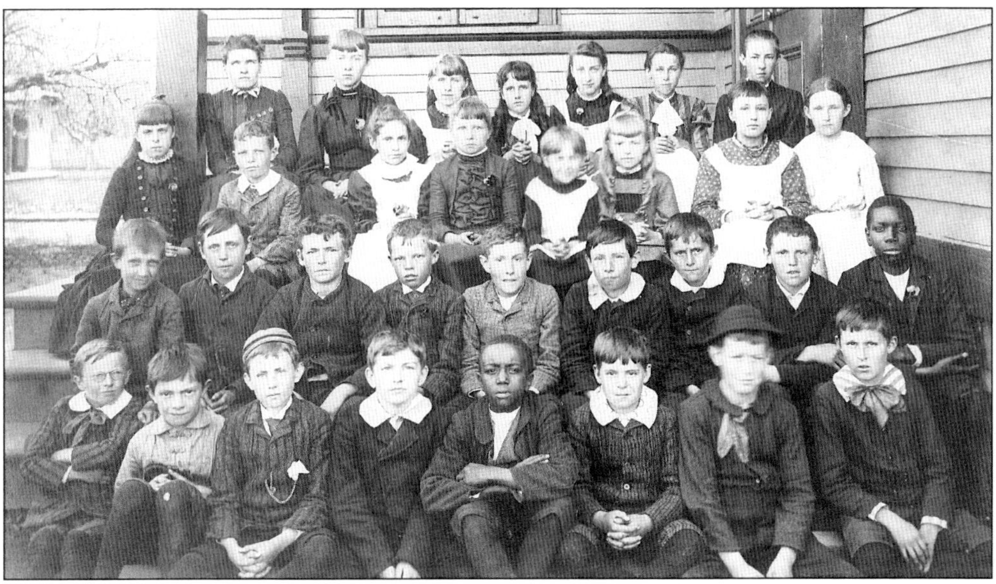

ON THE PORCH OF GRANT SCHOOL, *c.* 1895. The thirteen girls and eighteen boys in this picture also seem to be of different ages. At least eight of the children are wearing a flower on their dress or jacket, and they are all dressed up, leading one to suspect that this was a special occasion. The teacher can be seen in the top row on the left.

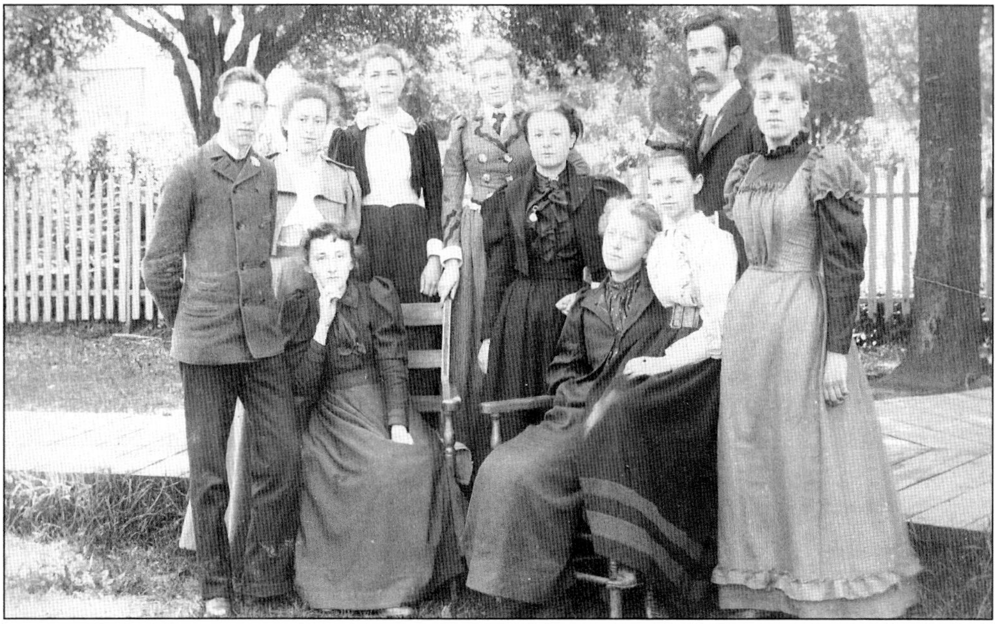

THE LONE MAN, 1894. The solitary male in the nearly all-female graduating class of 1894 was Ed Maroney, on the left. The gentleman on the right was the teaching principal, Richard Clement. This photograph was taken outside Grant School on May 29, 1894. Notice the boardwalk behind the group.

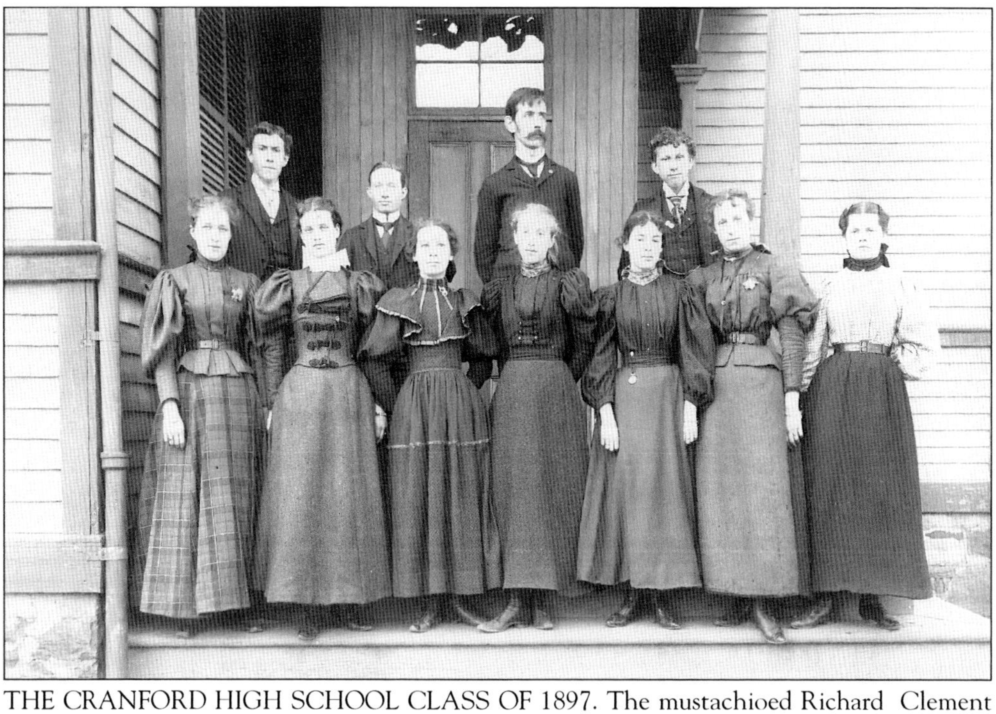

THE CRANFORD HIGH SCHOOL CLASS OF 1897. The mustachioed Richard Clement poses with his ten-member class, only half of whom graduated. From left to right are: (front row) M.J. Smock, C.D. Nix, M.E. Littell, M.K. Dohrman, L.E. Taylor, Virginia Marcus, and F.E. Peterson; (back row) C.R. Cox, William Howell, Clement, and William Becker.

SPECIAL

School Meeting

NOTICE IS HEREBY GIVEN, That a Special Meeting of the legal voters of the TOWNSHIP OF CRANFORD will be held at the

OPERA HOUSE,

in the VILLAGE OF CRANFORD, Union County, New Jersey, on the

12th Day of October, 1897,

at 8 o'clock P. M., for the purpose of considering and taking action upon the following propositions:

1st. A proposition to purchase a tract of land for a school site in said township on the south side of the Central Railroad of New Jersey, at a cost not exceeding $1,800.

Said proposed site described as follows: Being a tract of land 200 feet square, on the southerly side of Lincoln Avenue, opposite Grove Street, being part of a piece of property owned by Mrs. Mary R. Matthews.

2d. To accept a site for a school house in said township, on the south side of the Central Railroad of New Jersey, offered as a gift by F. E. C. Winckler,

being lots Nos. 20 and 21 on a map entitled, "Map of Oakwood, Cranford, N. J., 1896, surveyed by F. B. Ham," lying on the southwesterly side of Woodlawn Avenue, as laid down on said map, said lots being each 33 feet front and rear, and 197 feet deep, and to purchase lots Nos. 18, 19, 22 and 23 on said map, of about the same dimensions, said lots adjoining lots Nos. 20 and 21 mentioned above, said lots Nos. 18, 19, 22 and 23 to be purchased at a cost not exceeding $100 each.

3d. A proposition to expend the sum of $1,600,

or so much thereof as may be necessary, in inclosing the school house on Springfield Avenue with brick.

4th. To authorize the Board of Education to borrow money and issue bonds therefor in a sum not exceeding $10,900,

to bear interest at a rate not exceeding 5 per cent., and for such period as the legal voters at the meeting may determine, for the following or any of the following purposes: 1st, To repair and improve the school house on Springfield Avenue, in pursuance of a resolution passed at the special school meeting held on the 12th of July last; 2d, To construct a Primary School building on the south side of the Central Railroad of New Jersey, in pursuance of a resolution passed at said special meeting, held on the 12th of July last; 3d, To purchase either of the sites for a school house on the south side of the railroad mentioned above; and 4th, To inclose the school house on Springfield Avenue with brick.

5th. A proposition to rescind and annul so much of the resolution adopted at the special school meeting held July 12, 1897,

as authorized the expenditure of not exceeding $4,000 in repairing plumbing and indirect heating and ventilating the present school house.

6th. A proposition to authorize the erection and furnishing of a new school building in place of the present building,

on the present site, corner Holly Street and Springfield Avenue, at a cost not exceeding $24,700.

7th. To authorize the Board of Education to borrow money and issue bonds of the district therefor in the corporate name of the district,

in such sums and in such amounts, not exceeding $30,000 in the aggregate, and payable at such times as the legal voters at the meeting may determine, with interest at a rate not exceeding five per cent. per annum, payable half yearly, for the following or any of the following purposes, viz: 1st, To purchase either of the sites for a school house on the south side of the Central Railroad of New Jersey, mentioned above, (at a cost not exceeding $1,800 for the more expensive site); 2d, To erect on the site thus selected, at a cost not exceeding $3,500, a school house for primary purposes, pursuant to the resolution adopted at the special school meeting held July 12, 1897; 3d, To erect and furnish a new school building in place of the present building on the present site, corner Holly Street and Springfield Avenue, at a cost not exceeding $24,700.

By Order of the Board of Education of the Township of Cranford,

Dated Cranford, N. J., Sept. 25, 1897.

F. N. BRUNDAGE, District Clerk.

A SCHOOL MEETING BROADSIDE, OCTOBER 12, 1897. Cranford had about 1,800 residents in 1897 and that meant a considerable number of children. The Board of Education announced this town meeting to consider a number of items, including "inclosing the school house on Springfield Avenue with brick." This was Grant School, which once stood at the corner of Holly Street and Springfield Avenue.

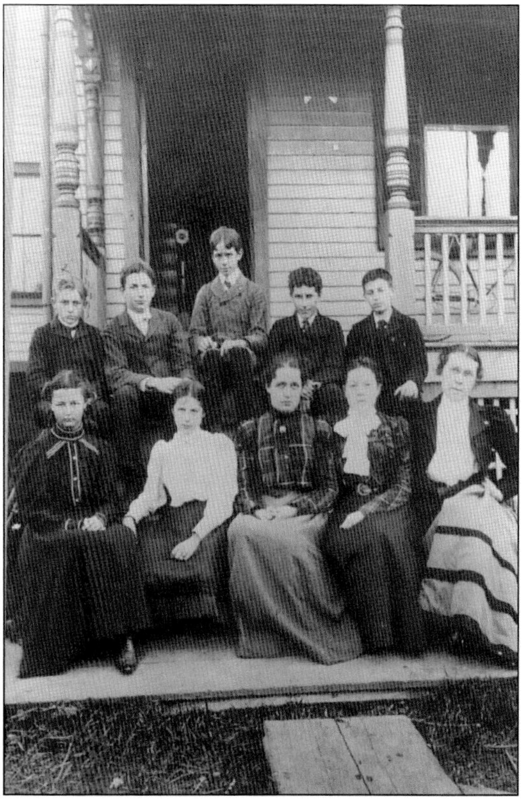

A CRANFORD HIGH SCHOOL CLASS, 1898. Miss Lutten (front row, right) sits with her class consisting of, from left to right: (front row) Marjorie Gilmore, Dolly Faitoute, Alice Vorhees, and Ethel Wood; (back row, looking much younger and smaller than their female counterparts) August Grube, Harry Swackhammer, Lester Ussing, Peter Jackson, and Alan Plume.

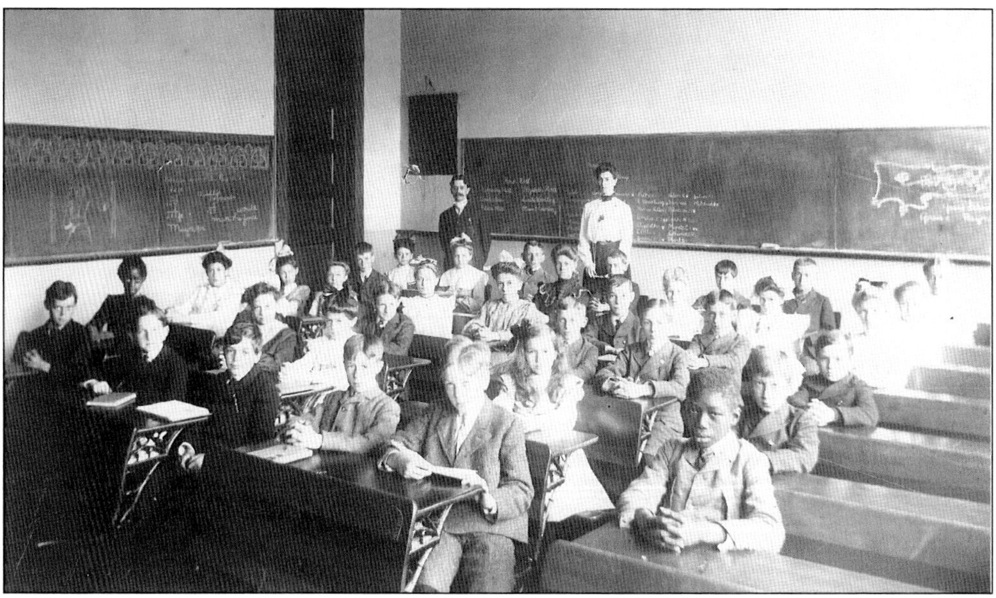

READIN', 'RITIN', AND 'RITHMETIC. These fifth graders sat, hands folded, for their formal class portrait in Grant School on May 12, 1903. Professor Wendell Thomas, the school principal, is in the back of the class with Miss Barnes, the teacher. Behind them on the blackboard are the names on the class honor roll: Katherine Hart, Amelia Klein, Rebecca Mix, Elizabeth Pierce, Lucille Woodling, and Stuart Connery.

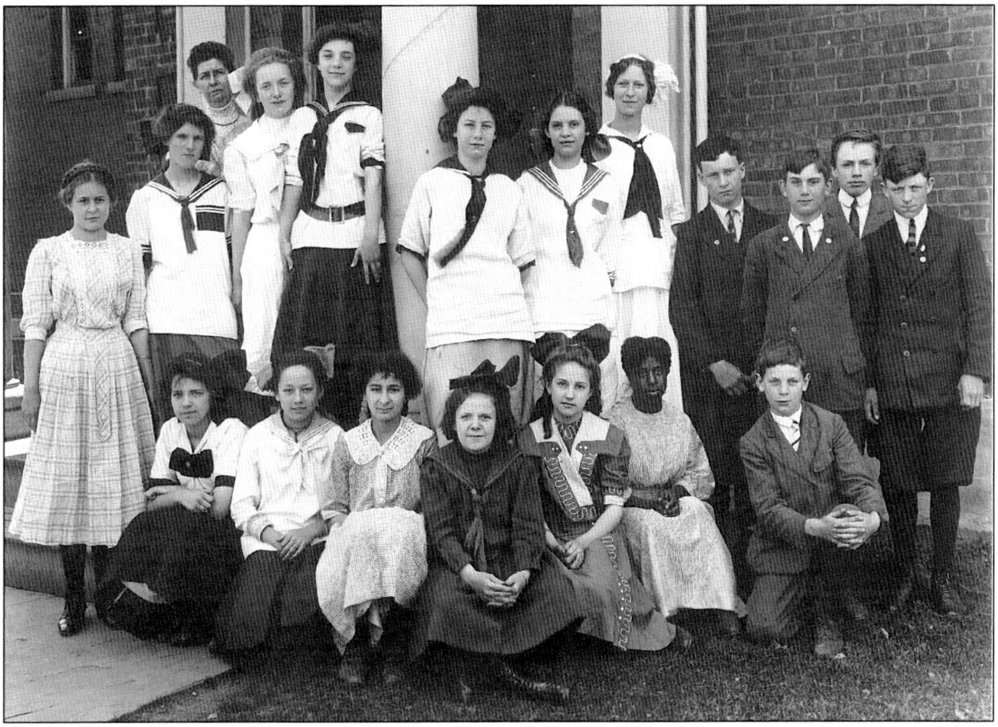

A CRANFORD HIGH SCHOOL CLASS, c. 1909. A class of thirteen girls and five boys in front of Grant School, which served as the high school. Obviously, white jumpers, middy blouses, and large bows for the hair were the rage among young ladies at the time.

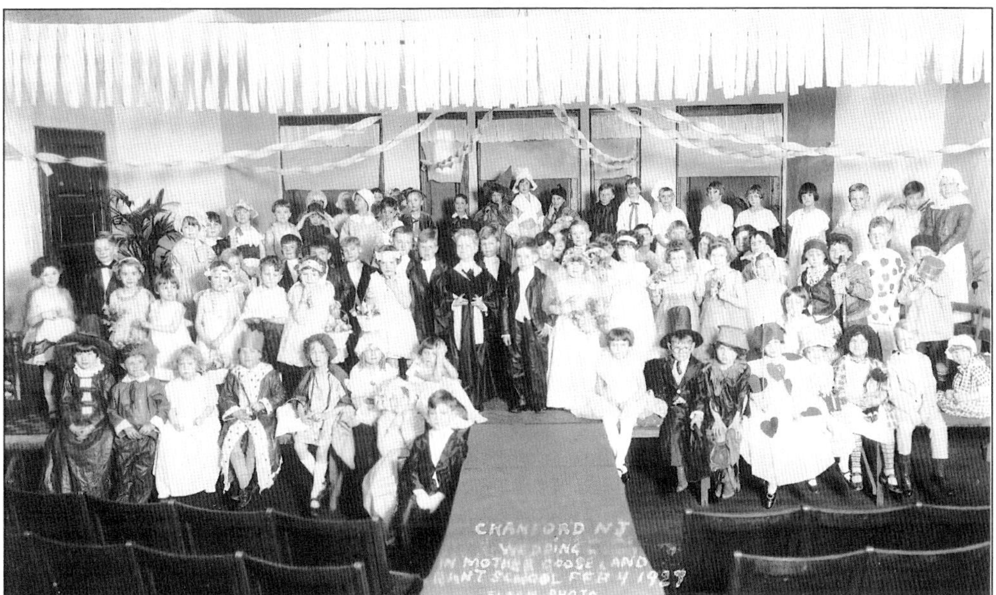

A "WEDDING IN MOTHER GOOSE LAND," FEBRUARY 4, 1927. This entertainment was given to raise funds for the purchase of a piano for the kindergarten at Grant School. This picture, which was placed in a box in the cornerstone of the school on February 8, 1927, was found in 1974, when the cornerstone was opened.

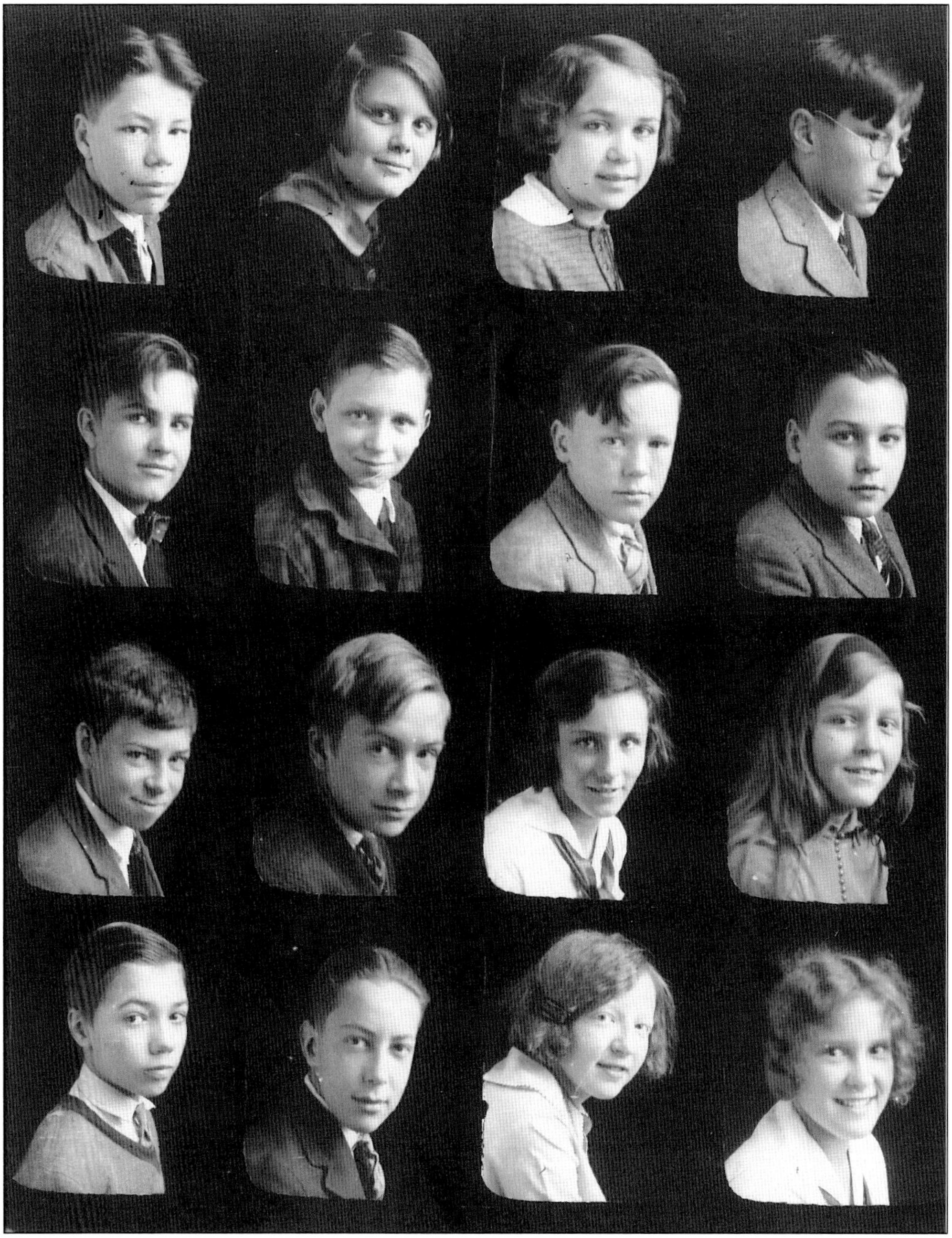

EIGHTH-GRADERS AT CLEVELAND SCHOOL, 1925. The faces of these young adolescents from the "Roaring Twenties" peer out at us from across a span of seventy years. Yet, time seems to stand still when one gazes at these eager, smiling youngsters. They look like schoolmates we all had back in the eighth grade.

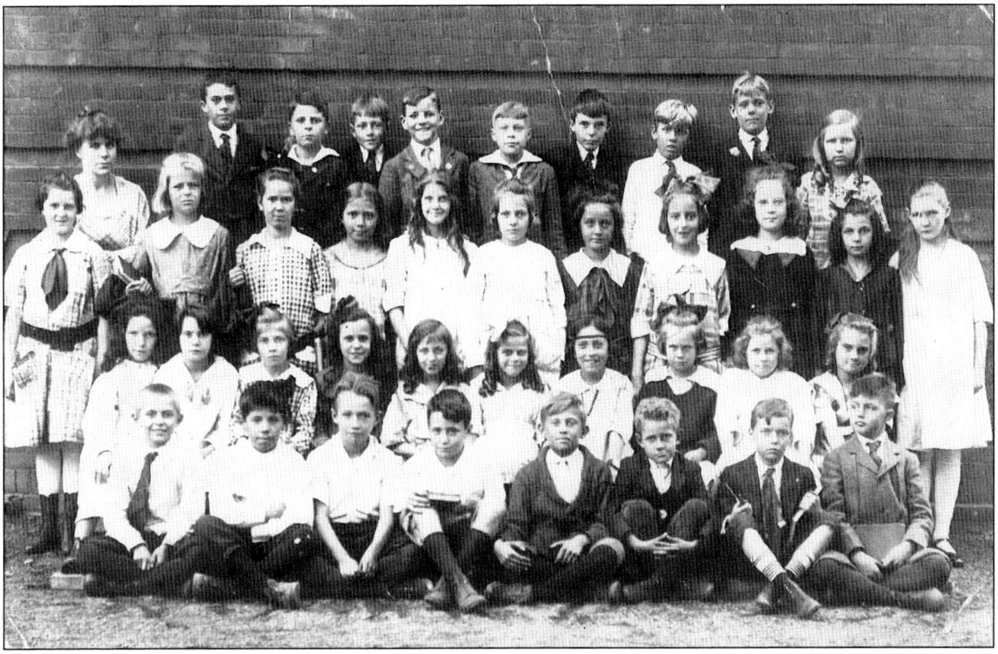

MISS COMSTOCK'S 5B CLASS, 1919. Miss Comstock (left) must have been proud of these well-dressed, well-scrubbed fifth graders at Grant School. As was the custom at the time, this class picture was made into a "real photo" postcard that could be sent to friends and relatives or kept at home in a family album.

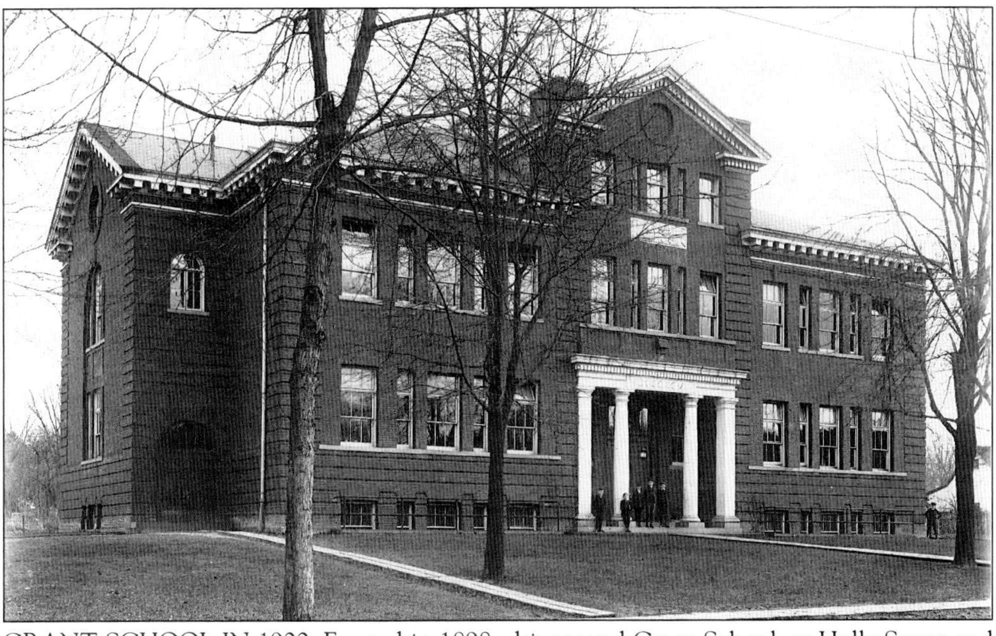

GRANT SCHOOL IN 1900. Erected in 1898, this second Grant School, at Holly Street and Springfield Avenue, replaced an earlier frame building at the same location. The school was abandoned in 1936, but in 1942 Union Junior College moved into the building and remained there until the college moved to its new campus in 1963. The "Old Lady of Holly Street," as the building was known, has since been demolished.

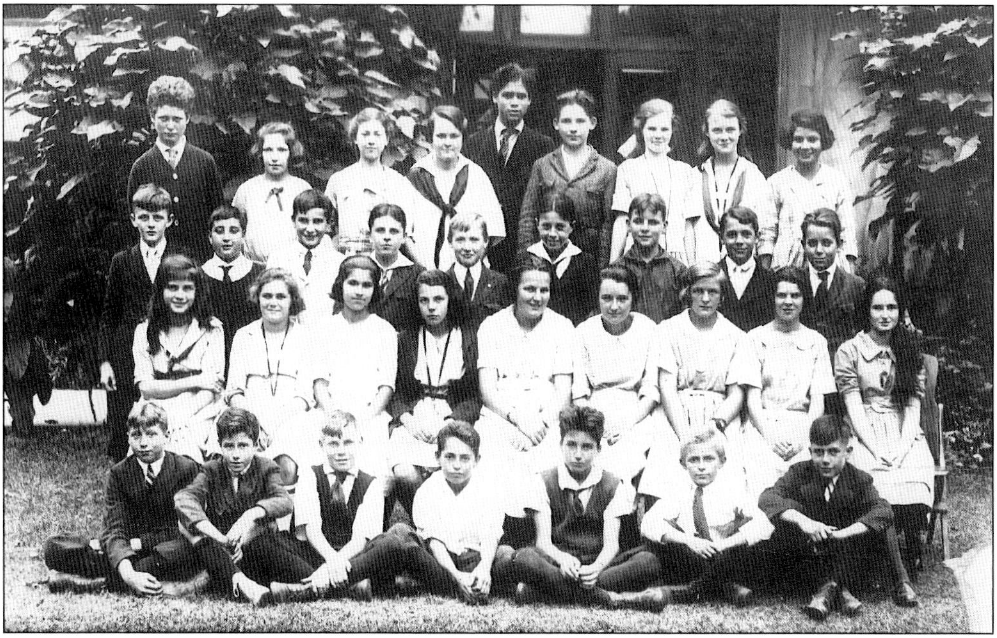

EIGHTH GRADERS AT CLEVELAND SCHOOL, 1921. The nineteen boys and fourteen girls in this class indicate a trend that was identified and widely debated in the 1920s. In the ninth grade the boy-girl ratio was basically even. But the percentage of boys decreased steadily until the twelfth grade, resulting in less than half as many boys as girls at graduation time.

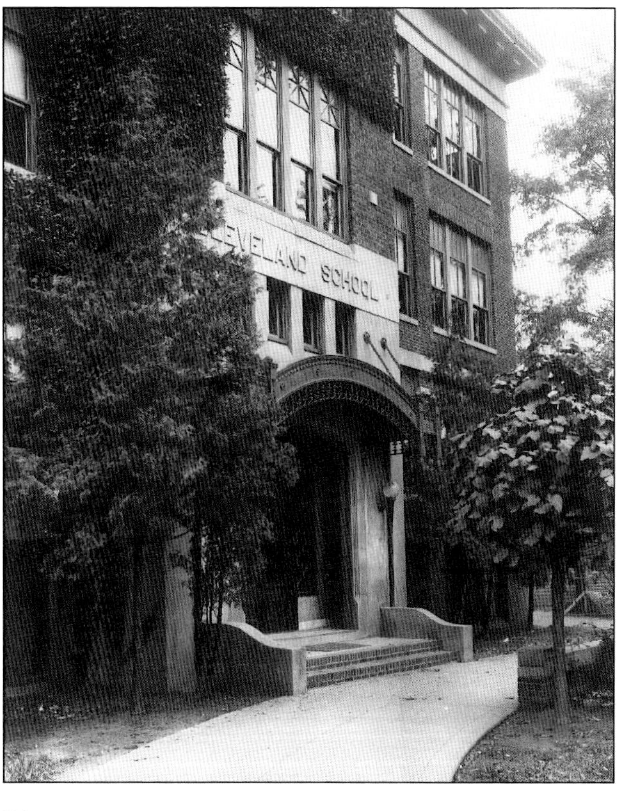

THE ENTRANCE TO CLEVELAND SCHOOL. Named for former President Grover Cleveland, this school was erected in 1914. At that time it was considered the most modern of schools because of its "fire proof" construction, consisting of interior tile walls, a brick exterior, steel-truss frame, and tile-covered concrete floors. Today, residents know the old school as Cleveland Plaza.

Six

The Sporting Life

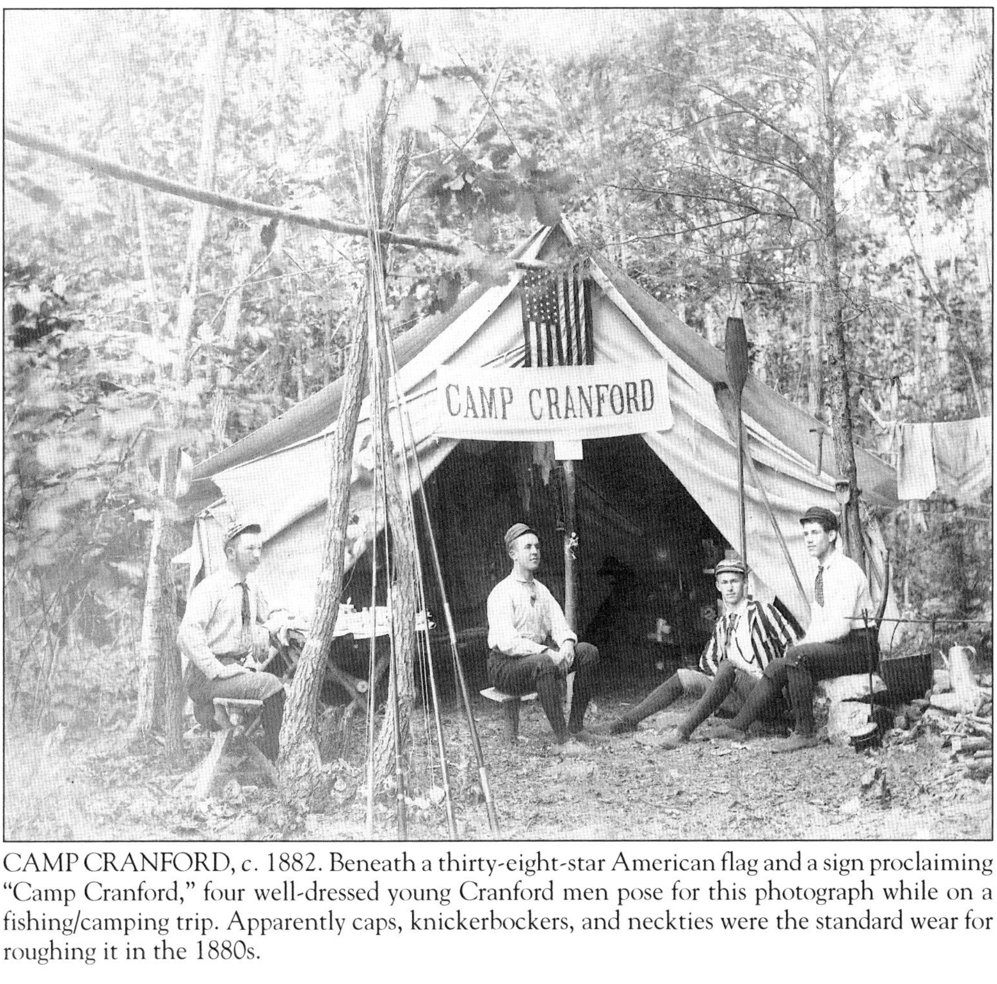

CAMP CRANFORD, c. 1882. Beneath a thirty-eight-star American flag and a sign proclaiming "Camp Cranford," four well-dressed young Cranford men pose for this photograph while on a fishing/camping trip. Apparently caps, knickerbockers, and neckties were the standard wear for roughing it in the 1880s.

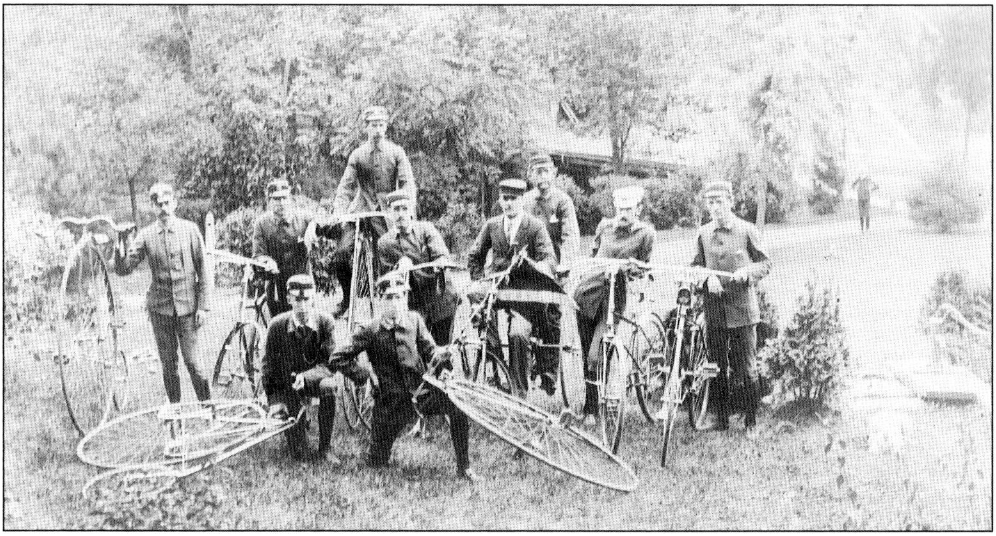

THE CRANFORD CYCLING CLUB, 1890. By the decade of the nineties, cycling clubs had become a national craze. The Cranford Club, organized in 1890, had one-hundred members. Riding both high-wheelers and the newer chain-driven "safety" bikes, ten uniformed members gathered at the North Union Avenue bridge. Led by Captain A.P. "Pathfinder" Folk (kneeling at left), the club won many prizes throughout the state. In 1891 the club opened its membership to women cyclists.

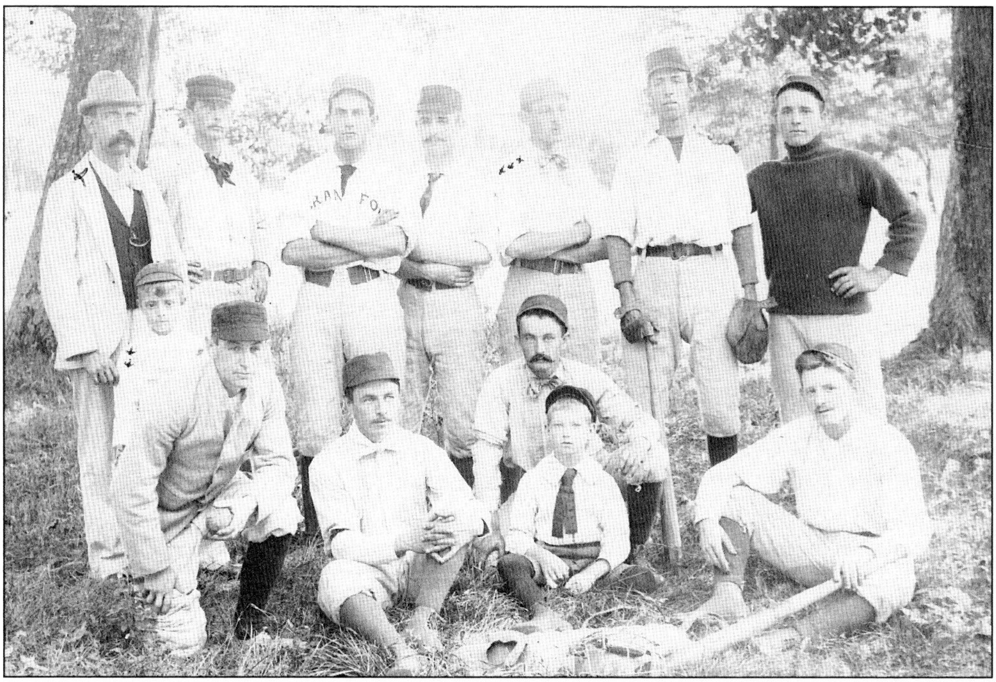

CRANFORD BASEBALL, c. 1892. During the nineteenth century, baseball became the national pastime, and every town organized a baseball team. Almost all of them had a young boy as a mascot. This Cranford team seems to have had two—or perhaps there was one mascot and one mascot-in-waiting. The boy on the left is Harry Sanderson Folk, who is standing with his father, Gus Folk.

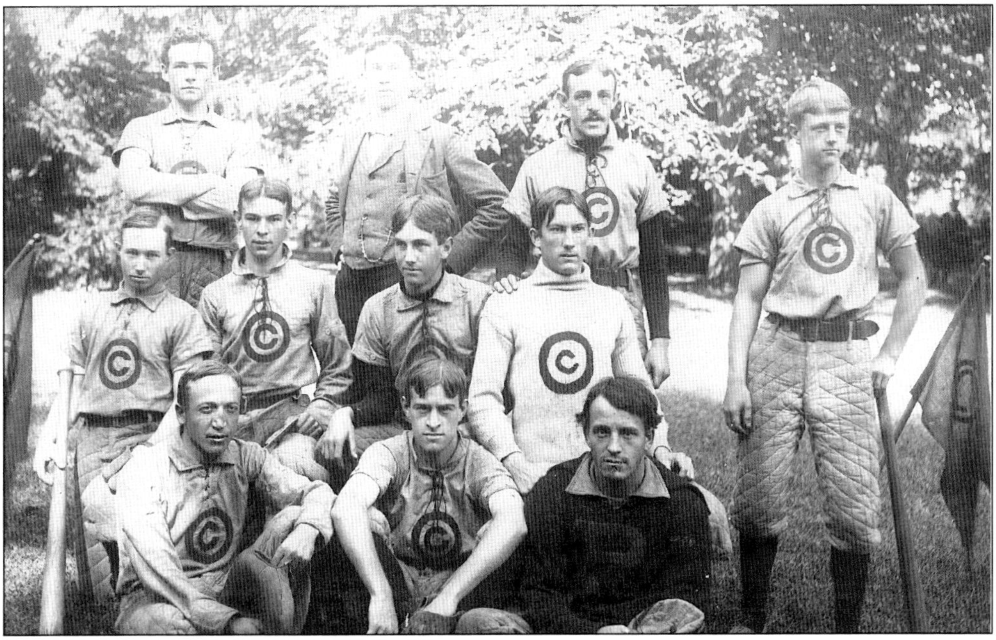

"PLAY BALL!", 1898. With hair parted in the middle and wearing the latest uniforms with quilted pants, the 1898 "C"s were ready to play ball. The roster included, from left to right: (front row) W. Bolich, C. Fox, and F. Bindenberger; (middle row) W. Howell, T. Klase, C. Park, and F. Cox; (back row) M. Hennessey, S. Cox, Alvin Denman, and G. Bates.

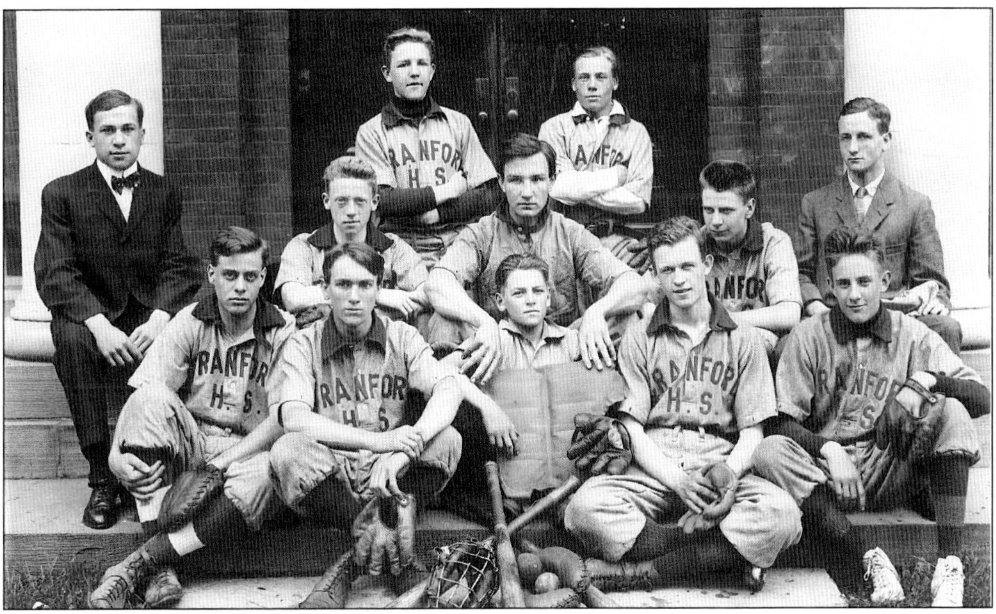

THE CRANFORD HIGH SCHOOL BASEBALL TEAM, 1911. All nine members of the high school baseball team showed up to have their picture taken. The handsome young man in the middle of the first row appears to be the omnipresent mascot. Manager Harry Heins (in bow tie) is at left and teacher/coach David Bennett is at right. In the center is William Bell, the team captain who was also captain of the football team. Notice the heavy, high-top boots worn by the players.

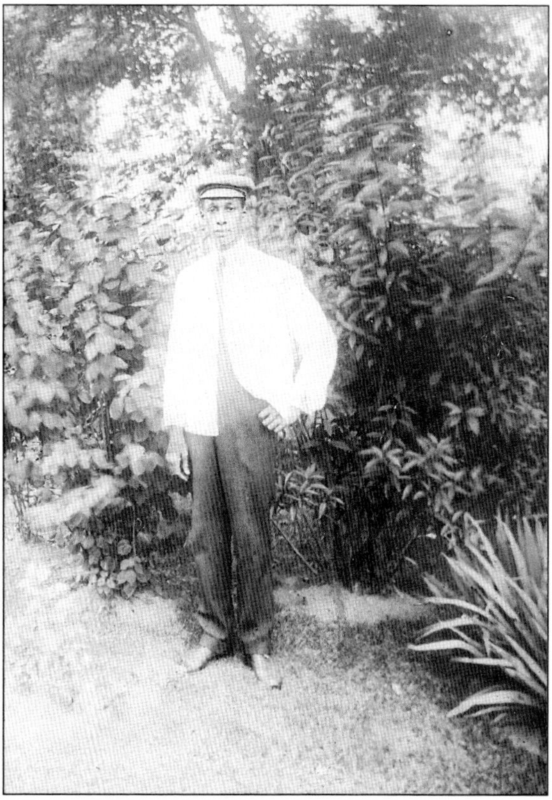

ERNEST E. TYREE, *c.* 1910. Born in 1882, Ernest Tyree became a Cranford caterer, but his first love was always baseball. After World War I, Tyree founded and then managed the Cranford Dixie Giants, an all-black team at a time when baseball was racially segregated. The Tyree home on Cranford Avenue served as the team's headquarters, locker room, and social center.

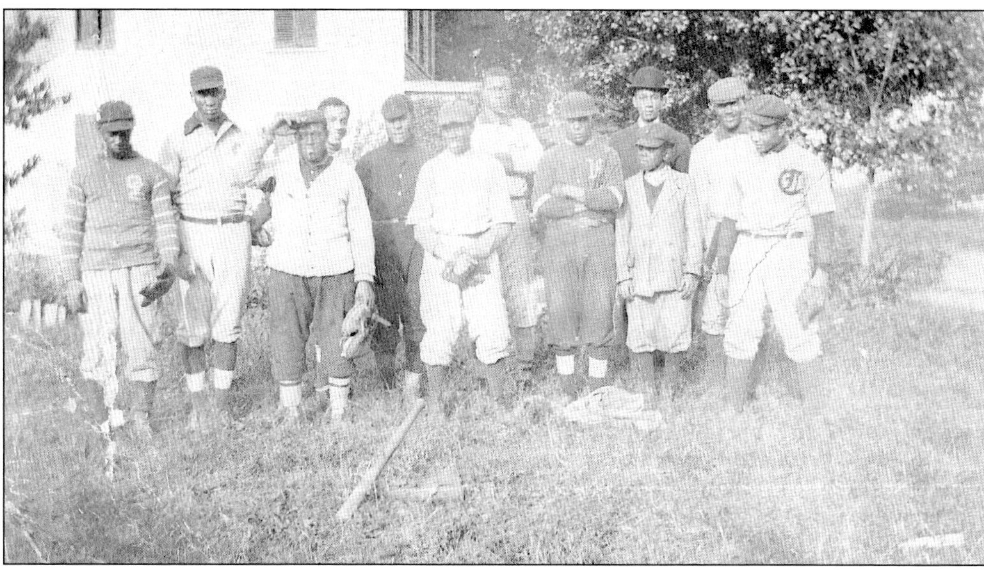

THE CRANFORD DIXIE GIANTS, *c.* 1925. The all-black Dixie Giants, formed after World War I, continued until the late 1930s. They played their home games at the old ball fields at Cranford and Elizabeth Avenues and at the B & O oval at Aldine. Although the "color line" of that day prohibited players of different races from playing on the same team, the line became quite blurred at times. The Dixie Giants regularly played and regularly beat all-white teams in the area.

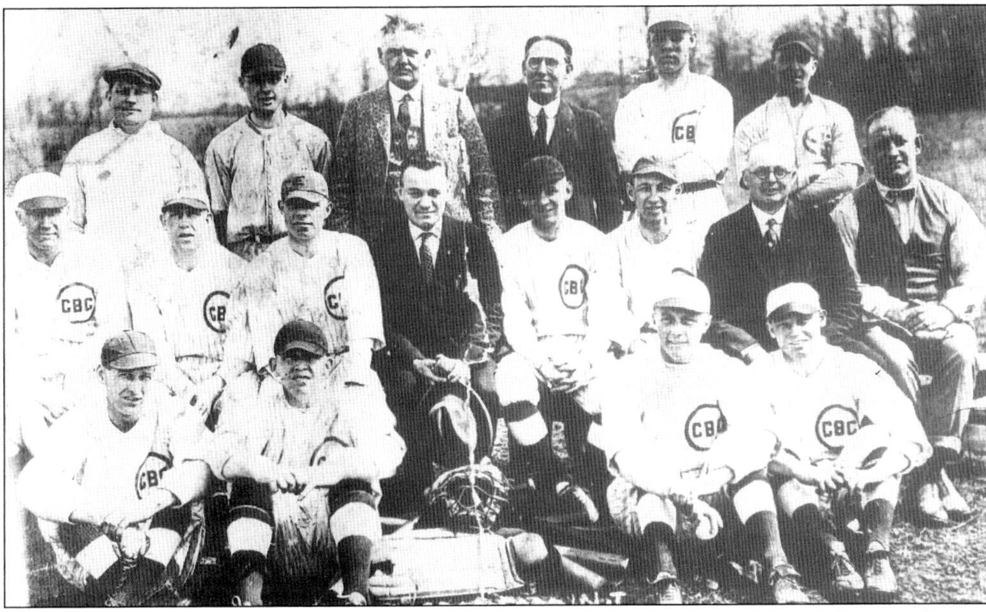

THE CBC. The Cranford Baseball Club posed for this picture in the summer of 1924. The two gentlemen seated on the right (not in uniform) are Ed McMahon (left) and Charles Kurtz. Seated in the center, with hat in hand, is coach J. Seth Weekly, who was a sports instructor or coach to a host of Cranford schoolchildren right up through the 1950s.

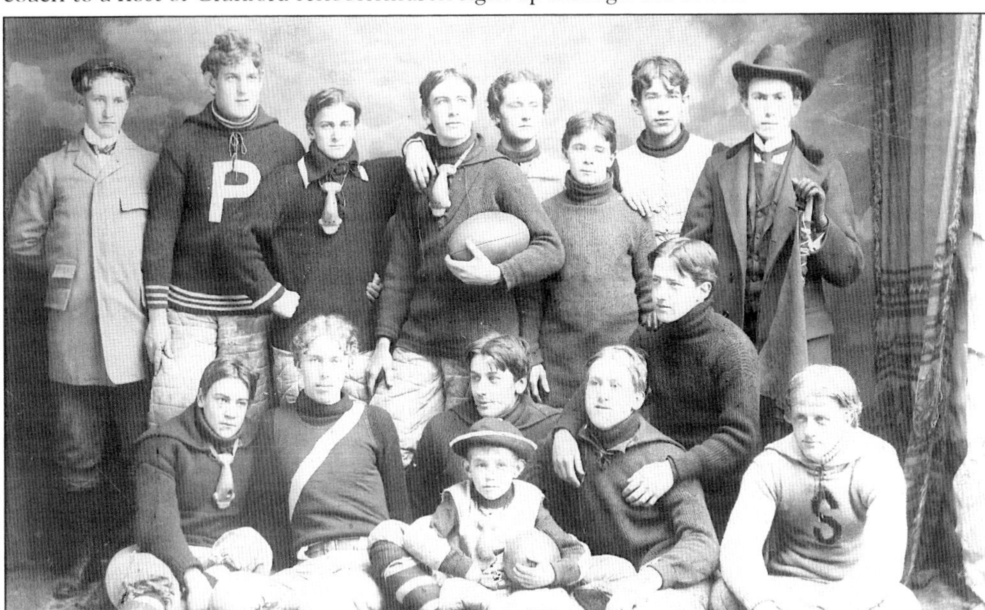

THE "ECHO CLUB," 1897. In the 1890s, football was played mostly by college students, but local groups had begun to organize teams. This early Echo Club team consisted of, from left to right: (front row) Will Johnson, James Miller, Clarence Heleker, Will Allen, Poggi, and George Bates, with "Crisp" the mascot (a young Dean Mathey); (back row) Bert Hibson, Blank, Will Moody, Worth Phillips, Mulford, Herrick, Day, and Clifton Cox. Four players wear nose guards around their necks.

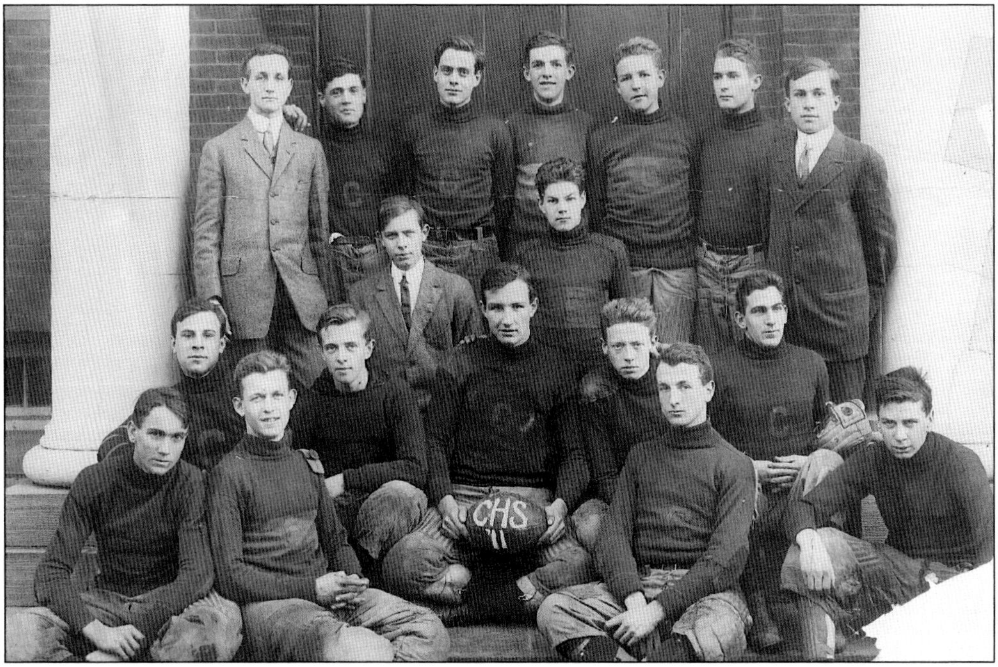

CHS FOOTBALL, 1911. Team members played both offense and defense, so the roster was small. From the left to right are: (front row) Walt Chamberlain, Raymond Toole, Harold Collins, and Edward Jeambey; (middle row) Fred Heins, Edward Smaney, captain William Bell, Charles Gilmore, and Pat Halsey; (upper center) Edward Hagen (in suit) and William Hale; (back row) coach David Bennett, Andrew MacConnell, Stephen Hopkins, Laton Wanser, Robie Droescher, Eugene Towler, and manager Harry Heins.

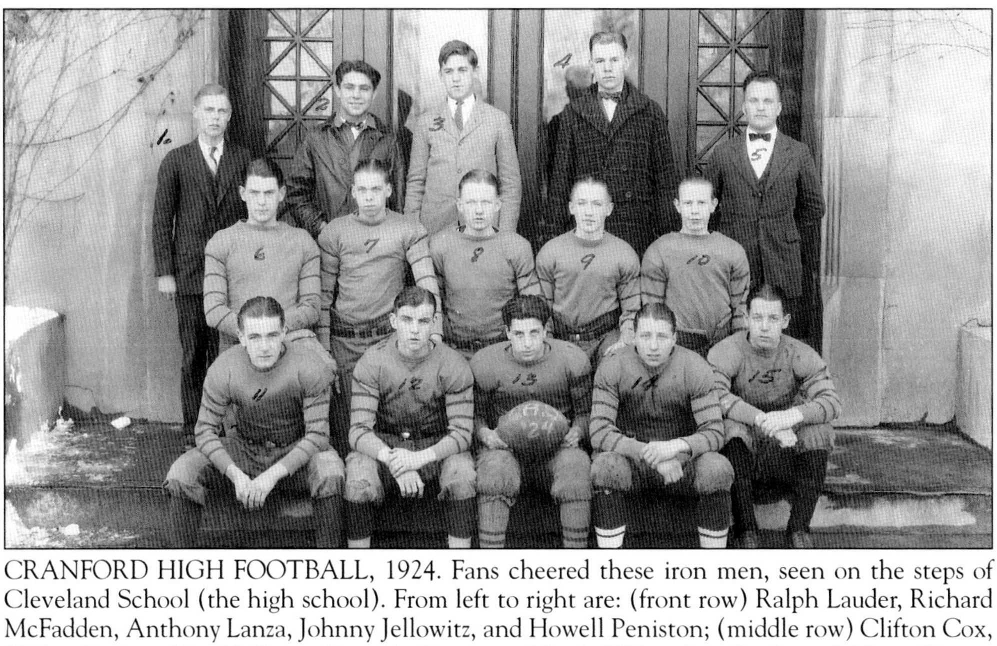

CRANFORD HIGH FOOTBALL, 1924. Fans cheered these iron men, seen on the steps of Cleveland School (the high school). From left to right are: (front row) Ralph Lauder, Richard McFadden, Anthony Lanza, Johnny Jellowitz, and Howell Peniston; (middle row) Clifton Cox, Walter Tarbox, Harold Cross, Quentin Frazer, and Rudy Wikander; (back row) Harry Sisson, Jake Mazzen, Charles Morris, Robert Morris, and coach Axel Holmes.

MATHEW DEAN HALL. Although football did not match baseball in popularity, neighborhood rivalries were strong and victory was sweet. Nineteen-year-old Mathew Hall played on the Orchard Street champions of 1923. At other times Hall was co-captain of the Pingry School Eleven. Compare Hall's football helmet with those worn by players today.

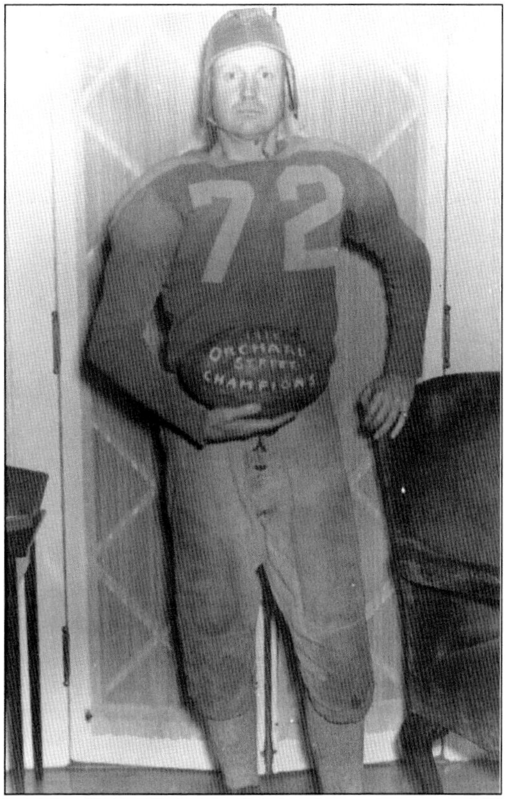

UNBEATEN BUT TWICE TIED, 1927. As this pocket schedule and score card shows, coach Sydney Souter's unbeaten Cranford High School football team posted an enviable record, outscoring opponents by a lopsided 128 to 18. Yet, the team was tied twice. Both Union High School and Cranford's own alumni withstood the steamroller.

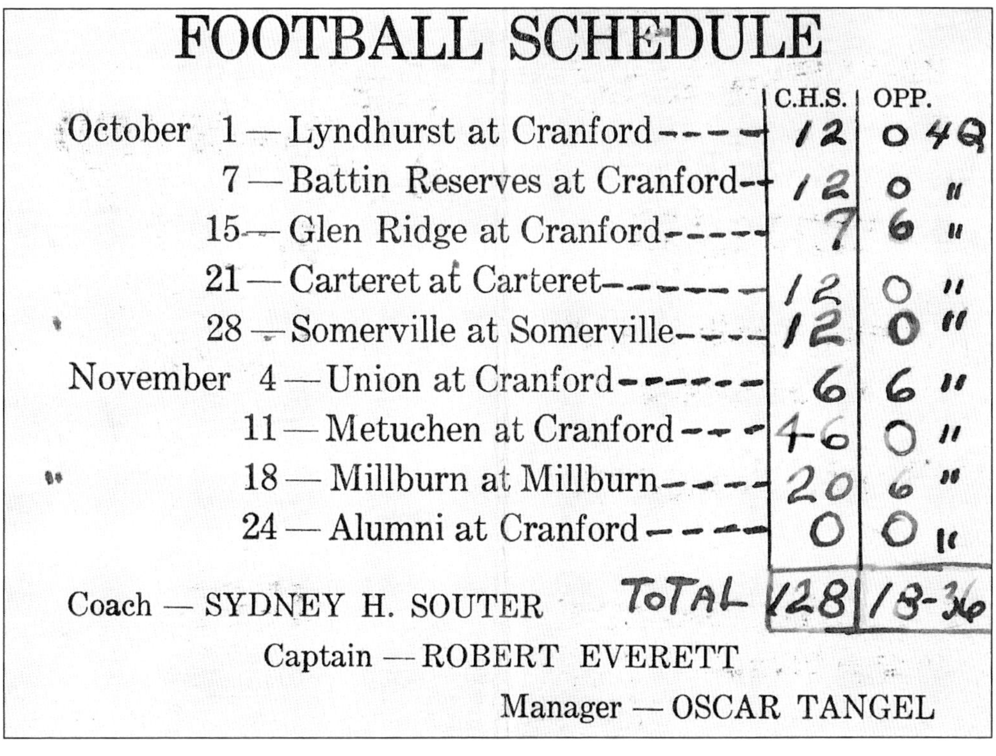

FOOTBALL SCHEDULE

	C.H.S.	OPP.
October 1 — Lyndhurst at Cranford	12	0 4Q
7 — Battin Reserves at Cranford	12	0 "
15 — Glen Ridge at Cranford	7	6 "
21 — Carteret at Carteret	12	0 "
28 — Somerville at Somerville	12	0 "
November 4 — Union at Cranford	6	6 "
11 — Metuchen at Cranford	46	0 "
18 — Millburn at Millburn	20	6 "
24 — Alumni at Cranford	0	0 "
TOTAL	128	18-36

Coach — SYDNEY H. SOUTER

Captain — ROBERT EVERETT

Manager — OSCAR TANGEL

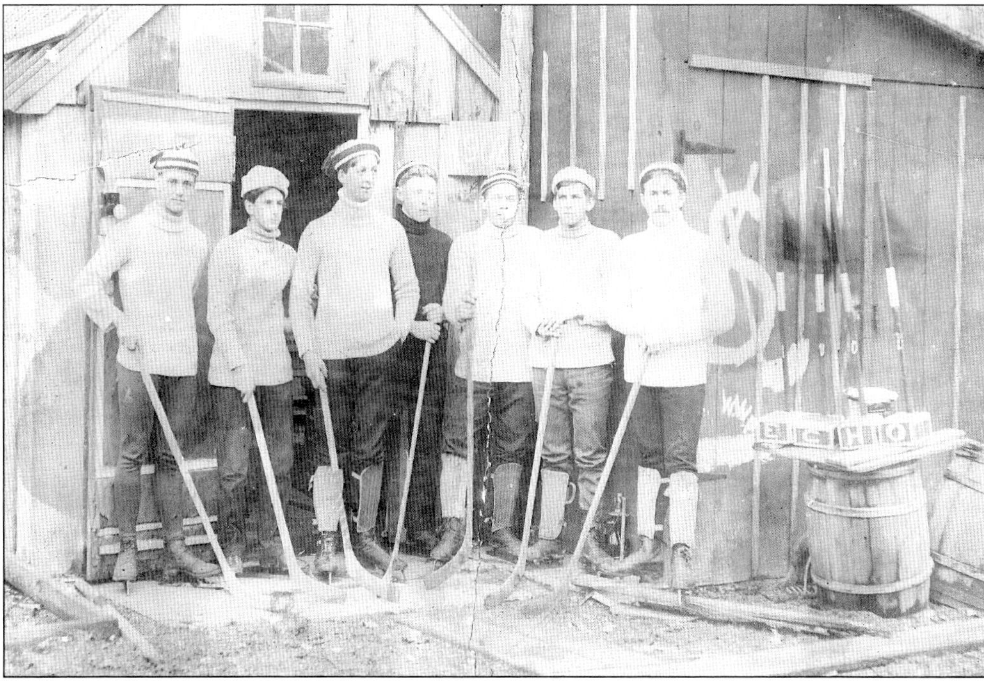

"THE SHANTY GANG," 1902. Described by a newspaper as "well behaved young men," the Shanty Gang engaged in all outdoor sports, from hunting to boating to football. Standing in front of their shanty clubhouse, on the west bank of the river opposite the foot of Alden Street, is the hockey team. Their logo, an "S" crossed by two hockey sticks, can be seen roughly painted on the door on the right.

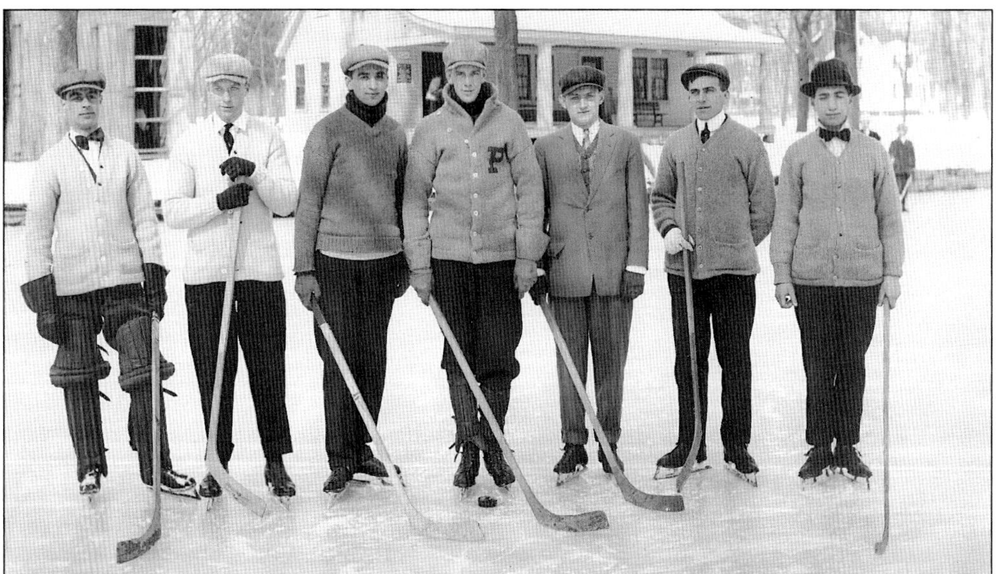

WHAT WELL-DRESSED HOCKEY PLAYERS WORE, *c.* 1912. Neatly dressed and wearing caps (one fedora) and ties, these gentlemen hockey players met in front of the Cranford Canoe Club at Springfield Avenue. From left to right are: Ed Beadle, Bob Miller, Herb Winckler, Max Marston, Eddie Wild, Joe Plummer, and Joe See.

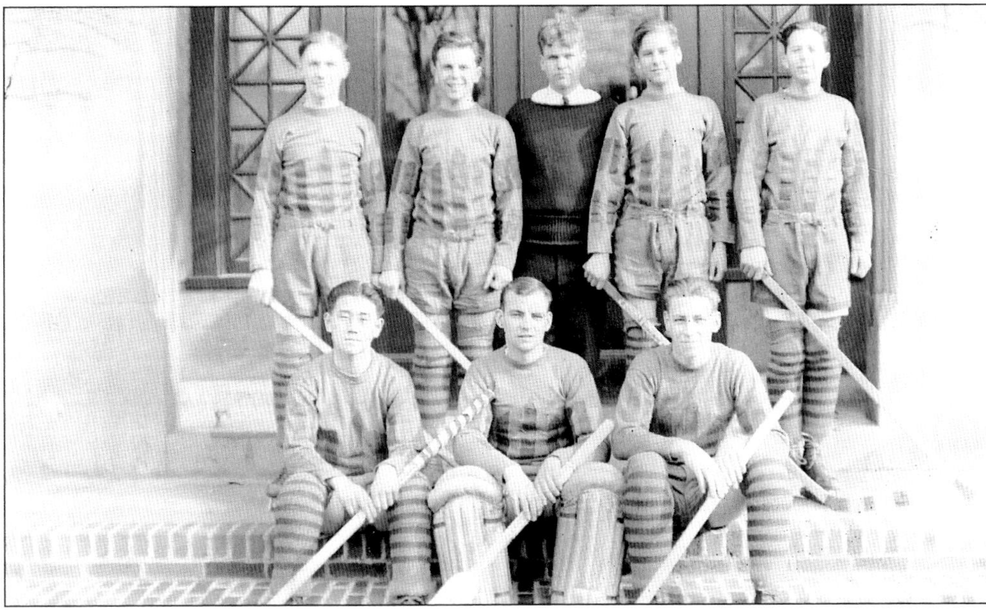

THE CHS HOCKEY TEAM, 1927. The first hockey team to represent the high school in interscholastic competition had "no coach and uncertain weather," but it posted a .500 season. Richard McFadden (center front) and George Larson (center back) have been identified, as well as Frank Hayashi (on the left), who also played on the football and basketball teams.

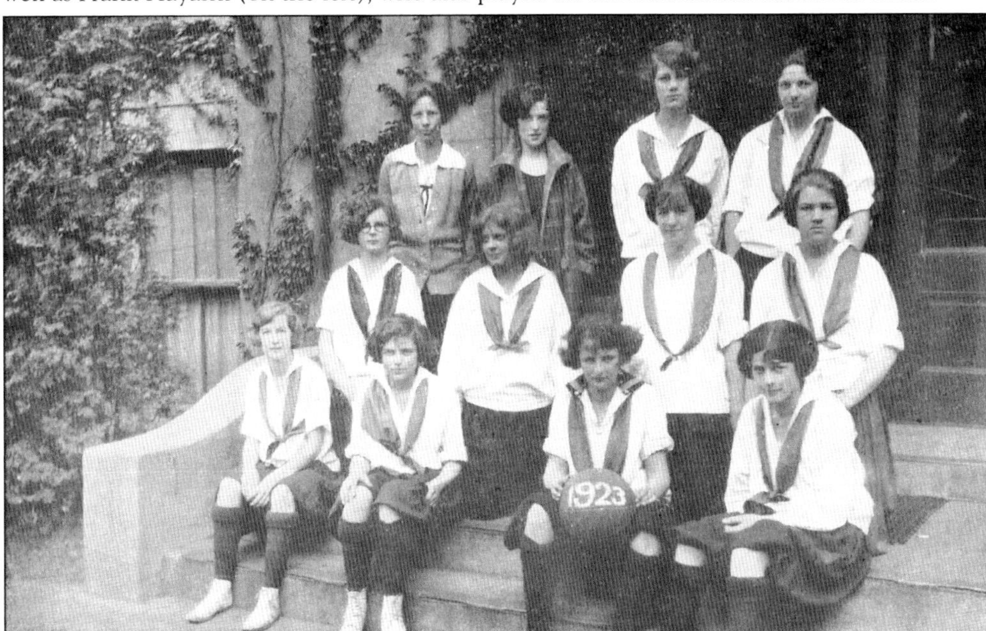

GIRL'S BASKETBALL, 1923. By the 1920s women were playing interscholastic schedules. This team posted a 9–6 record. The high school yearbook said that the girls wanted to win, but "in a fair and square way." The fair and square players are, from left to right: (front row) Margaret Jones, Marie Bremner, captain Judith Botts, and Dolores Kahl; (middle row) Phyllis Skillin, Florence Durling, Edna Waterson, and Ruth Torrey; (back row) Miss Achsah Lewis, Katherine Chadwick, Helen Taylor, and Mary Ninde.

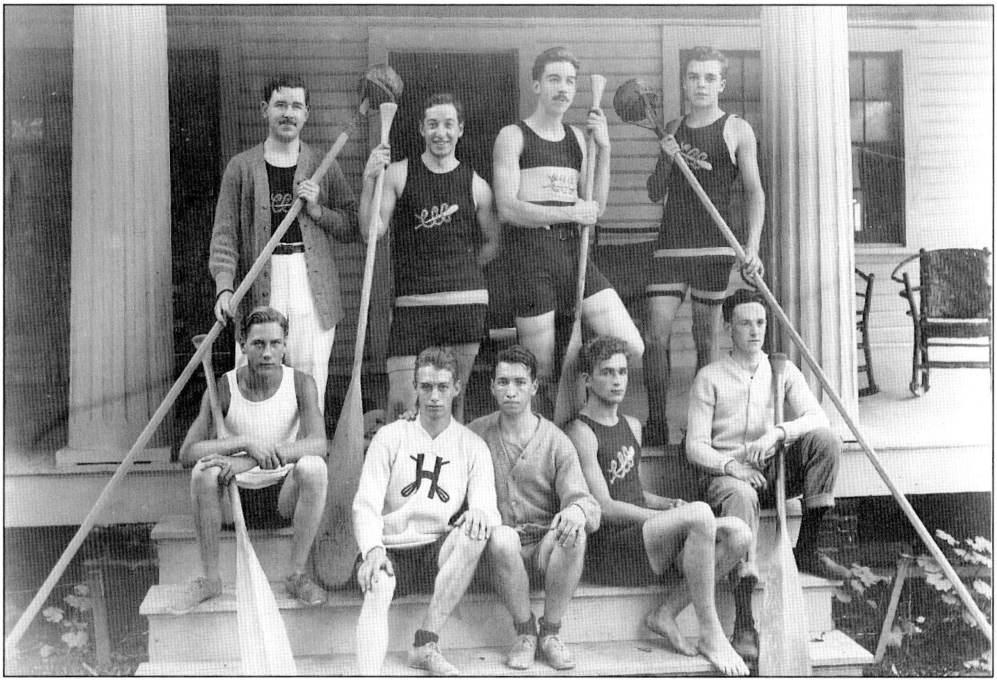

THE CRANFORD CANOE CLUB, 1910. Originally organized as the Shanty Gang, and later called the Skeeter Canoe Club, a group of young sports enthusiasts finally assumed the respectable name of Cranford Canoe Club about 1908. In front of the club are, from left to right: (front row) Kenneth Jones, Albert See, Joseph See, Herbert Winckler, and Walter Wagstaff; (back row) Roderick Smith, Juan Bargos, Vernon Baker, and Louis Coudert.

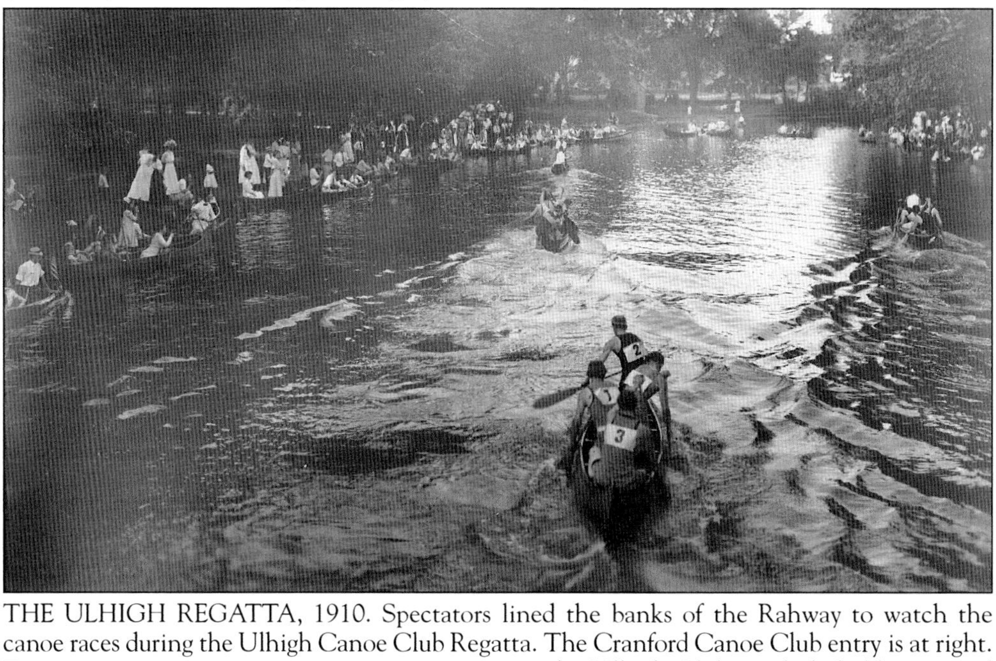

THE ULHIGH REGATTA, 1910. Spectators lined the banks of the Rahway to watch the canoe races during the Ulhigh Canoe Club Regatta. The Cranford Canoe Club entry is at right. To encourage canoe racing as a competitive sport, the Ulhigh Club regularly held races and regattas, inviting individuals and teams from throughout the state to compete.

DEAN MATHEY, *c.* 1924. One of Cranford's greatest athletes was Dean Mathey. In the course of a long tennis career he won a number of singles and doubles championships. In 1908 he won the National Interscholastic Singles Championship, and he later was twice Intercollegiate Doubles Champion. In 1919, with Watson Washburn, he won the French Doubles Championship.

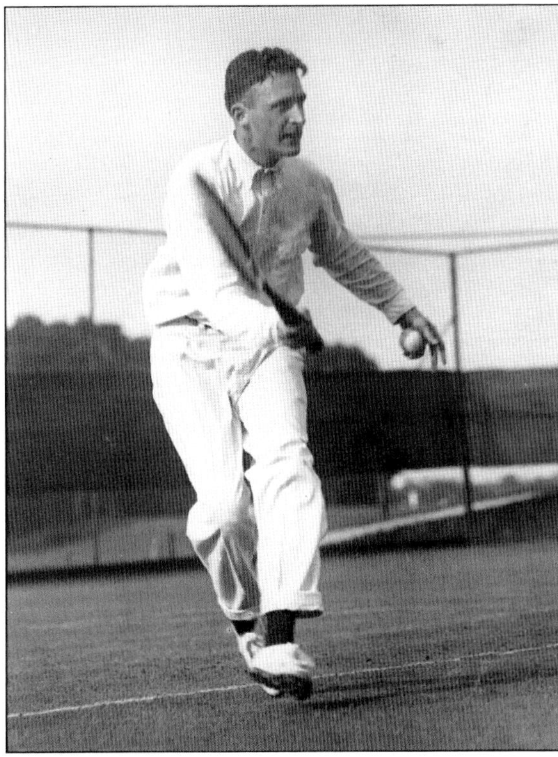

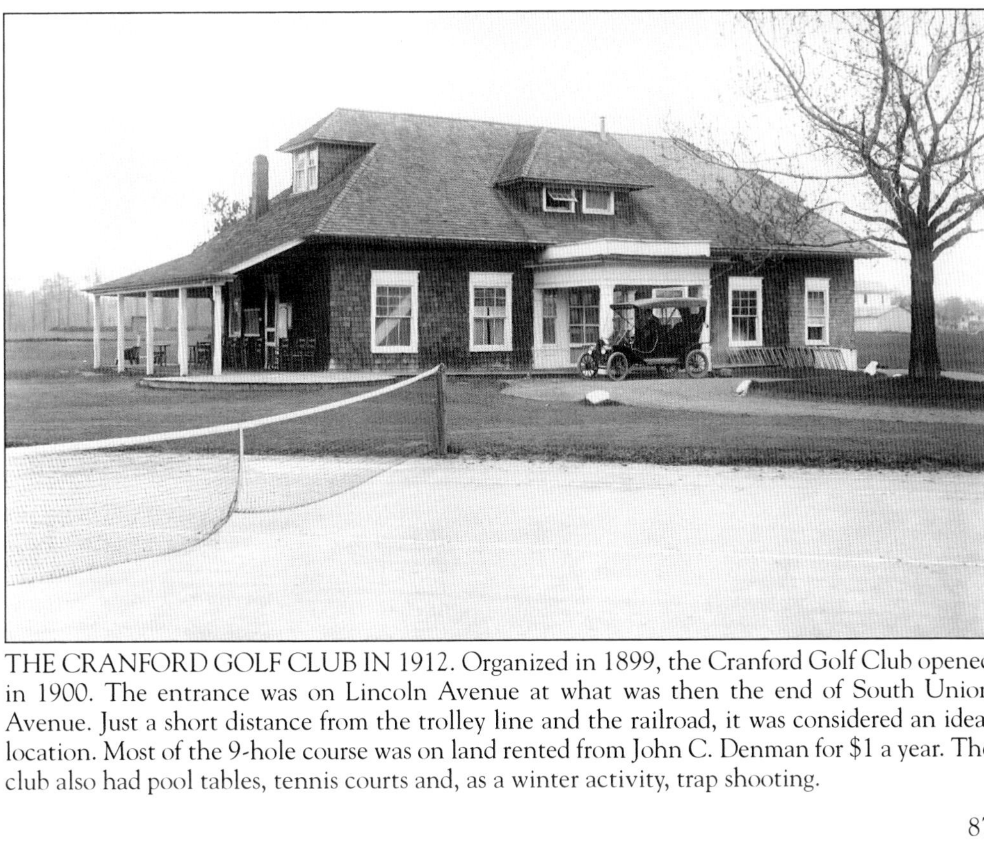

THE CRANFORD GOLF CLUB IN 1912. Organized in 1899, the Cranford Golf Club opened in 1900. The entrance was on Lincoln Avenue at what was then the end of South Union Avenue. Just a short distance from the trolley line and the railroad, it was considered an ideal location. Most of the 9-hole course was on land rented from John C. Denman for $1 a year. The club also had pool tables, tennis courts and, as a winter activity, trap shooting.

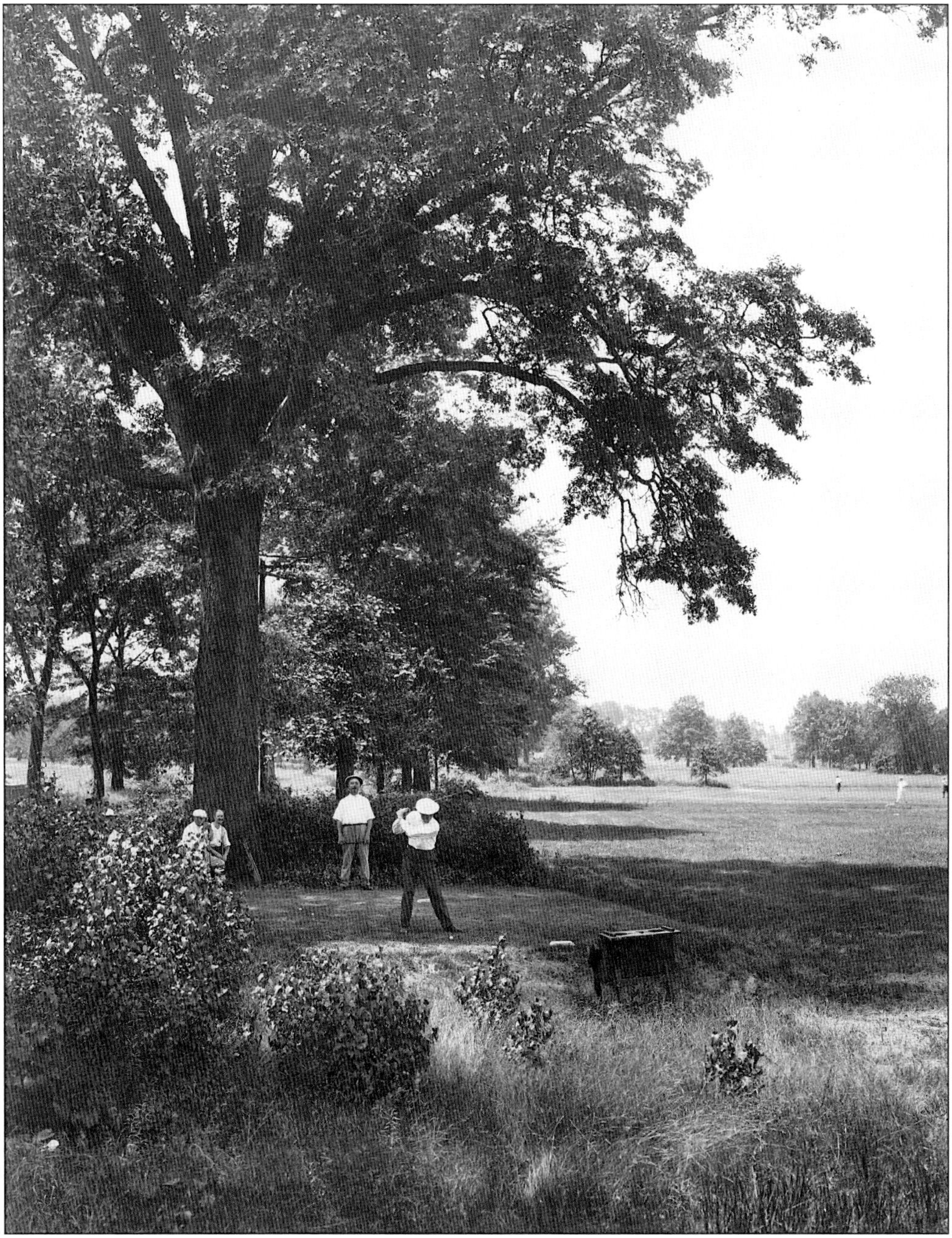

TEEING OFF. A foursome tees off at the Cranford Golf Club, just south of Lincoln Avenue West. The increasing popularity of the automobile meant that golf courses no longer needed to be near public transportation, so members of the Cranford Club began to look for a location where they could build an 18-hole course. In 1913 they moved to Westfield, and in 1921 changed the club's name to the Echo Lake Country Club.

Seven

On the Street Where You Live

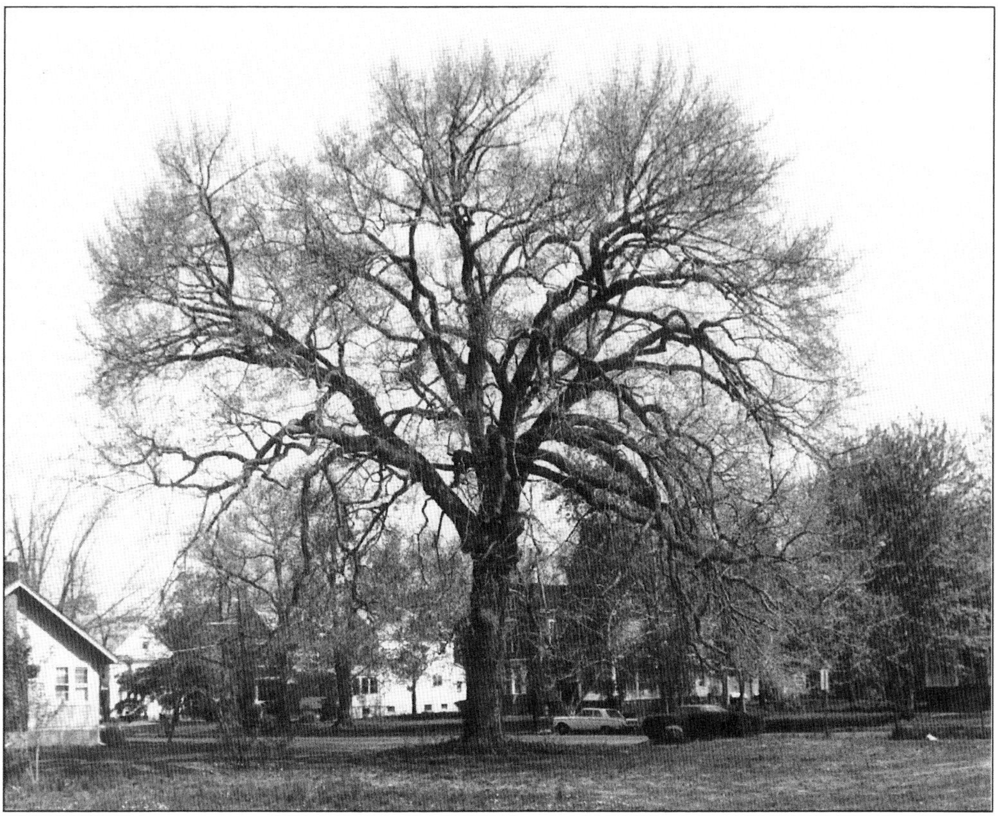

"OLD PEPPY." Cranford's gigantic pepperidge or sour gum tree was designated as the town's "official tree" by the Township Committee on March 10, 1964. At that time the tree was estimated to be two hundred years old. Known as "Old Peppy," it stands almost 80 feet high and its massive branches spread out for 90 feet. The tree is located next to the Lincoln Avenue Playground.

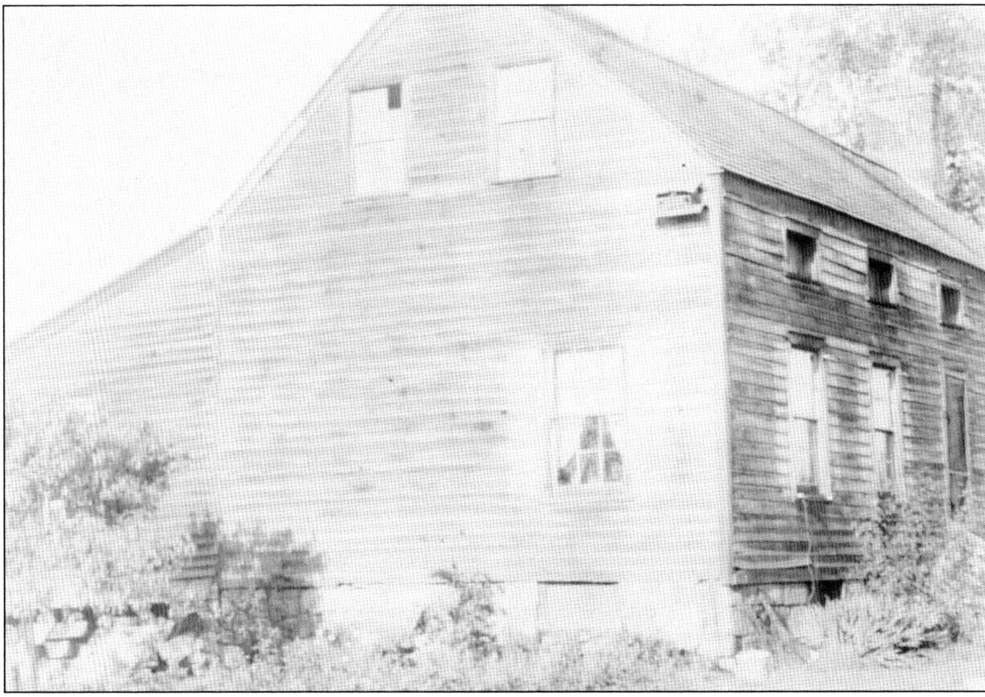

THE JOHN GRANT CRANE HOUSE IN 1875. This farmhouse, with its "cat-slide" roof in the rear, was built around 1800. It stood on the northeast side of Springfield Avenue, just where Hampton Road enters today. Extensively remodeled and Victorianized in the early 1880s by Edward Beadle, its new owner, the house was finally razed in the early 1900s, and its large farm was divided for residential development.

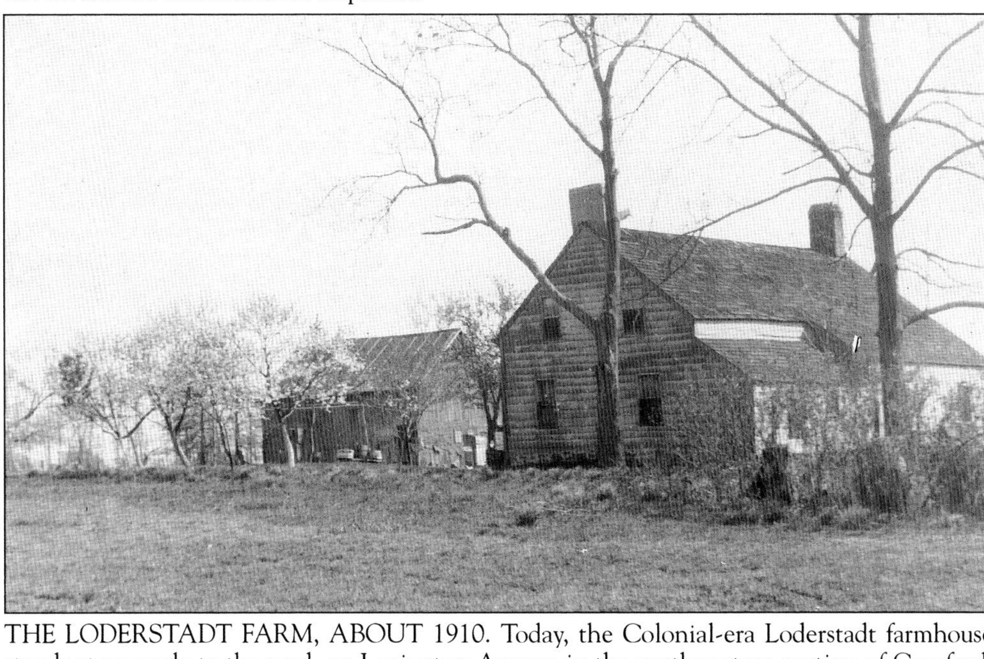

THE LODERSTADT FARM, ABOUT 1910. Today, the Colonial-era Loderstadt farmhouse stands at an angle to the road, on Lexington Avenue in the southwestern section of Cranford. This house was home to Squire Williams in the 1820s.

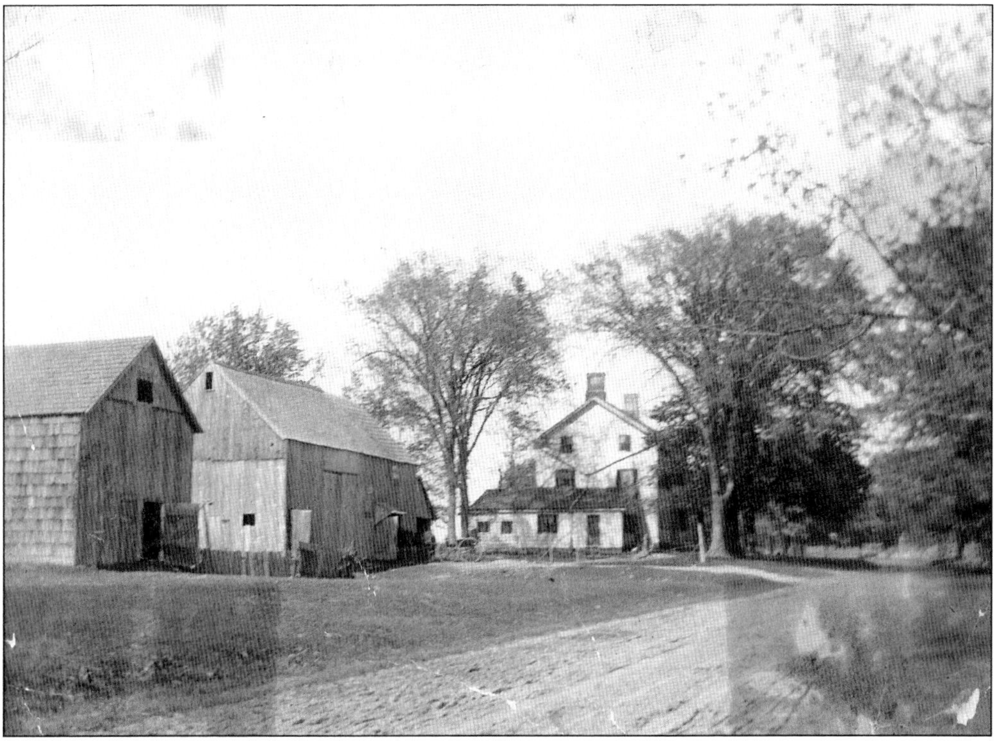

THE NORRIS-OAKEY HOUSE AND FARM IN 1895. Built about 1750 by Nathaniel Norris, this house today stands in a quiet suburban neighborhood on Orange Avenue near the Cranford-Kenilworth line. It is one of the oldest houses in Cranford. Substantially enlarged in the mid-nineteenth century, it became the home of Civil War veteran William Oakey in the early twentieth century.

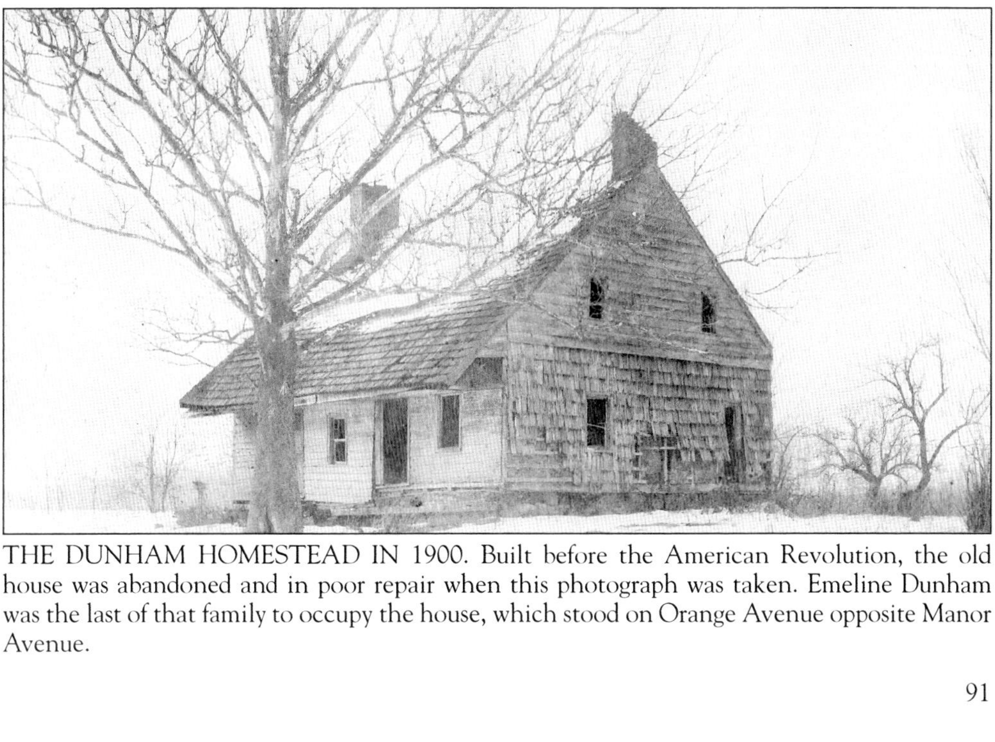

THE DUNHAM HOMESTEAD IN 1900. Built before the American Revolution, the old house was abandoned and in poor repair when this photograph was taken. Emeline Dunham was the last of that family to occupy the house, which stood on Orange Avenue opposite Manor Avenue.

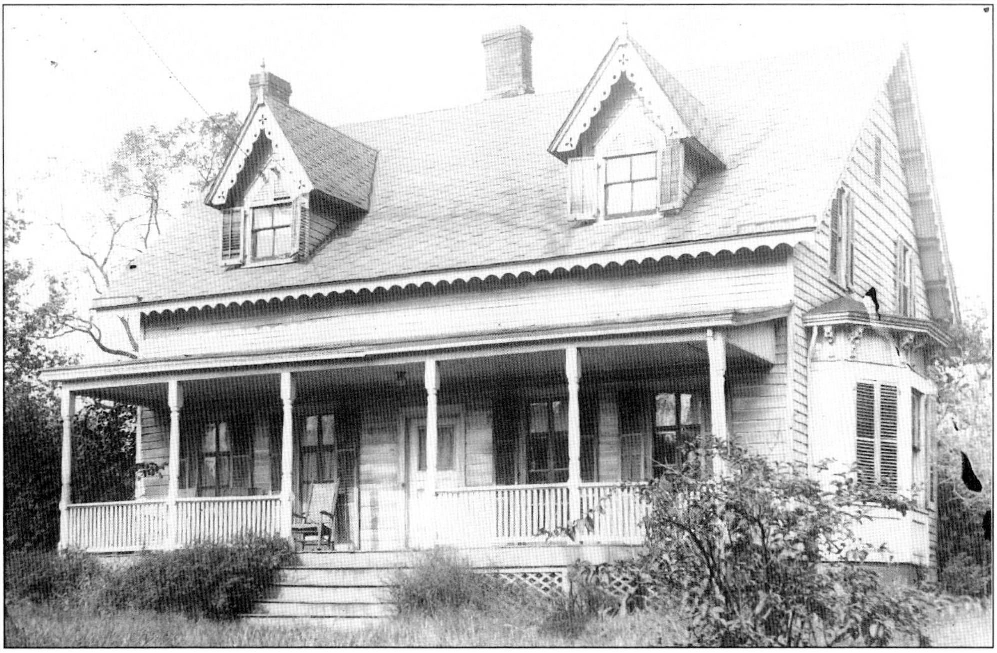

THE CORY HOUSE, ABOUT 1920. Built *c.* 1735, this was the oldest house in Cranford when it was demolished in 1971. Formerly located at 321 North Avenue East (the site of condominiums today), the house was famed for a tunnel supposed to have been used in the Revolutionary War to aid the escape of soldiers. More likely, the tunnel provided New England-style winter passage from the house to the barn. This picture shows the house with added Victorian architectural details.

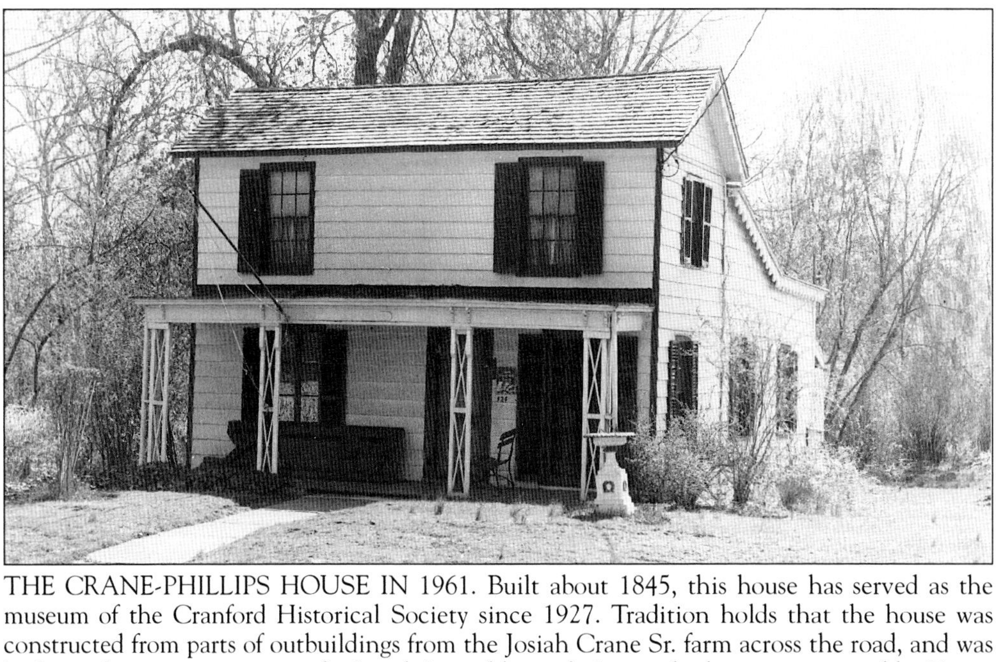

THE CRANE-PHILLIPS HOUSE IN 1961. Built about 1845, this house has served as the museum of the Cranford Historical Society since 1927. Tradition holds that the house was constructed from parts of outbuildings from the Josiah Crane Sr. farm across the road, and was built as a honeymoon cottage for Josiah Jr. and his wife. Later, the house was owned by Henry Phillips, a sometime inventor. The house stands at 124 North Union Avenue.

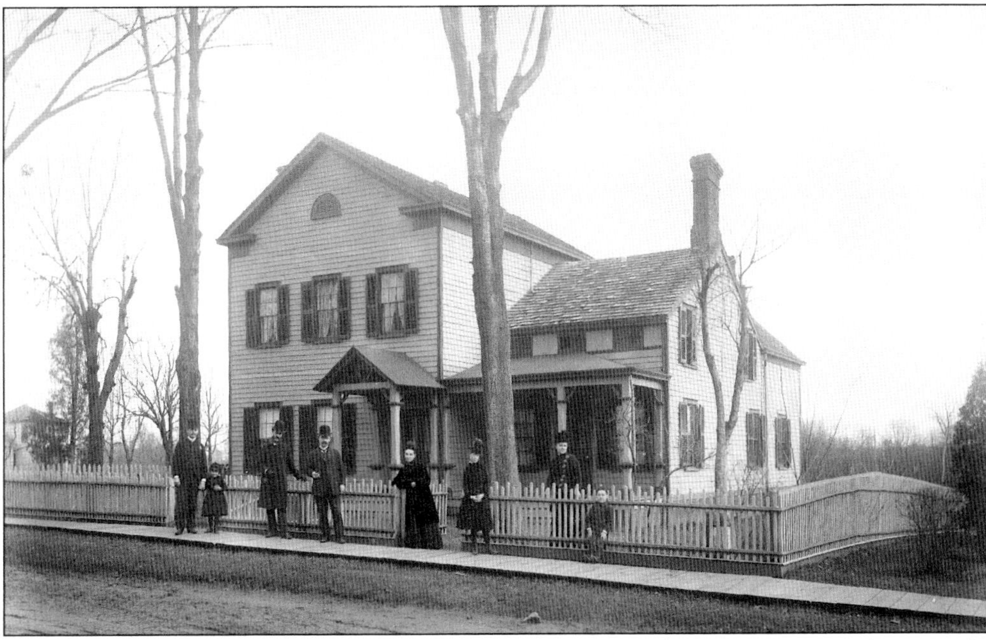

AN 1880 VIEW OF THE JAMES FERGUSON HOUSE. The Fergusons pose here on the boardwalk in front of the house, built in the 1860s as a larger gable-roofed attachment to an earlier colonial house (on the right). Located on North Union Avenue, the house was torn down in 1922 and replaced by the Shapiro Building.

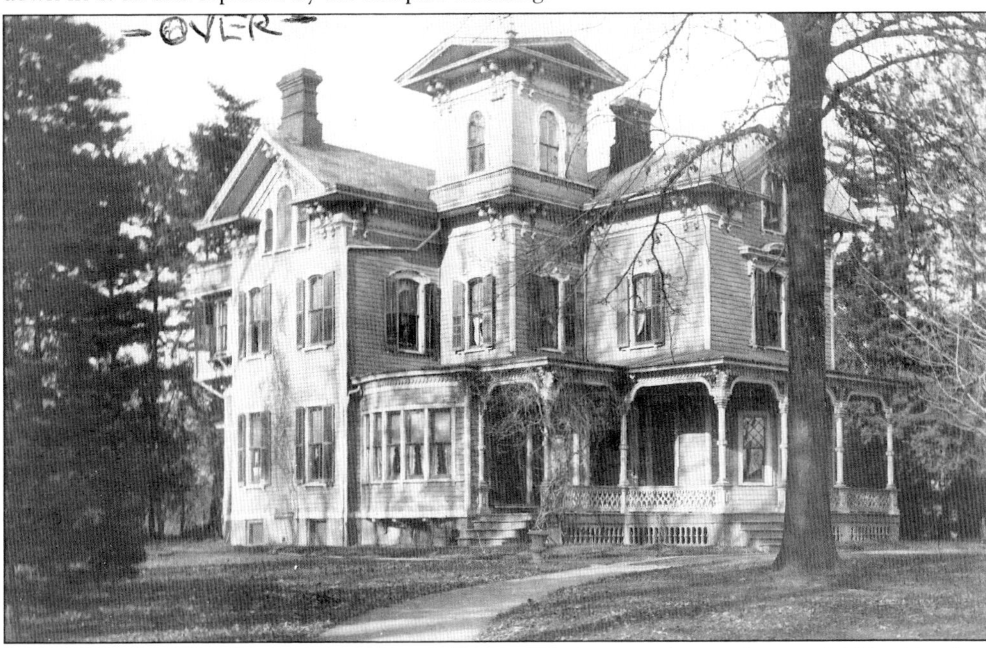

MARLBOROUGH PLACE IN 1910. Built in 1863, this was the residence of Alden Bigelow, one of Cranford's town fathers. Named for the Massachusetts town where Bigelow was born, the house stood at 111 North Union Avenue. The grounds included a coach house, a hen yard, hundreds of fruit trees, and an enormous garden. Sold to the township in 1913, it became the site of Cleveland School, today's Cleveland Plaza.

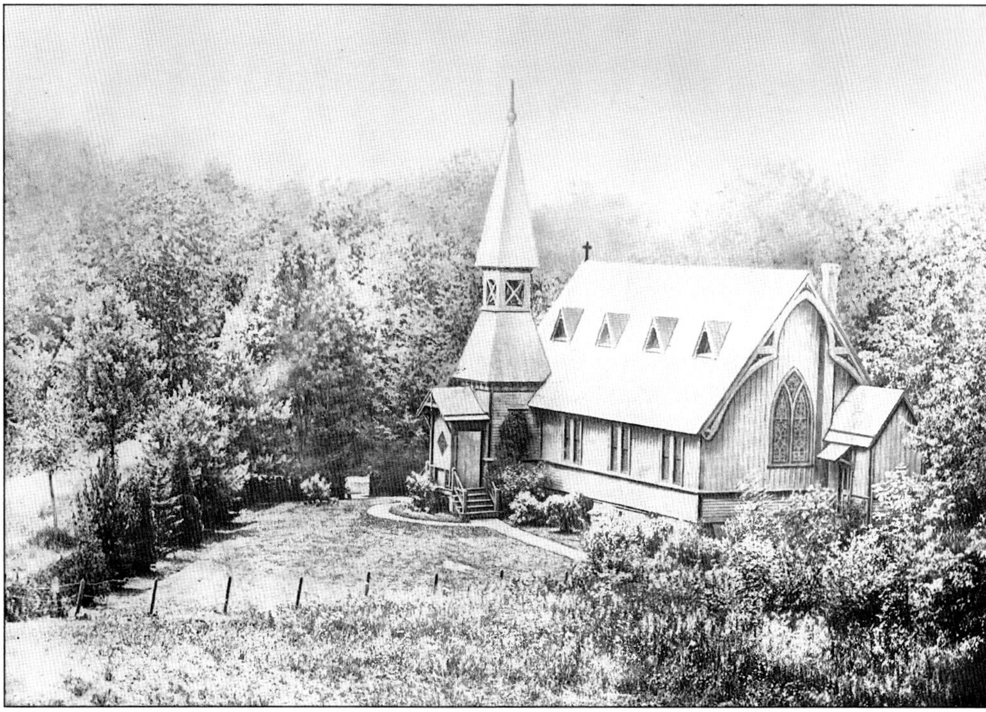

TRINITY EPISCOPAL CHURCH IN 1886. The first Episcopal service in Cranford was held in 1872, but it was not until 1875 that Trinity Church was erected on Forest Avenue, near the corner of North Avenue, on land donated by John M. and Harry E. Atwater. Today's building, although extensively altered, follows the same structural lines as the original wooden church.

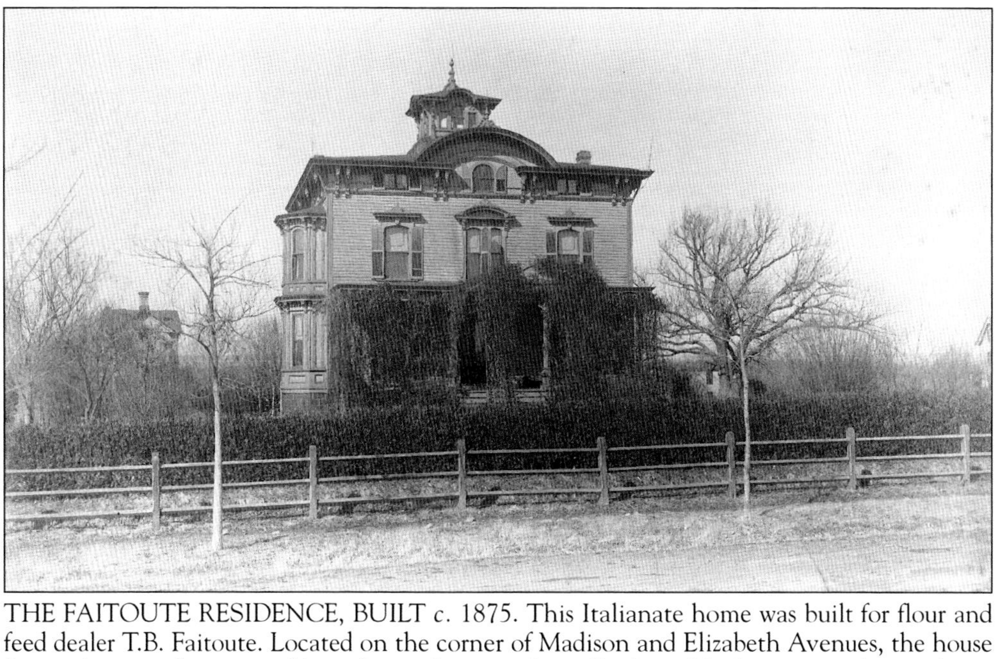

THE FAITOUTE RESIDENCE, BUILT *c.* 1875. This Italianate home was built for flour and feed dealer T.B. Faitoute. Located on the corner of Madison and Elizabeth Avenues, the house featured a curved center gable and a rooftop cupola or "lookout." In later years the residence became a boarding house. It was finally torn down in 1915.

THE SITE OF THE FIRST CATHOLIC MASS IN CRANFORD. St. Michael's Roman Catholic Church was established in 1872, and for a time the small congregation met in the home of Terrence Brennan on South Avenue, where Reverend G.I. Misdziol ("Father Mitchell") celebrated Mass every second Sunday.

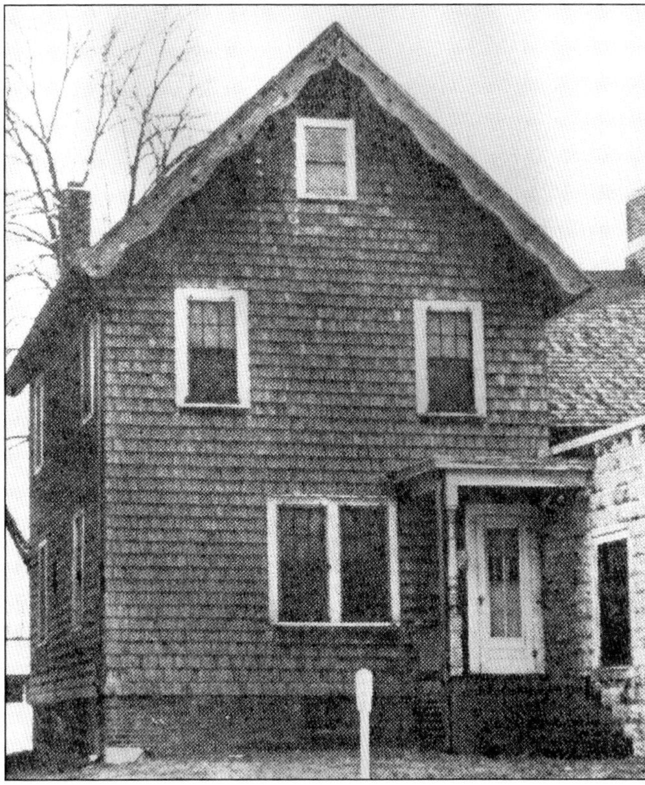

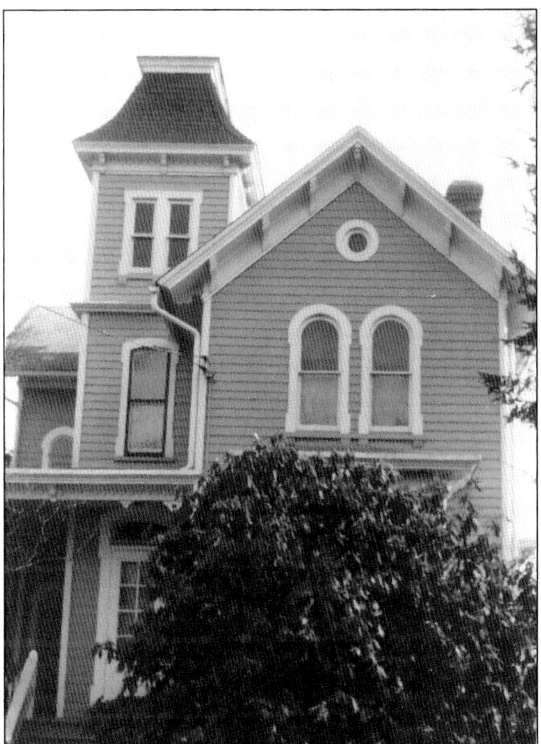

THE OLD ST. MICHAEL'S RECTORY. Built around 1870 on Bloomingdale Avenue, this attractive Italianate house, with its square tower and round arched windows, served as the rectory for St. Michael's Roman Catholic Church.

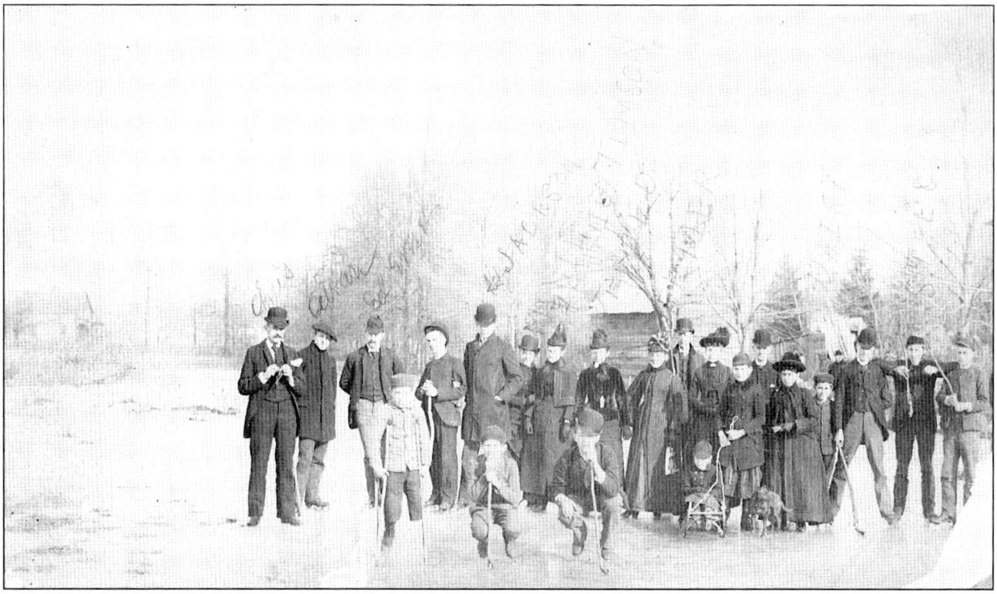

SKATING ON PARMENTIER'S POND, 1887. Since filled in, Parmentier's Pond was located in a marsh along a brook that fed the Rahway River, in the area of Grove Street and Lincoln Avenue. Neighborhood skating parties were very popular in late nineteenth-century Cranford. The boy on crutches grew up to be Cranford's township clerk.

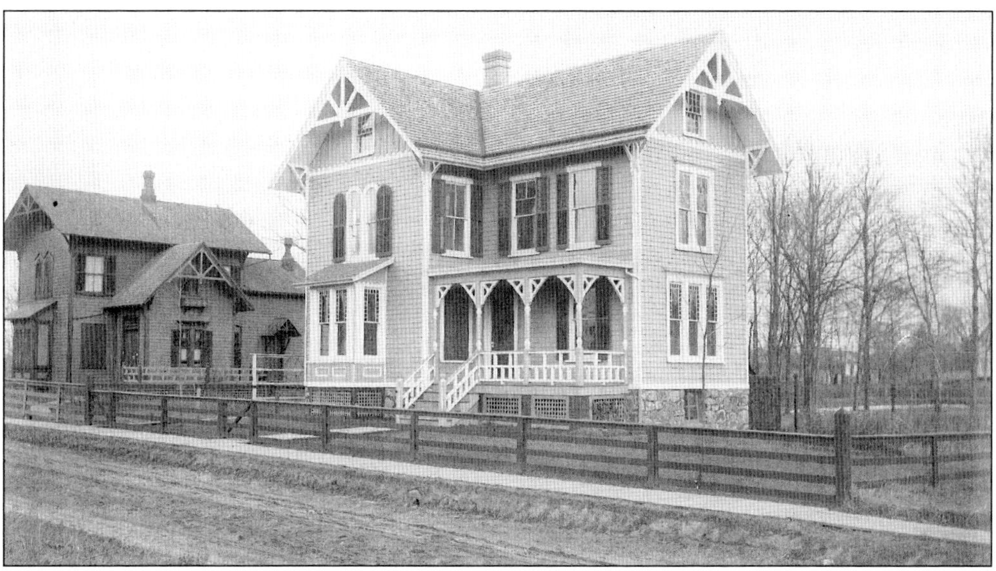

A BRAND NEW CRANFORD HOME IN THE 1880s. Located at 12 Orange Avenue, this was the first Cranford home of the Brundage family. Typical of upper middle class town and country homes of the time, it features an uncoursed rubble foundation, ornate barge boards and brackets at the roof, and a painted board fence.

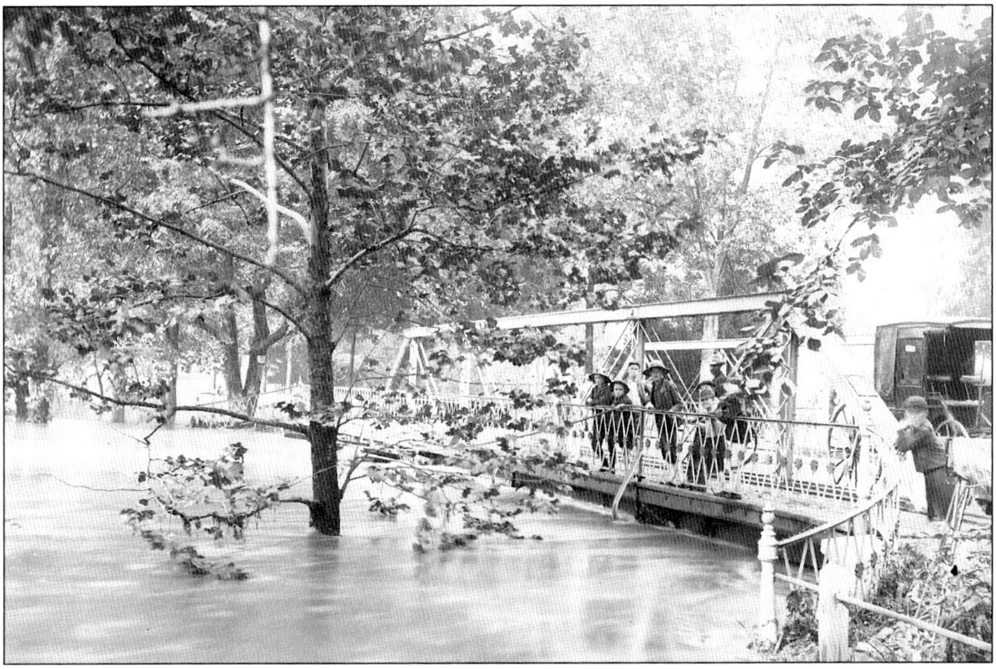

THE GREAT FLOOD OF JULY 1889. The Rahway River in Cranford is not always the tranquil stream that canoeists love. Young "Huck Finns" viewed the rising waters from the temporary safety of the North Union Avenue bridge.

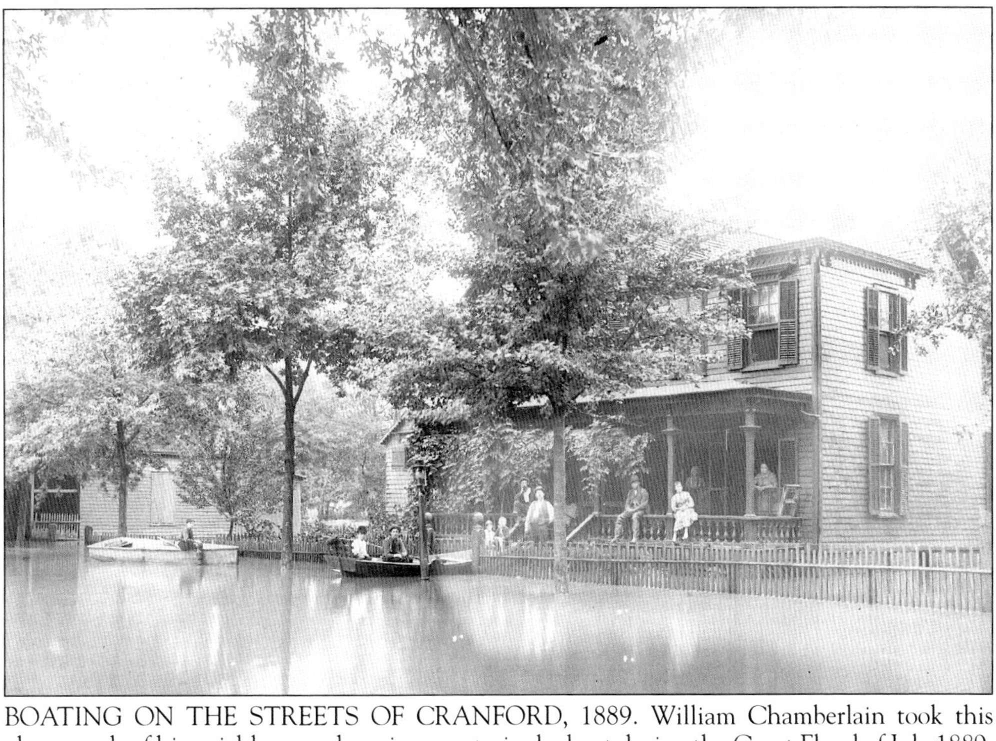

BOATING ON THE STREETS OF CRANFORD, 1889. William Chamberlain took this photograph of his neighbors exchanging courtesies by boat during the Great Flood of July 1889, caused by the breaking of the Echo Lake Dam.

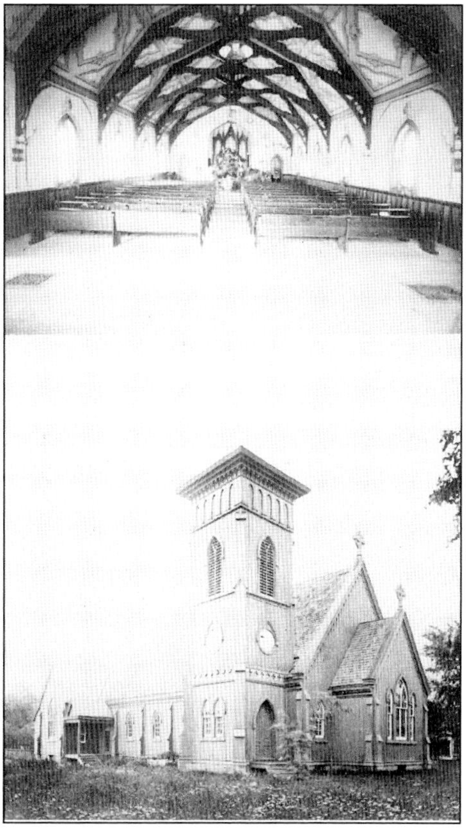

THE METHODIST CHURCH, 1871. This souvenir card was published to mark the dedication of the Reverend John Hancock Methodist Episcopal Church on Walnut Avenue, the site of the present Cranford Public Library. The Gothic frame church cost $16,000 to erect, and it seated three-hundred people.

THE FIRST BAPTIST CHURCH. The First Baptist Church had its beginnings in 1887 at 104 High Street. The cornerstone for the present church building was laid on June 6, 1897, and the first service in the new structure was held the following October. In 1987 the Cranford Historical Society presented its first Century Award to the First Baptist Church on the occasion of its 100th anniversary.

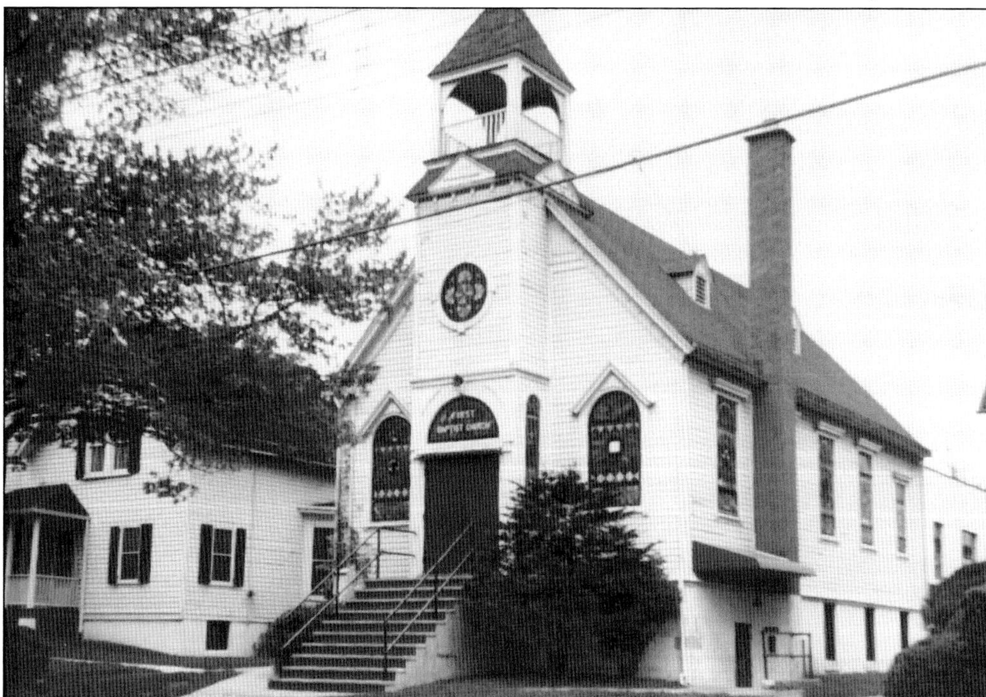

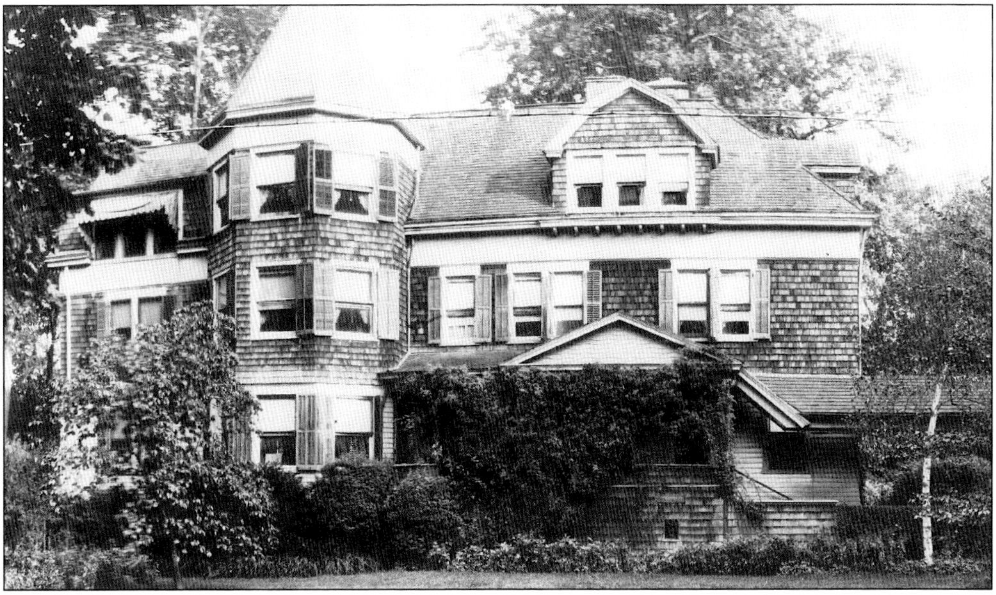

THE HAMPTON HALL ANNEX IN 1900. Hampton Hall was built in 1892 by Fannie Bates as an elegant residential hotel fronting on the Rahway River. The annex was added to accommodate an increasing number of guests. The hotel faced Hampton Street, near the corner of Eastman and the second Eastman Street bridge. The building was demolished in 1969 and the site is now Hampton Park.

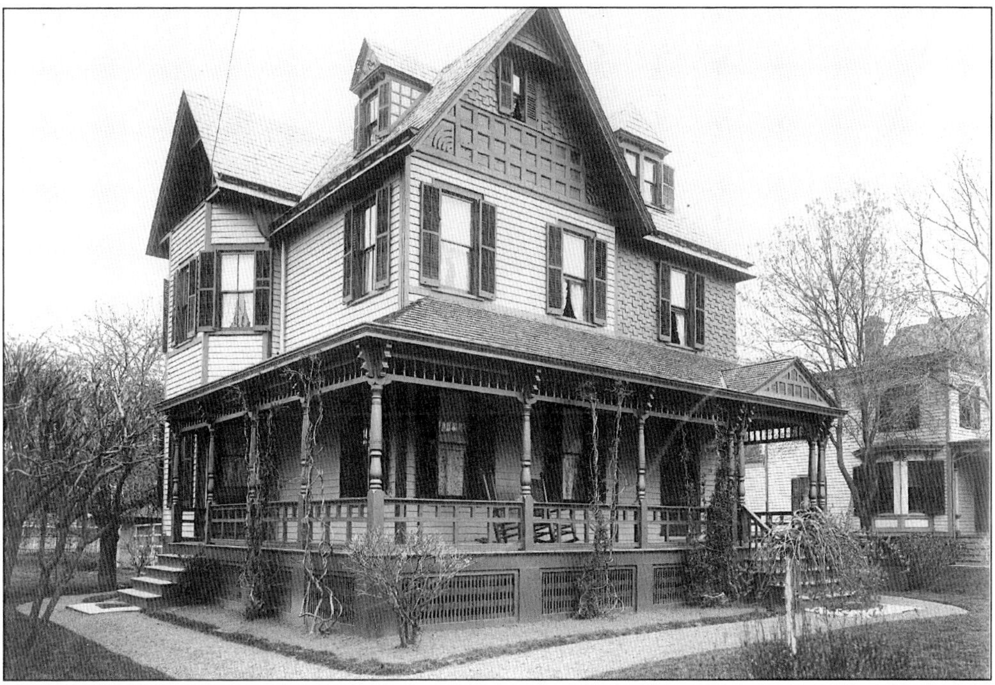

THE JAMES FERGUSON HOUSE, ABOUT 1885. Considered the father of the modern Cranford school system, James Ferguson was a banker and realtor. This is the second of two Ferguson homes (see p. 93). Minus its porch and stripped of its decoration, the house still stands at the northwest corner of North Union Avenue and Claremont Place.

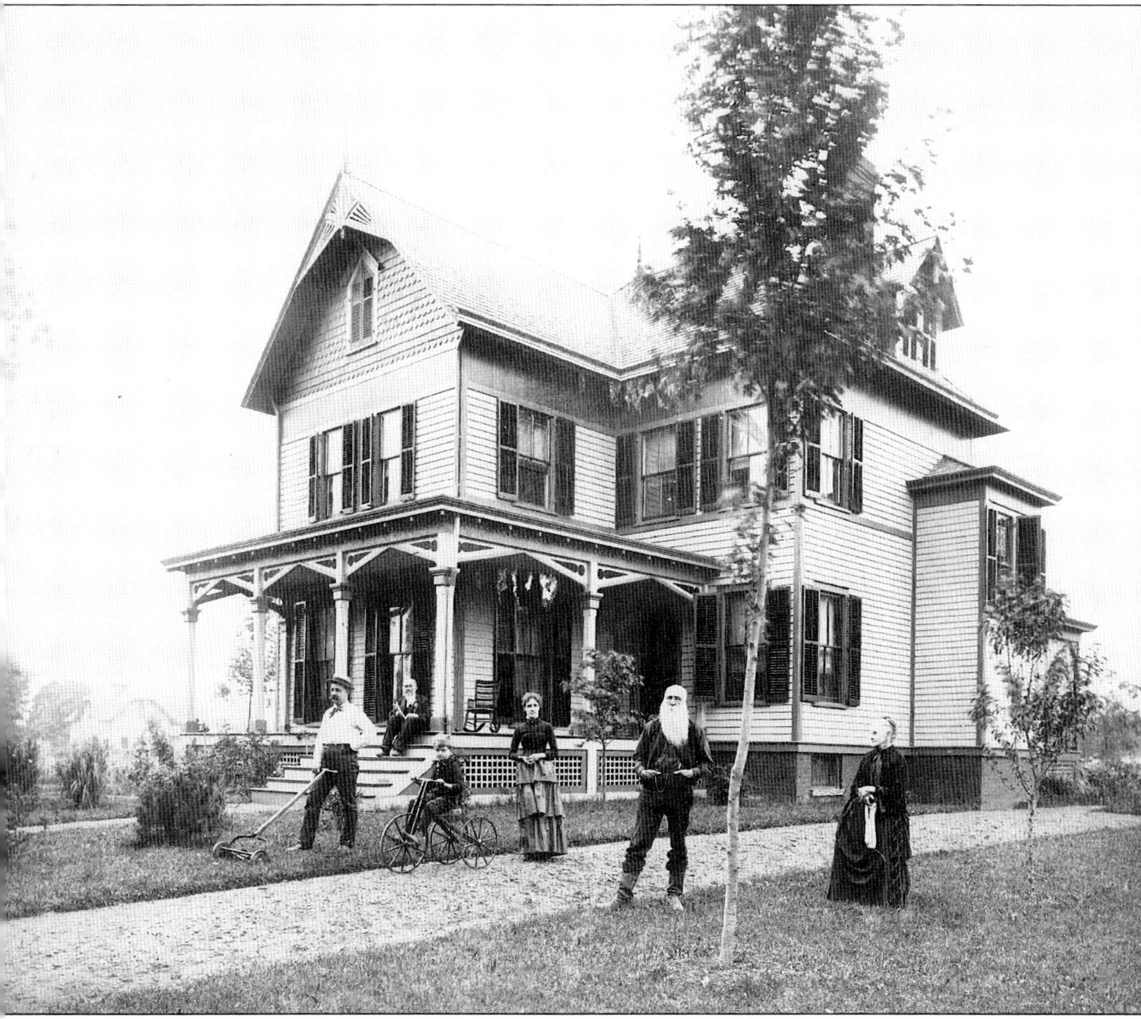

"HOME SWEET HOME" ON WALNUT AVENUE, 1888. Three generations of a Cranford family posed proudly in front of their home at 322 Walnut Avenue. The young trees indicate that the house was quite new when this photograph was taken. Note the beards on the two grandpas, father with his straw hat and lawn mower, and the boy's wooden tricycle.

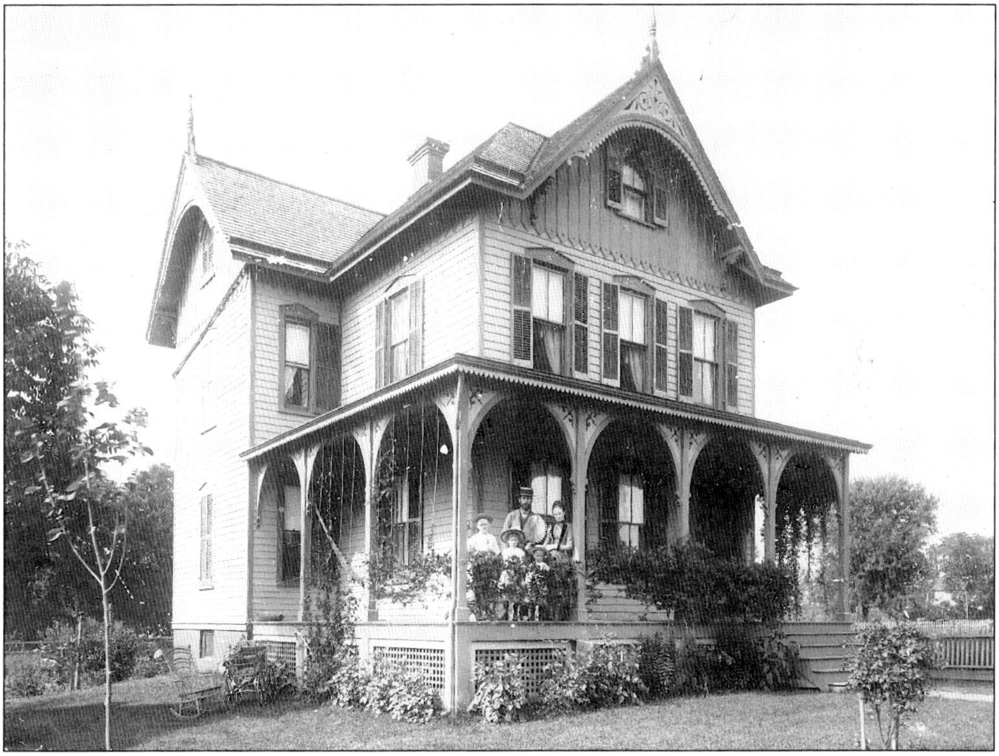

THE CHAMBERLAINS AT HOME, 1889. In this perfect image of Victorian tranquility, five members of the Chamberlain family gather for a portrait on the porch of their new home. Note the wicker rocker and baby carriage on the lawn at left. The house still stands at 215 North Avenue near Arlington Road.

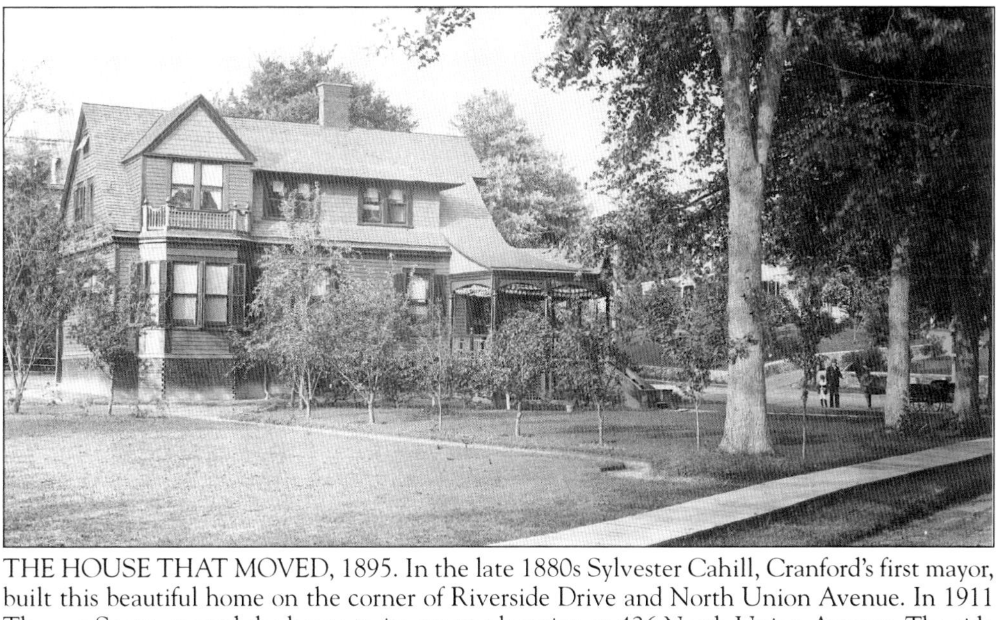

THE HOUSE THAT MOVED, 1895. In the late 1880s Sylvester Cahill, Cranford's first mayor, built this beautiful home on the corner of Riverside Drive and North Union Avenue. In 1911 Thomas Sperry moved the house to its present location at 426 North Union Avenue. The side of the house now faces the street, and some structural changes have been made.

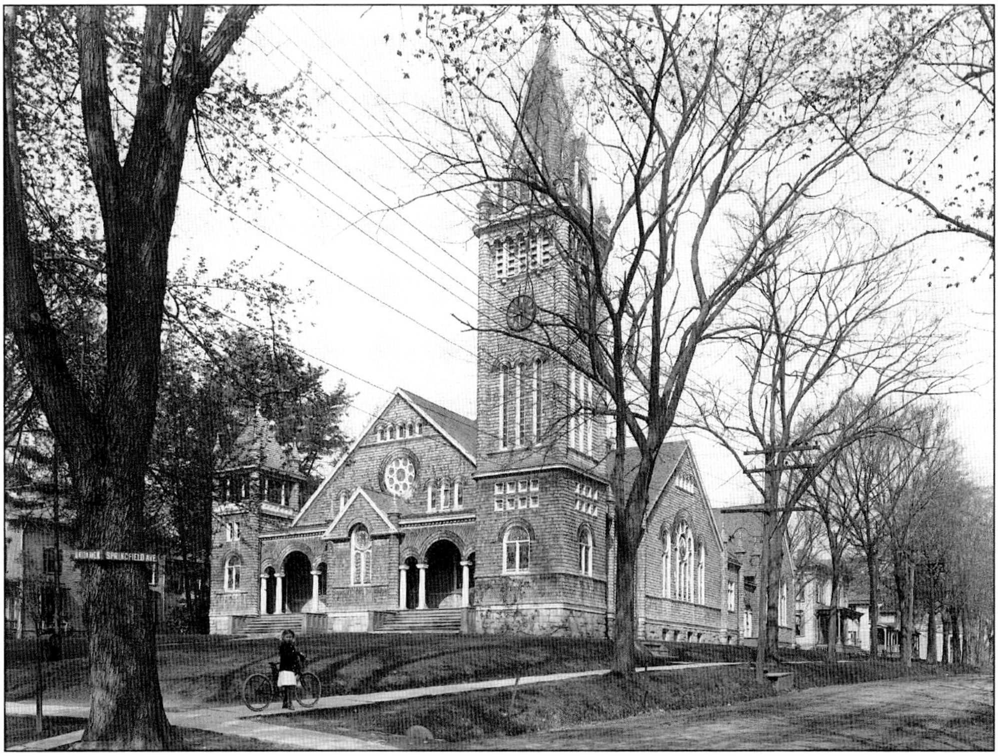

THE FIRST PRESBYTERIAN CHURCH, ABOUT 1900. Established in 1851, the First Presbyterian Church is the oldest congregation in Cranford. In 1893–94 the members built this magnificent Romanesque church on the corner of North Union and Springfield Avenues. It has stood as a Cranford landmark for more than a century.

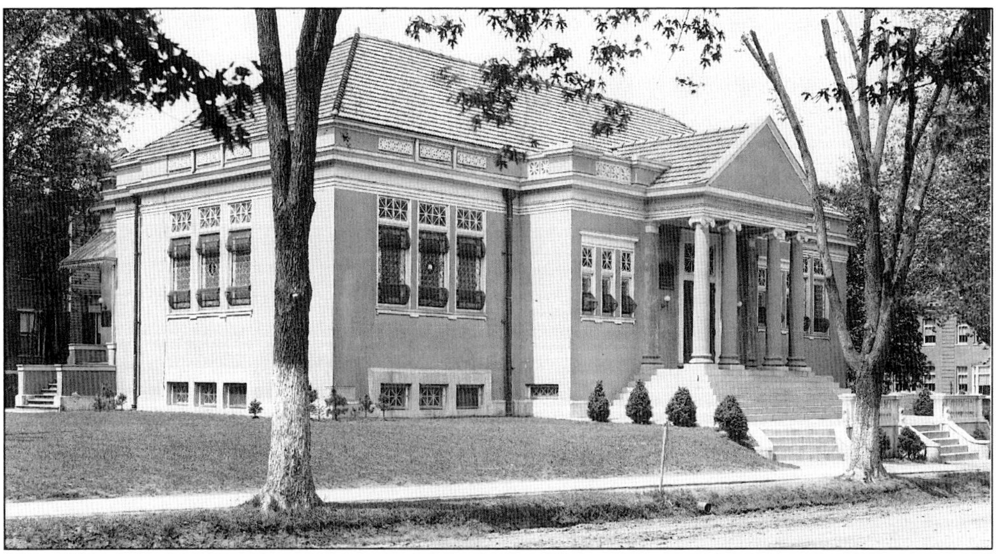

THE FIRST CHURCH OF CHRIST SCIENTIST, 1908. Local Christian Scientists organized their church in 1898, meeting in the old township offices on North Avenue and Eastman Street. This photograph was taken upon completion of the new church on Springfield Avenue in 1908.

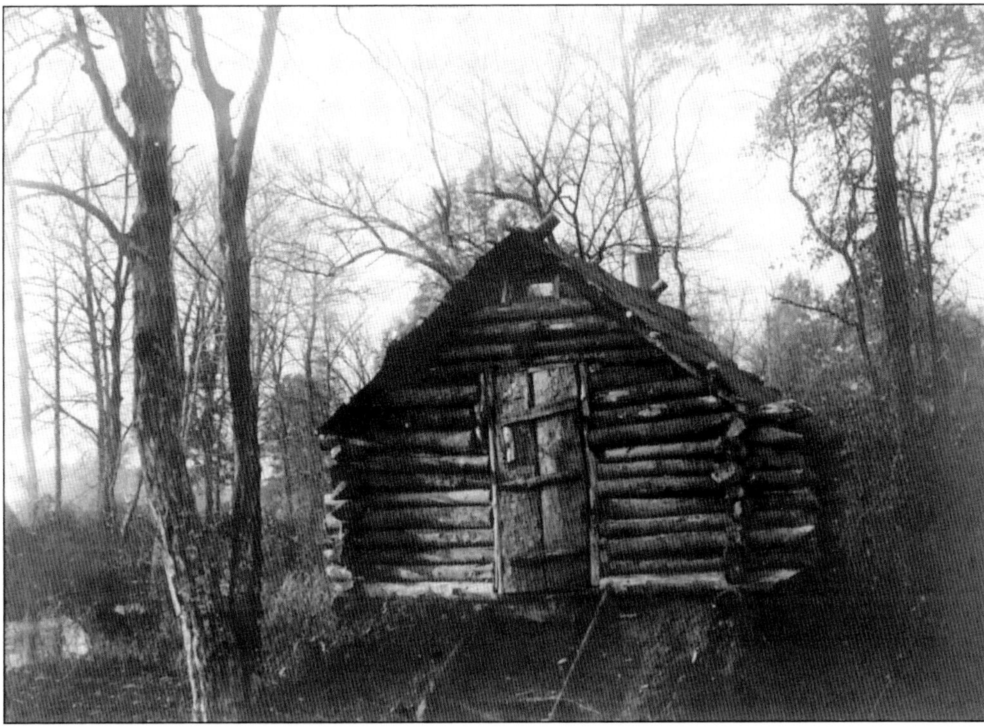

JOE PLUMMER'S RIVERSIDE LOG CABIN, 1895. During the time when "civilization" stopped at the second Springfield Avenue bridge, every boy in Cranford dreamed of having his own log cabin on the bank of the river deep in the woods. Joe Plummer did something about it—he designed and built his dream house.

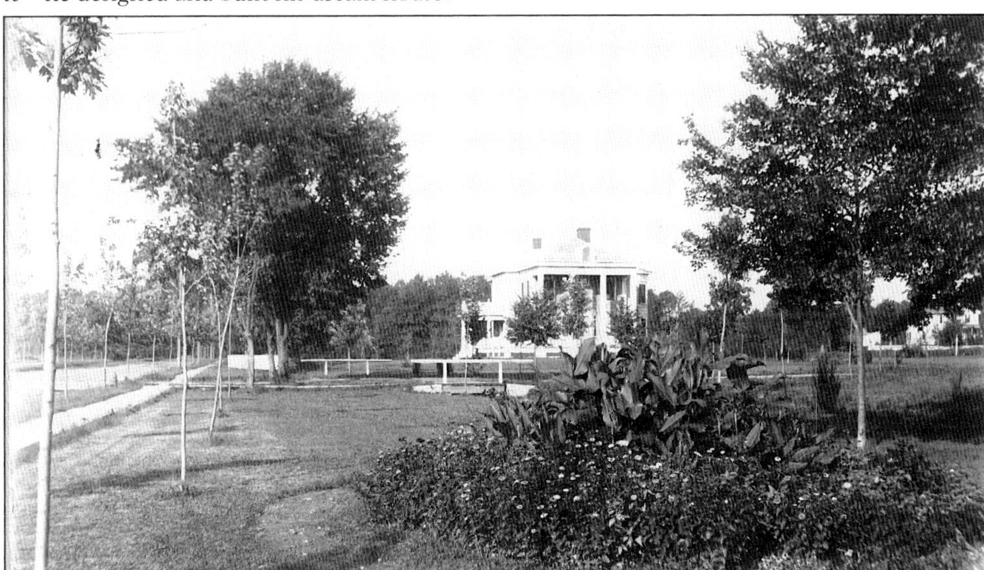

JOHN ROSS BATES' ESTATE, 1900. Formal garden plantings, young trees, and a bridge over a brook characterized the grounds of this great house at 406 Casino Avenue. Bates bought the house from its original owner, Carl Breckenridge. Estates of this size and larger were scattered throughout northern Cranford in the late nineteenth and early twentieth centuries.

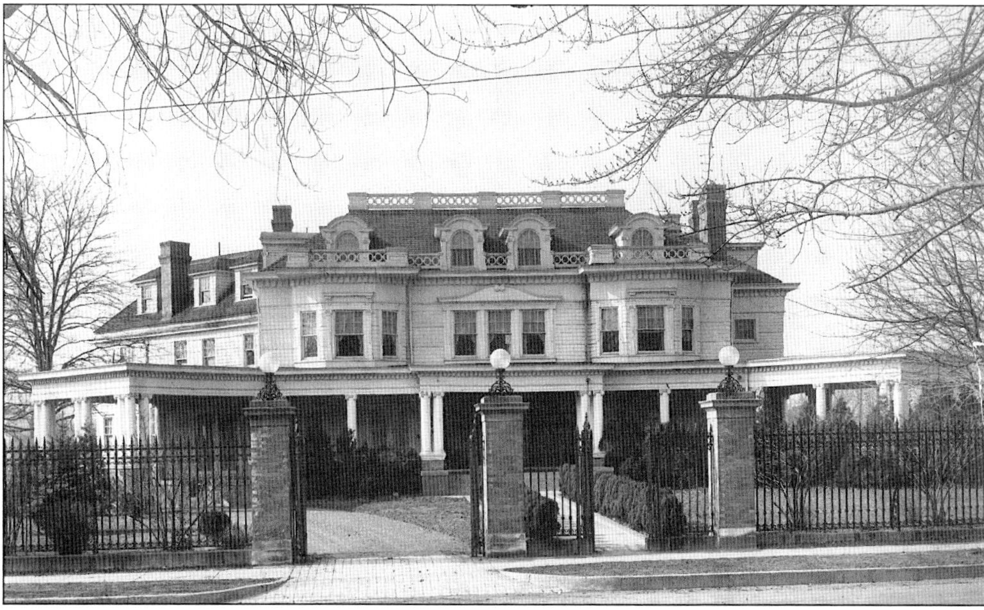

THE THOMAS SPERRY HOME IN 1905. The founder of the nation's largest trading stamp company, Sperry & Hutchinson (S & H Green Stamps), built this great house in 1903. It stood at Prospect Avenue and Claremont Place. The iron fence seen in this picture still exists on the site today, surrounding the English Village Condominiums.

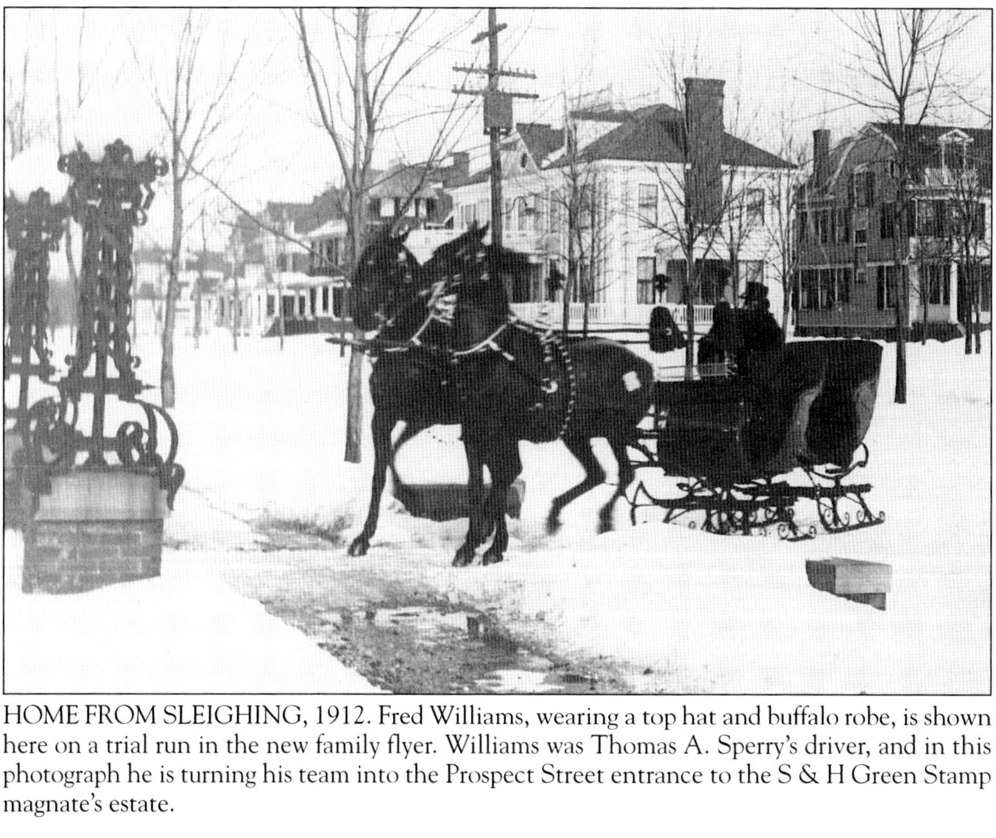

HOME FROM SLEIGHING, 1912. Fred Williams, wearing a top hat and buffalo robe, is shown here on a trial run in the new family flyer. Williams was Thomas A. Sperry's driver, and in this photograph he is turning his team into the Prospect Street entrance to the S & H Green Stamp magnate's estate.

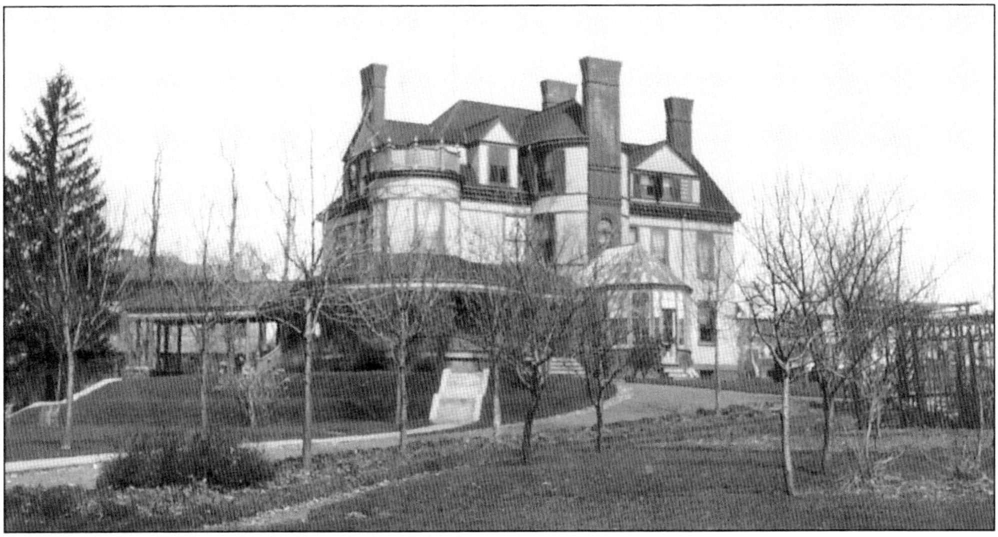

THE WILLIAM SPERRY HOUSE, ABOUT 1910. Standing on the northwest corner of North Union Avenue and Riverside Drive, this palatial house was home to Sperry from 1907 until his death in 1927. Sperry's favorite spot in the house was the glass conservatory, seen below the large chimney near the center of the photograph. The Riverside Condominiums occupy the site today.

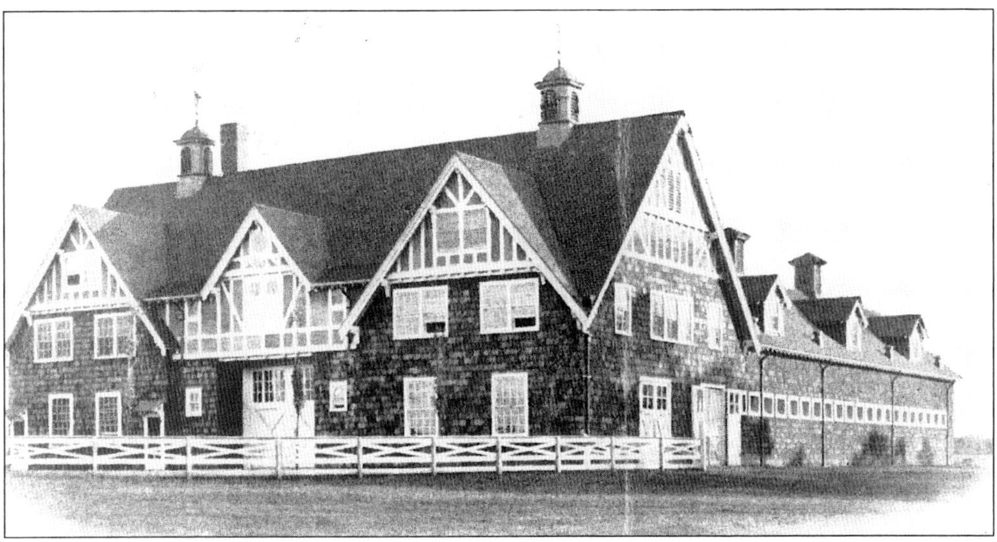

SPERRY'S BARN IN 1913. Thomas Sperry built this magnificent dairy barn on his Osceola Farms in southern Cranford in 1913. The building included herdsmen's apartments and a club room. Sperry died only four months after the barn was completed. The building burned to the ground twenty-eight years later, on February 22, 1941.

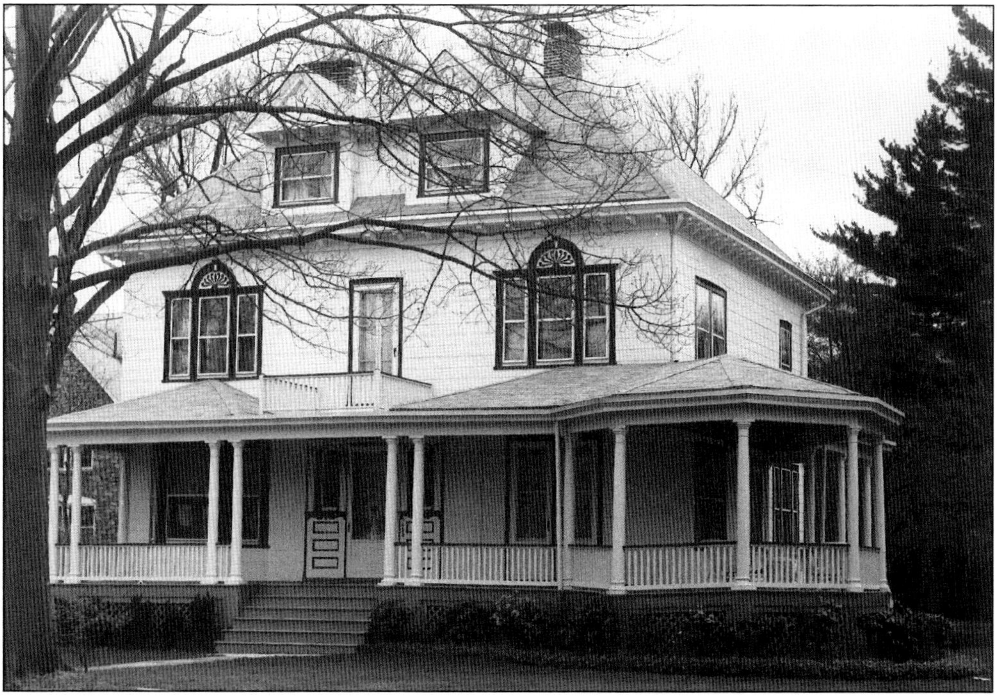

THE SANDERSON HOUSE. Facing Crane's Ford, this spacious home at 405 Springfield Avenue was built in 1894 by Harry Sanderson. Family descendants lived in the house until 1968. A carriage house (now a garage) behind this home was built for an earlier house on the site that was destroyed by fire. The former carriage house served as the Blue Bird Tea House and Dance Studio in the 1920s.

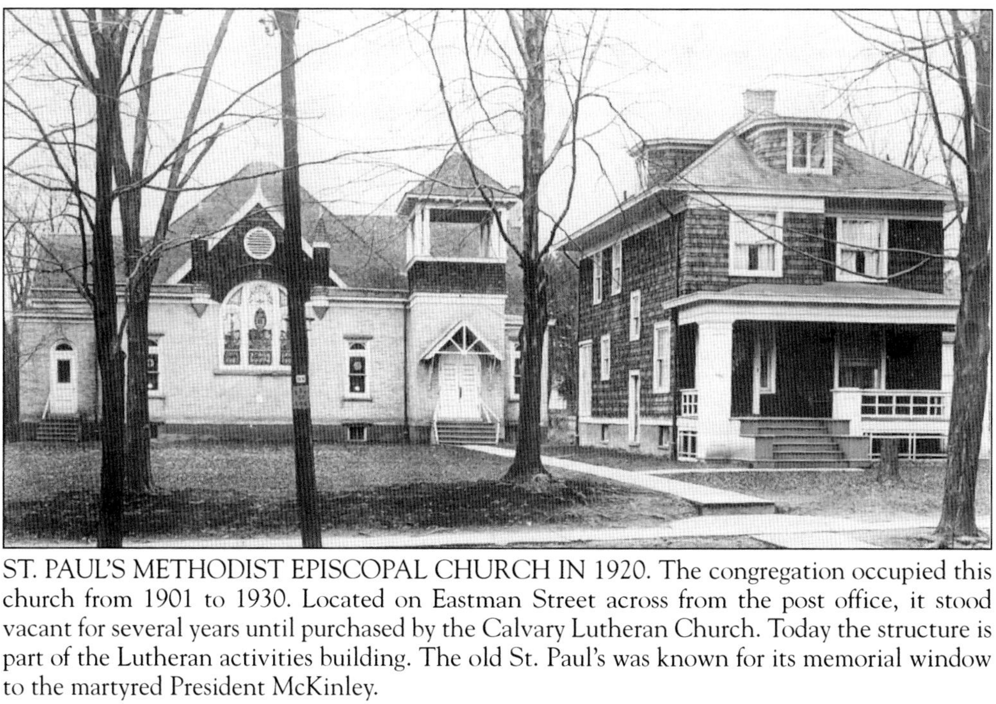

ST. PAUL'S METHODIST EPISCOPAL CHURCH IN 1920. The congregation occupied this church from 1901 to 1930. Located on Eastman Street across from the post office, it stood vacant for several years until purchased by the Calvary Lutheran Church. Today the structure is part of the Lutheran activities building. The old St. Paul's was known for its memorial window to the martyred President McKinley.

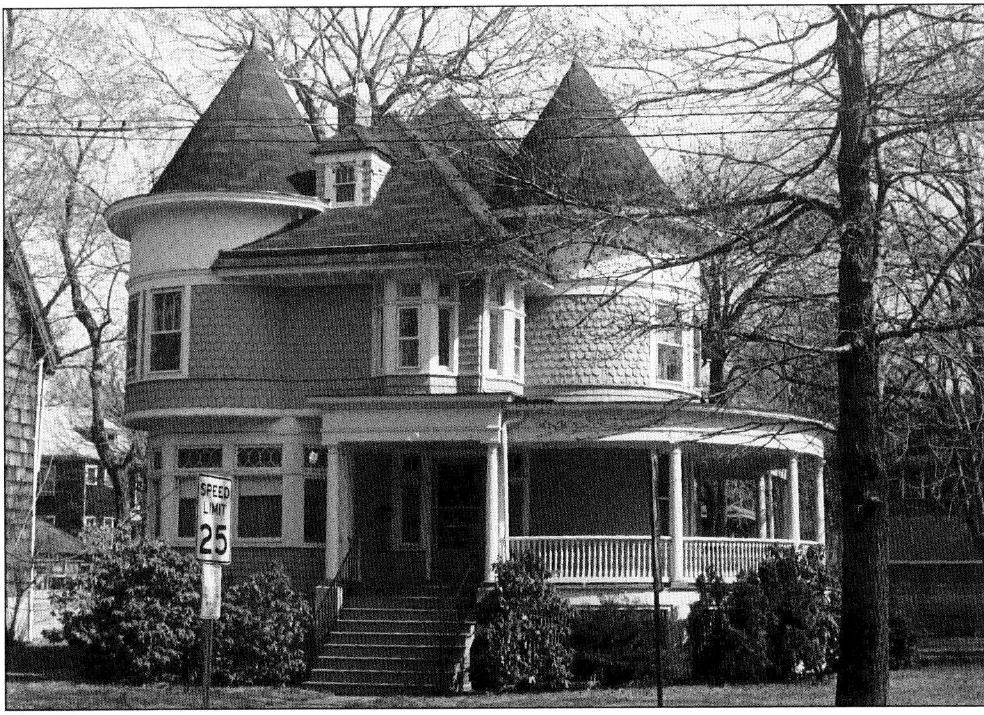

THE WATSON HOUSE, 117 FOREST AVENUE. In 1905 Eugene Austin built this Queen Anne-style house with its twin towers and curving porch. Austin sold the house in 1920 to Herbert and Frances Farrell. Their daughter, the late Florence Farrell Watson, acquired the house in 1979.

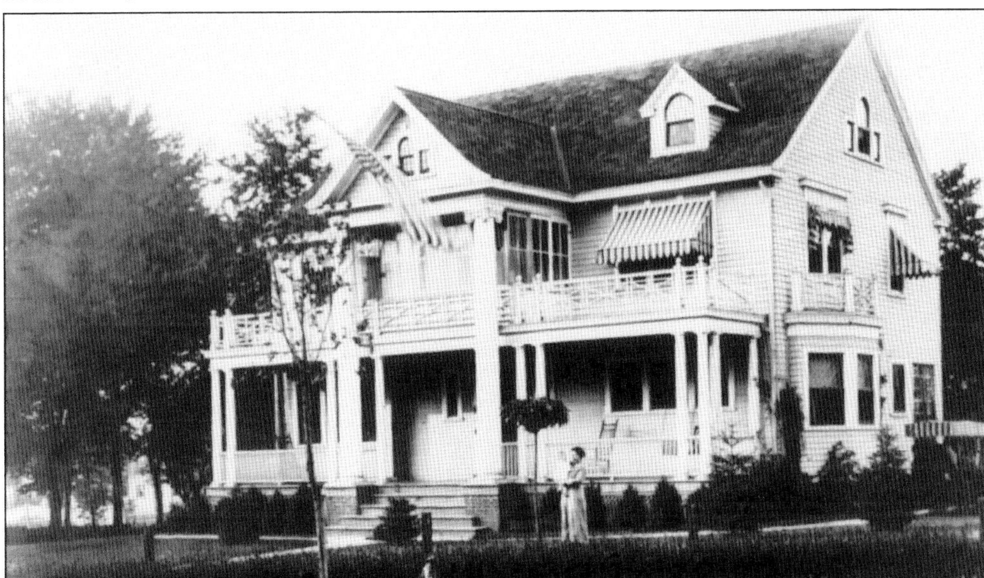

THE HIBSON HOUSE, 300 ELIZABETH AVENUE. Mrs. Lilly Hibson and her two daughters can be seen in front of the Hibson house, built on the site of the original St. Michael's Roman Catholic Church. In this 1915 view the house boasts striped summer awnings and a large American flag.

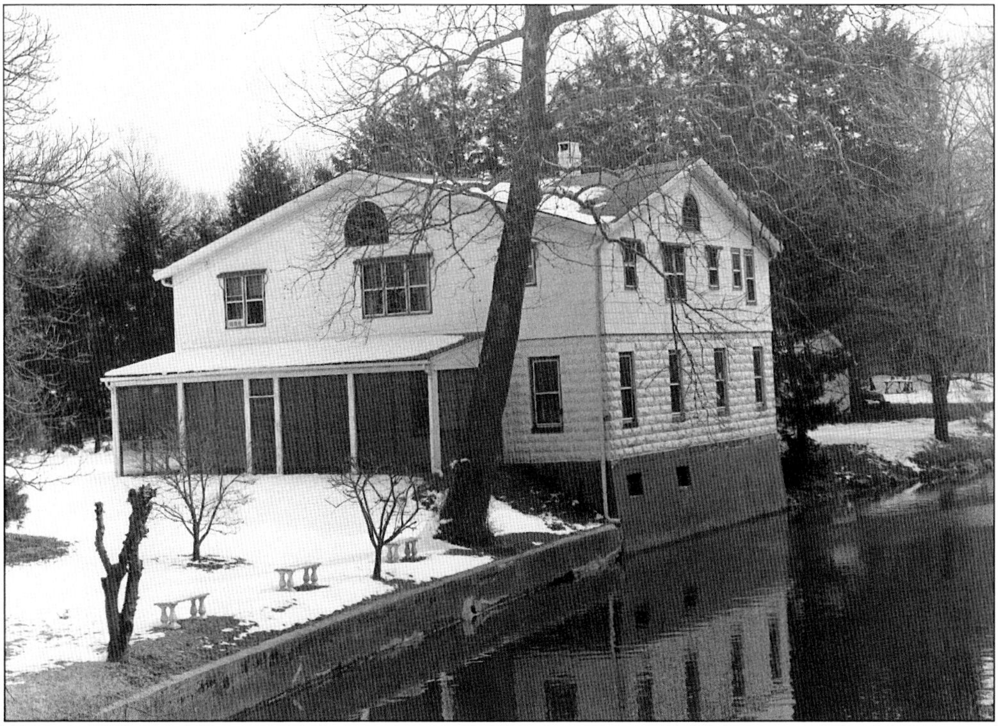

A CARRIAGE HOUSE ON THE RIVER. This striking frame and concrete-block house can be seen from the North Union Avenue bridge. Built in the early 1900s, it is one of only two local structures built directly into the river. Local tradition maintains that the building once had a dock and was the scene of gala River Carnival parties years ago.

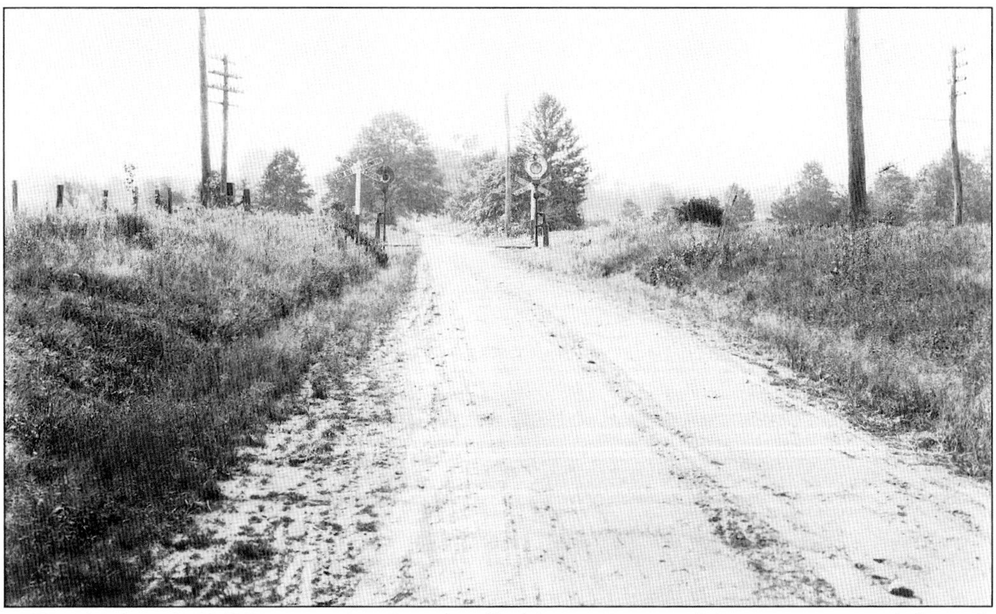

LEXINGTON AVENUE, 1922. Looking hardly like an "avenue," Lexington passed through farm fields in southwestern Cranford as it headed toward the Lehigh Valley Railroad crossing. Signs here warned "Look Out—Railroad Locomotive Crossing."

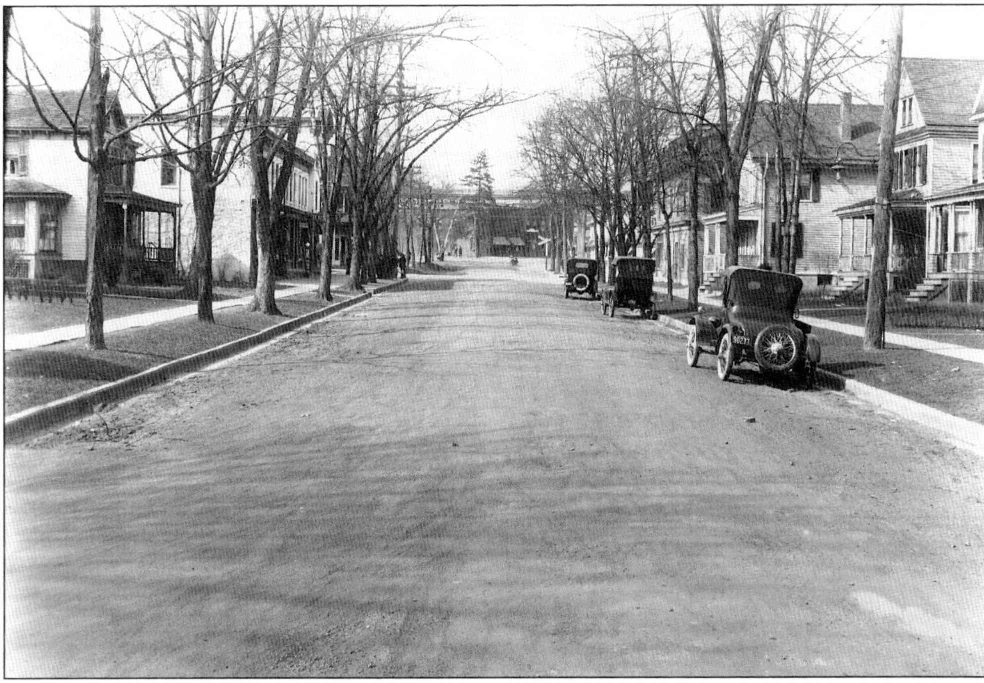

WALNUT AVENUE LOOKING NORTH, 1922. The road has new concrete curbs, gutters, and sidewalks, but it still has only a hard-packed dirt surface. The railroad crossing in the distance has not yet been elevated. The view of the downtown is blocked by the Chronicle Building, located where Eastman Plaza is today.

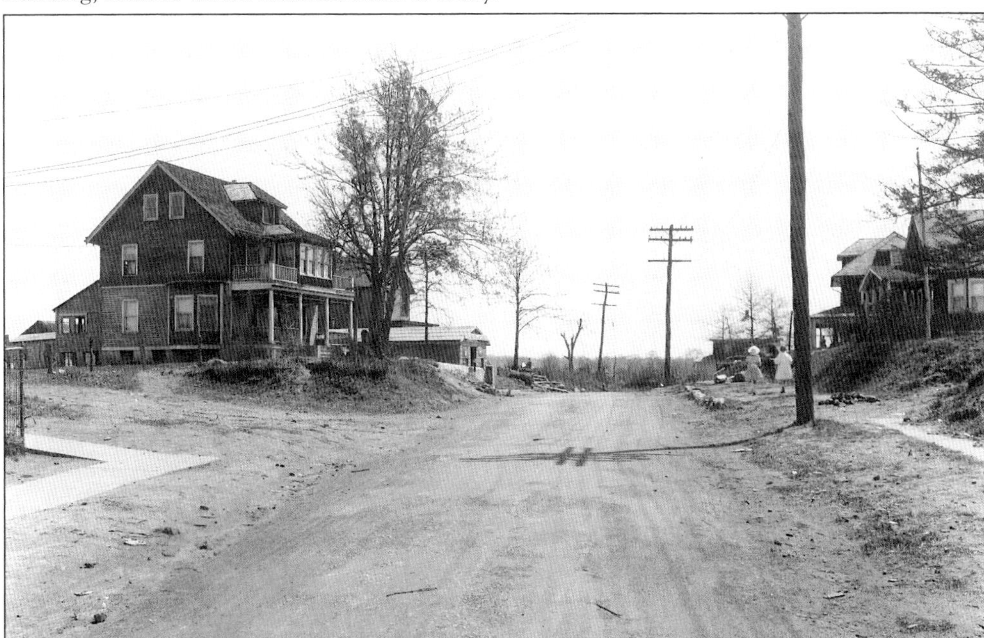

CENTENNIAL AVENUE LOOKING SOUTHEAST, 1922. In the early 1920s Centennial was just a dirt road heading for Linden and the area that later became Winfield. The long, low building in the left center of the picture is a general store.

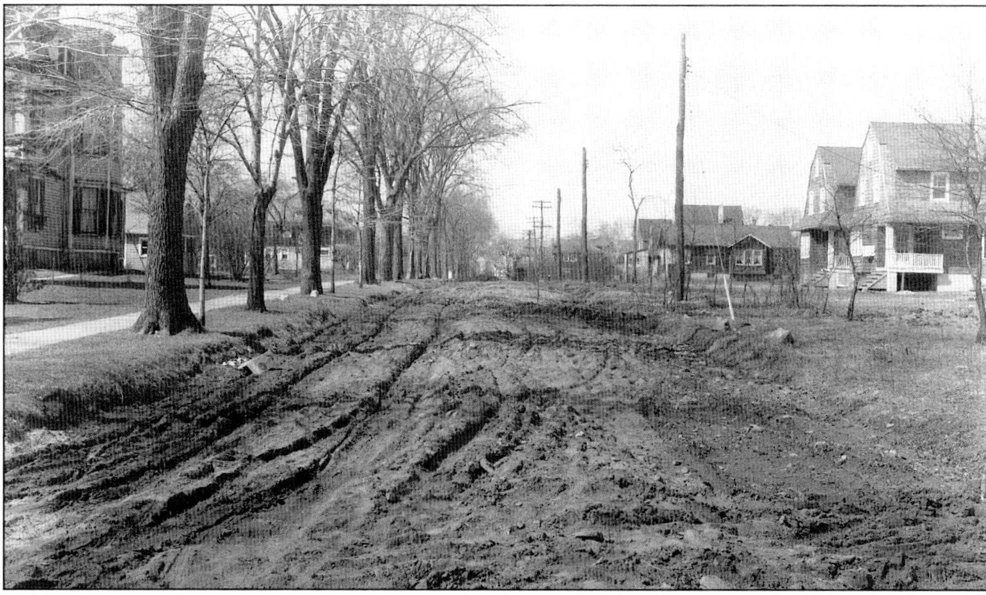

THE MUD OF JOHN STREET, 1926. It may look like a World War I battlefield, but incredibly this scene is of a Cranford street in the 1920s, after the spring thaw. Conditions like this motivated Township Engineer D.C.N. Collins to embark on a massive road building campaign, causing him to remark, "I wonder how many of us realize the magnitude of changes about to made in Cranford."

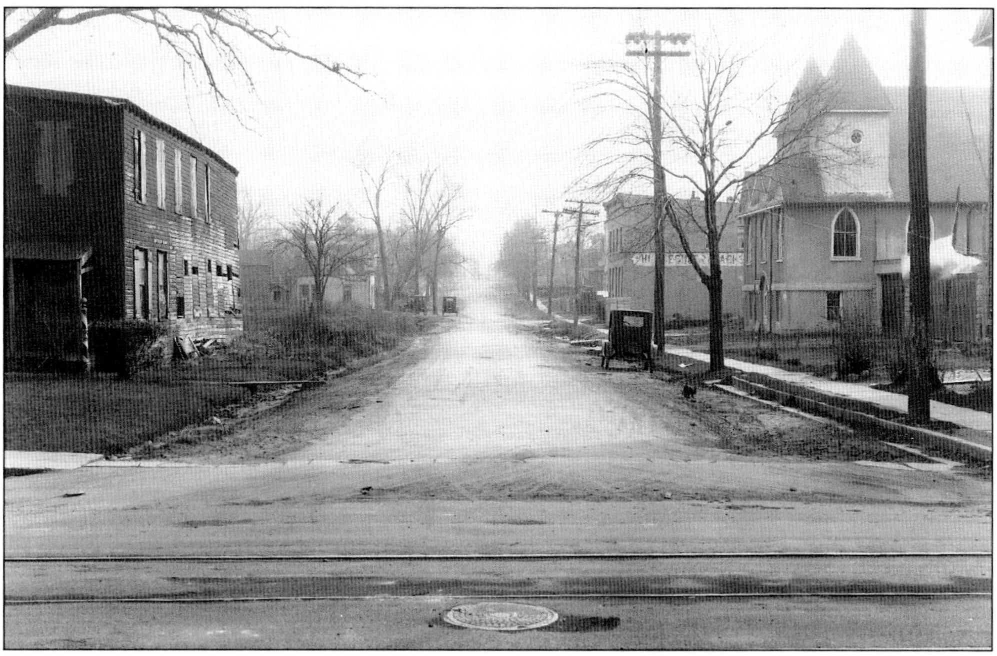

HIGH STREET SEEN FROM SOUTH AVENUE, 1927. On the right stands the brand new St. Mark's AME Church, which was destroyed by fire in 1988. The ramshackle building on the left was demolished shortly after this picture was taken. If you look closely, you can see an old wooden barber pole in front. Further up on the left, barely visible, is the Virginia Grocery. The South Avenue trolley tracks are in the foreground.

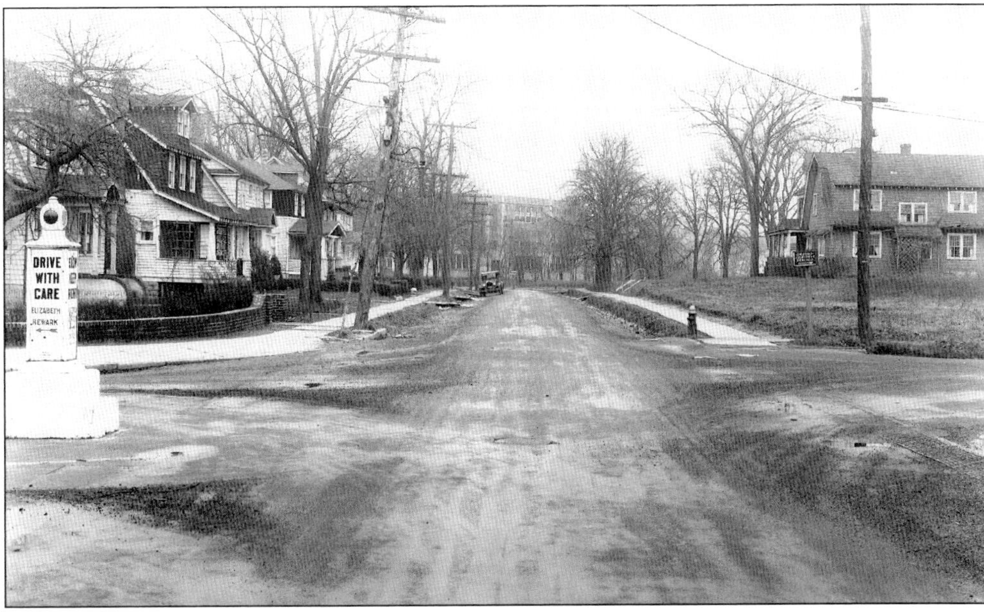

LINCOLN AVENUE, LOOKING EAST FROM RETFORD, 1927. Lincoln Avenue had a hard-packed dirt and cinder surface when this photograph was taken. The new Sherman School can be seen in the distance. The "Drive With Care" traffic signal on the left was gas-powered. The device was made by the American Gas Accumulator Company of Elizabeth, N.J.

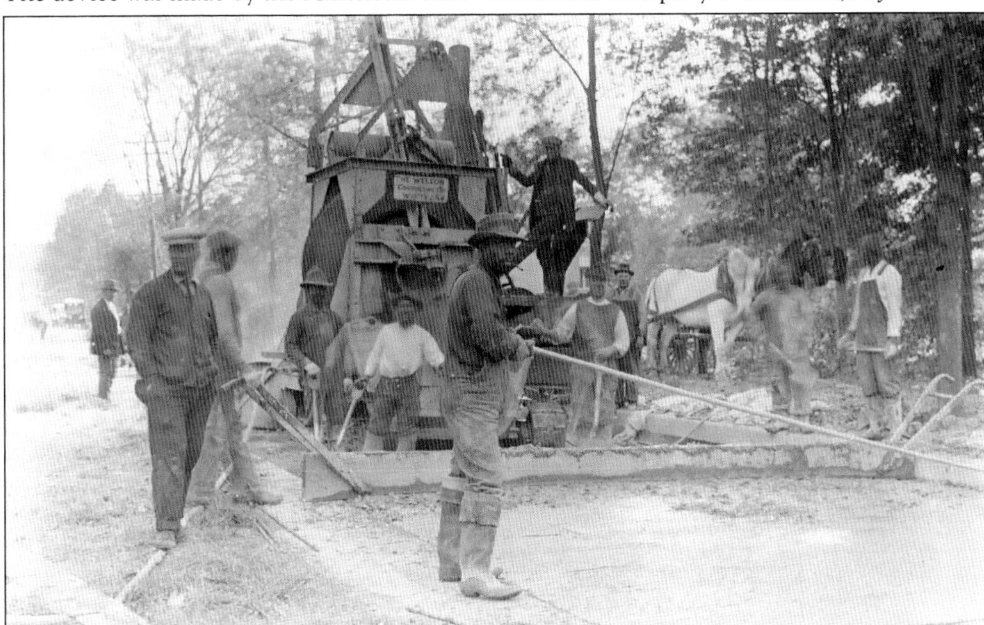

PAVING LINCOLN AVENUE, 1928. A crew from the Weldon Contracting Company in Westfield lays down a reinforced concrete surface and new curbing. The cement mixer in the picture moved on steel caterpillar treads. Two horses, which were still used, can be seen in the background. Cranford was a pioneer in planning annual programs of street improvements.

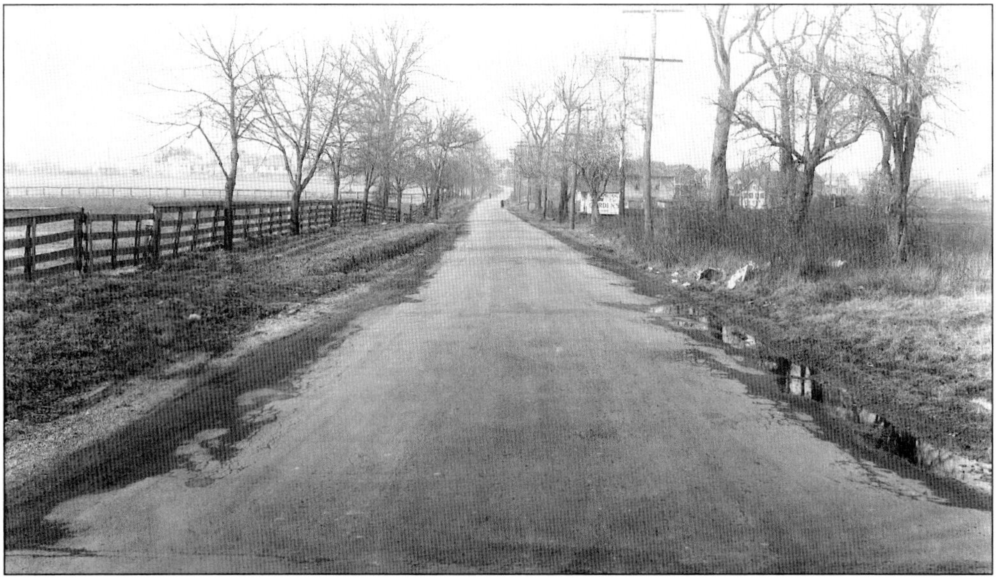

RUSTIC CENTENNIAL AVENUE, 1930. This photograph was taken looking north from Raritan Road toward the town center. Centennial Avenue, named for the United States Centennial in 1876, was still a country lane in 1930. A horse farm can be seen on the left, and the American Gardens Corporation is on the right.

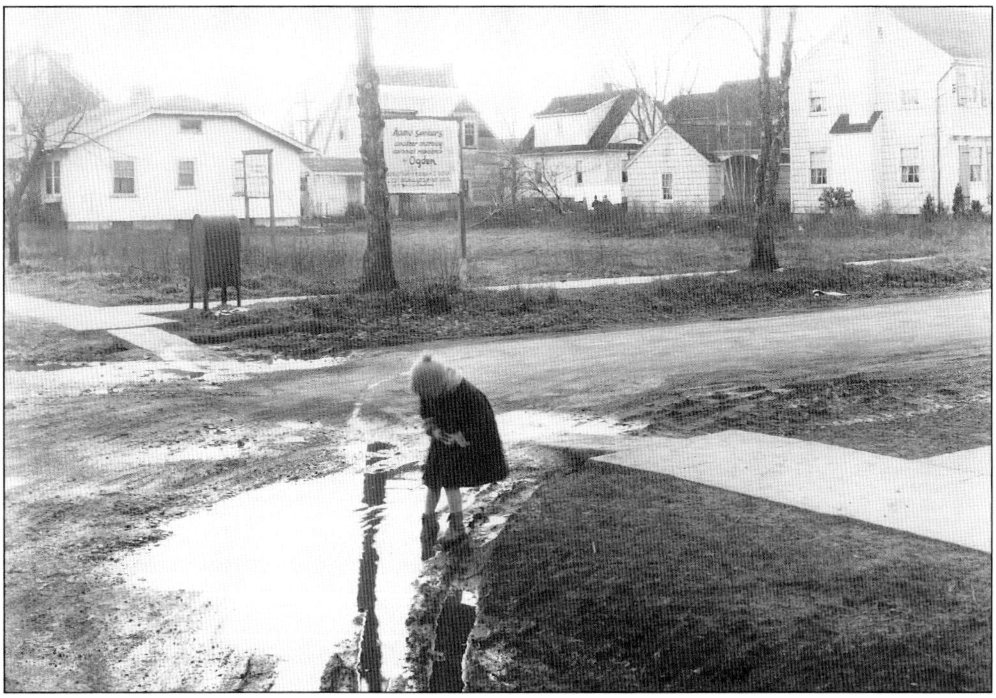

TESTING THE WATERS AT CRAIG PLACE, 1930. She could, of course, have walked around it. Here we are at Craig, looking west from Orange Avenue. The sign in the corner lot advertises, "Home Seekers: another charming colonial residence by Ogden." The house included a "center hall, 7 rooms, 2 baths, 2-car attached garage, open porch." One wonders what it cost in this second year of the Great Depression.

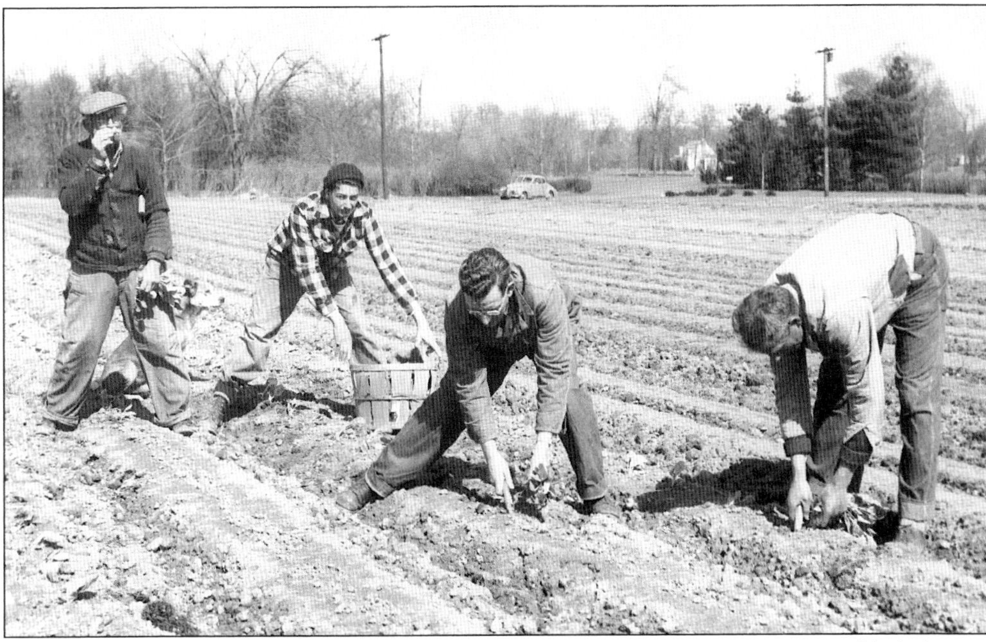

DREYER'S FARM, 1940. This farm on Springfield Avenue is Cranford's last tangible link to its agricultural past. It is much smaller now than it was when the Dreyers settled there nearly one hundred years ago. Union County College and split-level homes occupy the old pasture. Shown planting cabbage where today's Yale Terrace joins Penn Road are, from left to right: Gus Dreyer, Don Dreyer, Will Piegelbeck, and Henry Dreyer Sr. Nomahegan Park is in the background.

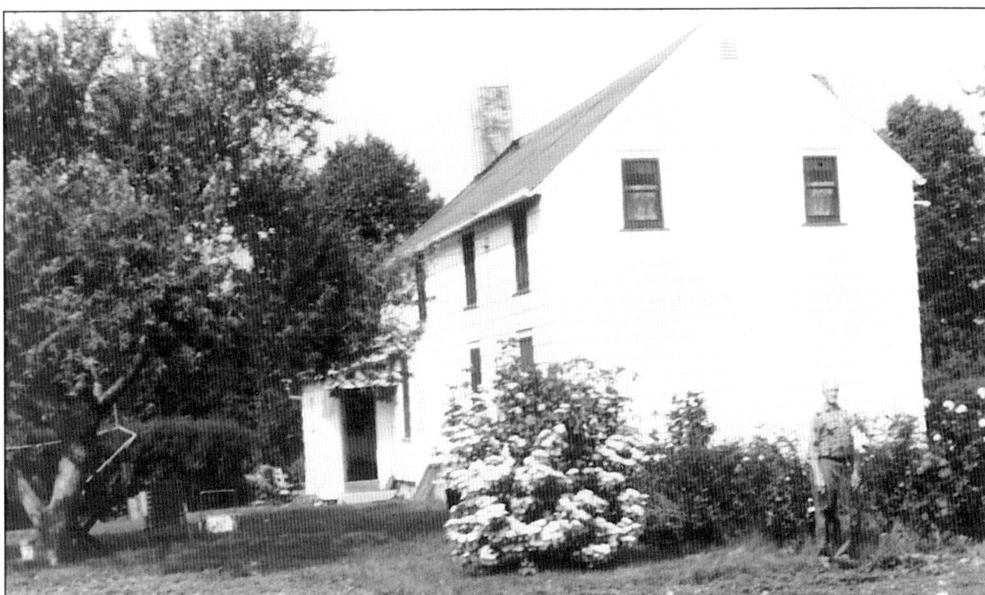

DITZEL'S FARM. Harry Herbert Ditzel at his home on Denman Road in the 1960s. Ditzel's farm was one of the last two farms to survive in Cranford, and was a favorite attraction for area schoolchildren. Five generations of Ditzels lived here between 1866 and 1984, when the last of the farmland was sold. Where corn grew not so long ago, residents now tend manicured lawns.

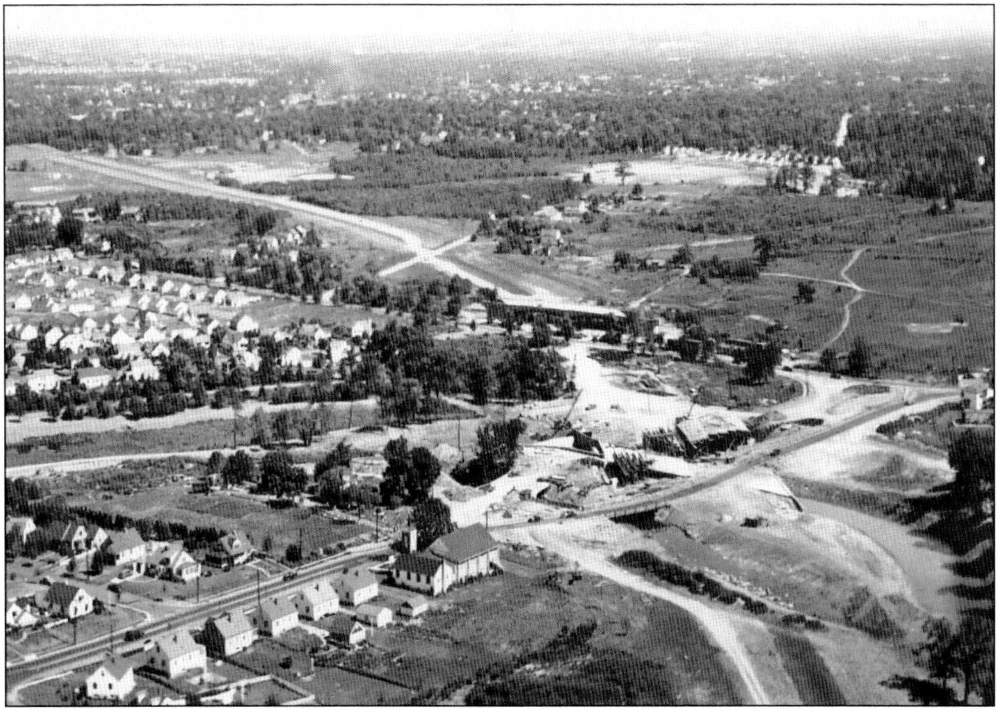

CONSTRUCTING THE PARKWAY, 1949. This aerial view shows work in progress on the new Garden State Parkway at exit 136 at the southern tip of Cranford. The Osceola Presbyterian Church on Raritan Road is just below center in the picture. At one time, the southern portion of Cranford threatened to secede and form the independent municipality of South Cranford.

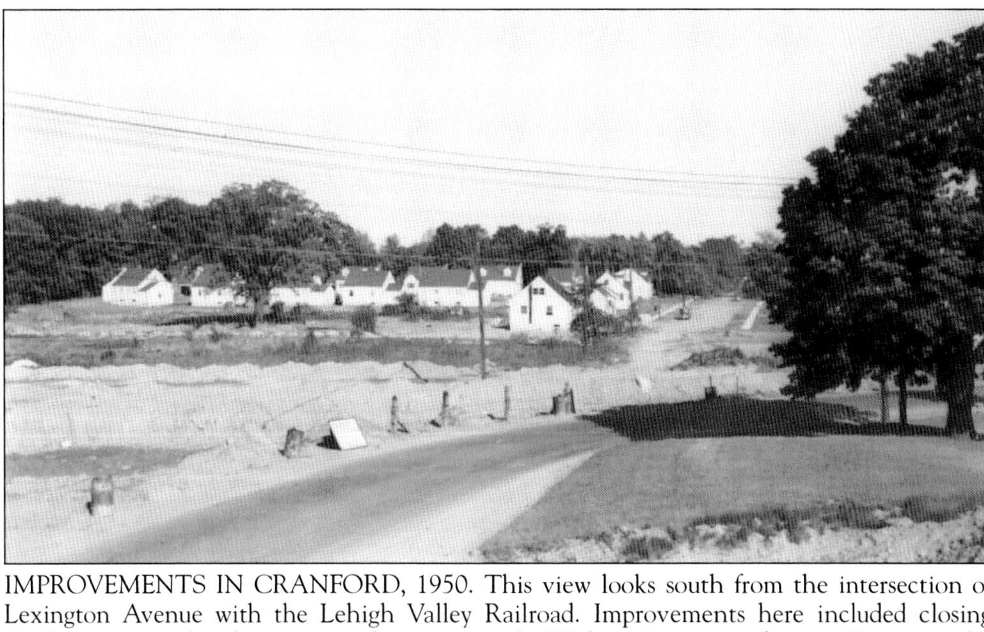

IMPROVEMENTS IN CRANFORD, 1950. This view looks south from the intersection of Lexington Avenue with the Lehigh Valley Railroad. Improvements here included closing the Lexington railroad crossing and excavating the Walnut Avenue underpass. Houses in the distance are along Roger Norton Place.

Eight

The Finest

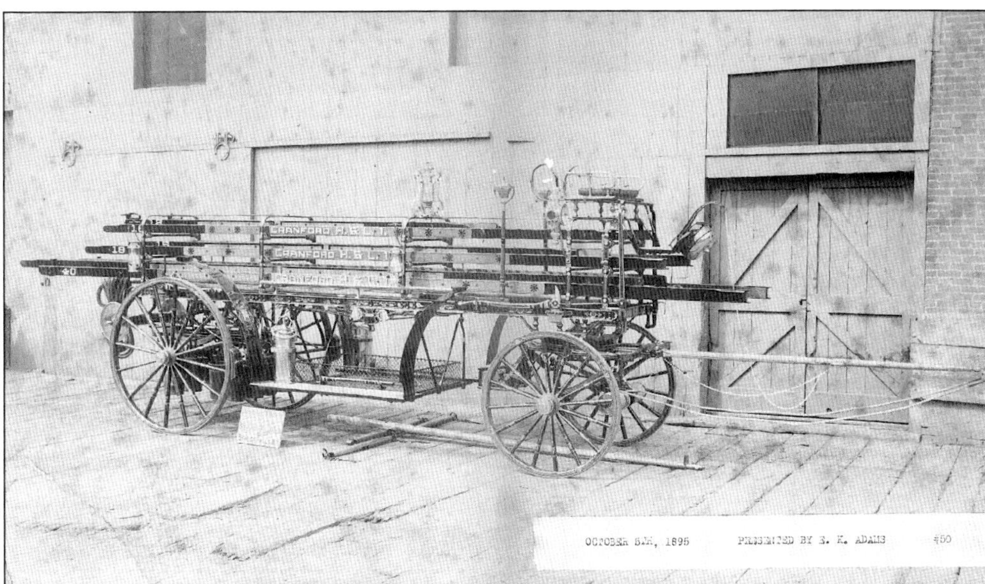

CRANFORD'S NEW HORSE-DRAWN LADDER TRUCK, 1895. Hook and Ladder Company No. 1, organized on April 17, 1893, became the proud possessor of this apparatus two years later. Built in Seneca Falls, N.Y., by Gleason and Baily, the truck carried 12, 15, 18, and 40-foot ladders, as well as rope, four axes, two fire extinguishers, four lanterns, two sledge hammers, fire hooks, and ten fire buckets.

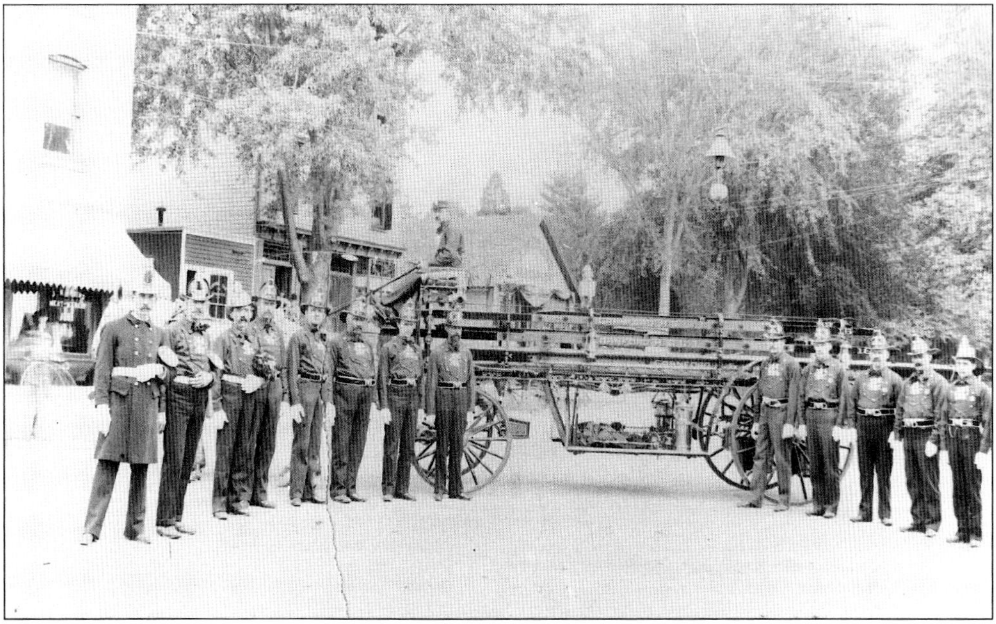

THE CRANFORD HOOK AND LADDER COMPANY NO. 1, 1895. Standing tall, Cranford's second fire company poses with their new horse-drawn truck. The first man on the left is Chief Daniel Torbush, and next to him is E.K. Adams Jr., founder of the company. In the background can be seen, from left to right, J.N. Irvings' Meat Market, the Central Cab Office, and Crane's Grocery store (the building with the peaked roof).

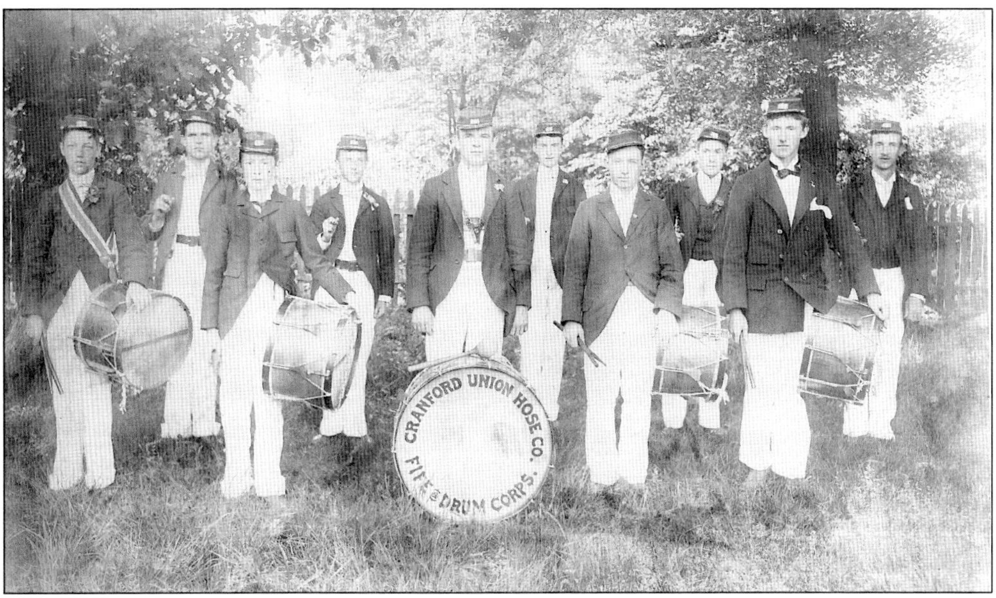

CRANFORD'S UNION HOSE COMPANY FIFE & DRUM CORPS, *c.* 1897. Volunteer fire companies were intensely competitive, not only in extinguishing fires but in social and civic activities as well. This volunteer company boasted its own fife and drum corps. The Union Hose music makers are, from left to right: Robert Crane, Robert Wakefield, Wilbur Baylis, Ed Burley, Harry Kirkman, Elmer Wheeler, Tot Howell, Ray Cox, Jesse Wheeler, and Walter Crane.

EMMOR K. ADAMS JR., 1892. Adams was the captain of the Thief Detecting Society, the deputy sheriff, a township committeeman, and a Union County freeholder, and he happily became involved with any group that aimed at civic betterment. Rightfully called "The Father of the Cranford Fire Department," he is shown here in the uniform of the Cranford Hose Company No. 1, a volunteer company he helped to found in 1892.

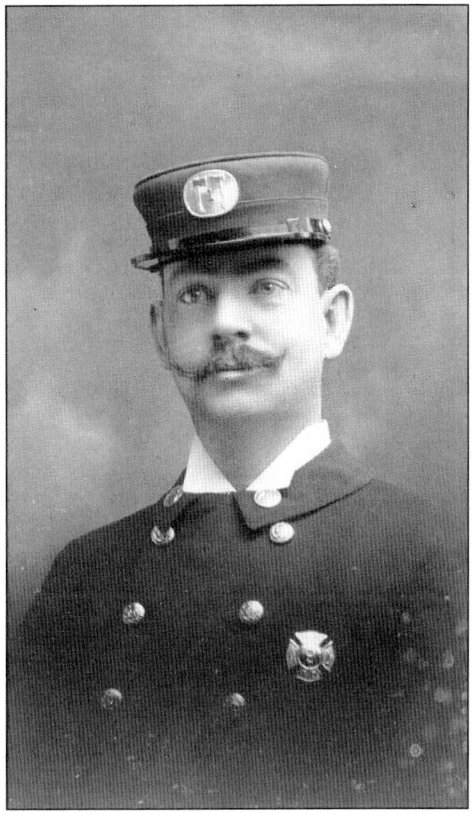

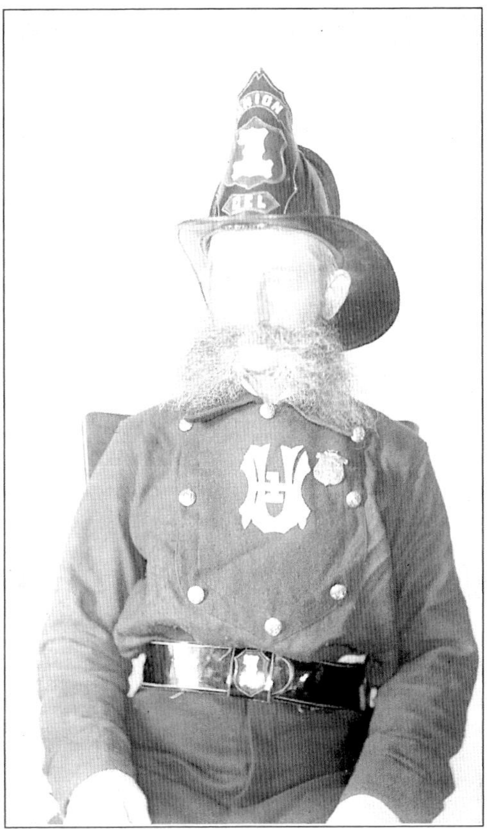

YOU COULDN'T TAKE HIM TO A FIRE. Gideon Ludlow's whiskers were a standing joke. His fellow firefighters would not stand near him at a blaze, they said, because his whiskers might go up at any time. In this 1893 portrait Ludlow is wearing his red fireman's shirt with the logo of the Union Hose Company No. 1. Before his fire department service, he served on the Township Committee, and he was Township Assessor from 1873 to 1881.

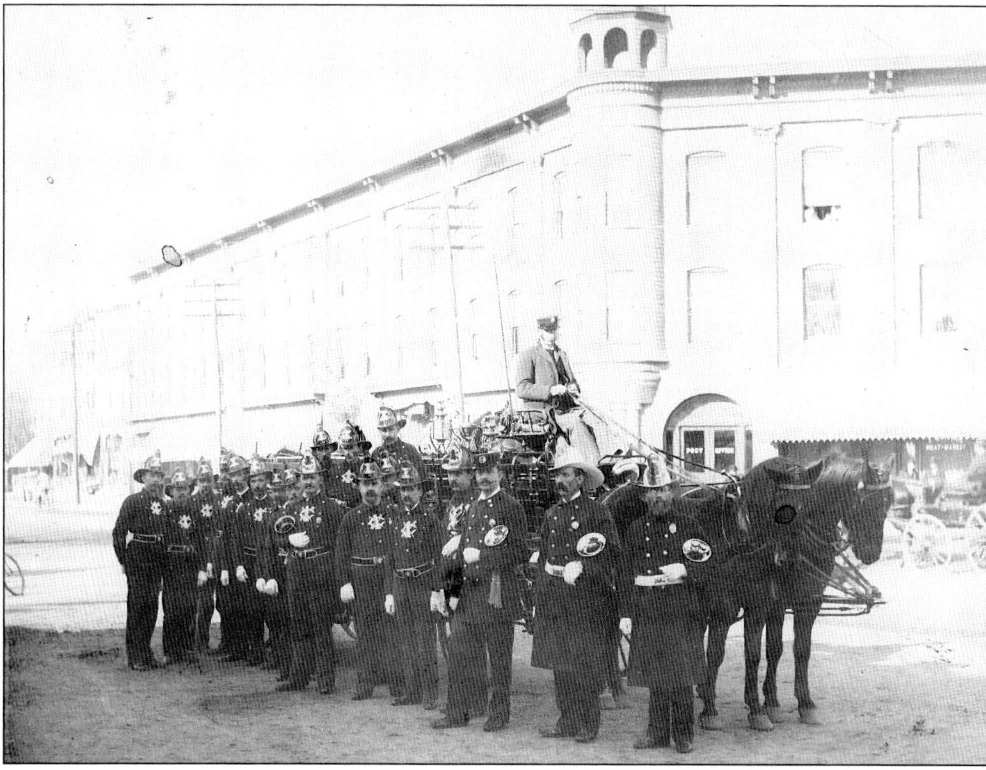

ONE-HALF OF THE CRANFORD FIRE DEPARTMENT, 1895. Resplendent in their blue woolen shirts and black leather helmets, Cranford's Hook and Ladder Company No. 1 posed with their new horse-drawn ladder truck, purchased by the township for $375. The man standing third from right is E.K. Adams Jr.

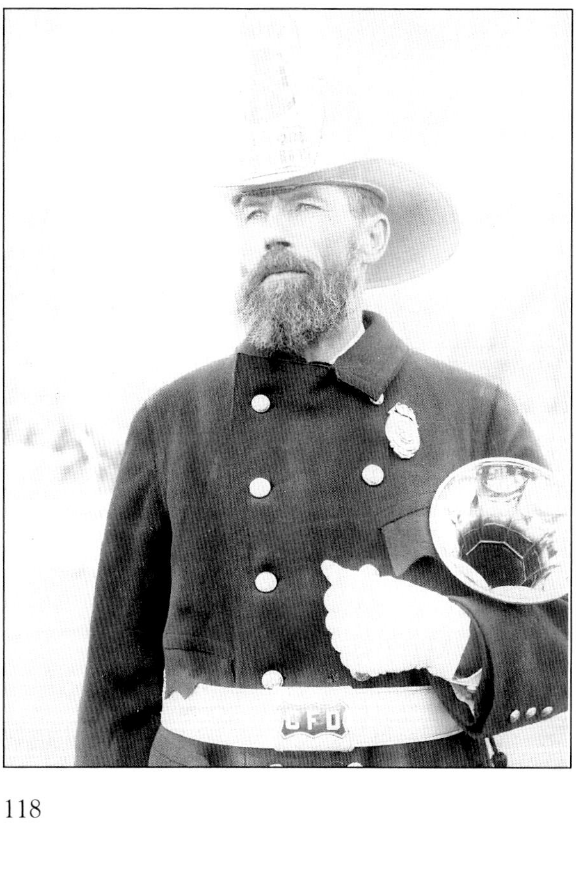

FIRE CHIEF JOHN WATERSON, c. 1895. Steely-eyed and stalwart, with his speaking trumpet tucked under his arm, Cranford Fire Chief John Waterson stands ready to answer the call.

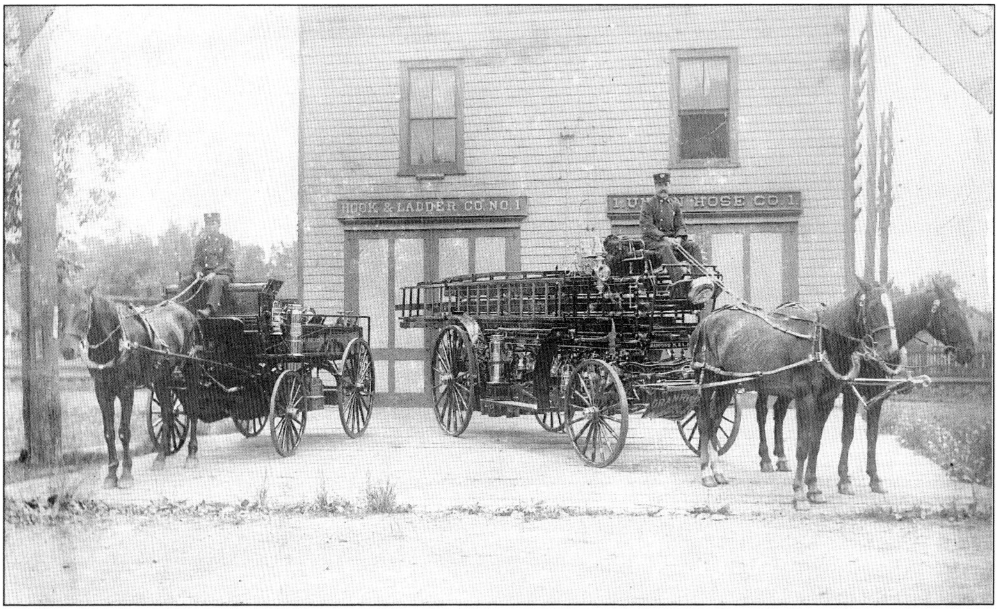

CRANFORD'S HORSE-DRAWN FIRE TRUCKS, *c.* 1900. The fire department had two companies, each with a total of three vehicles. Both companies were headquartered in this wood-frame, two-bay firehouse until 1909. Union Hose Company No. 1 was organized on November 10, 1892, and was followed by Hook and Ladder Company No. 1 on April 17, 1893. The Hose Company wore red shirts and the Hook and Ladder Company wore blue shirts.

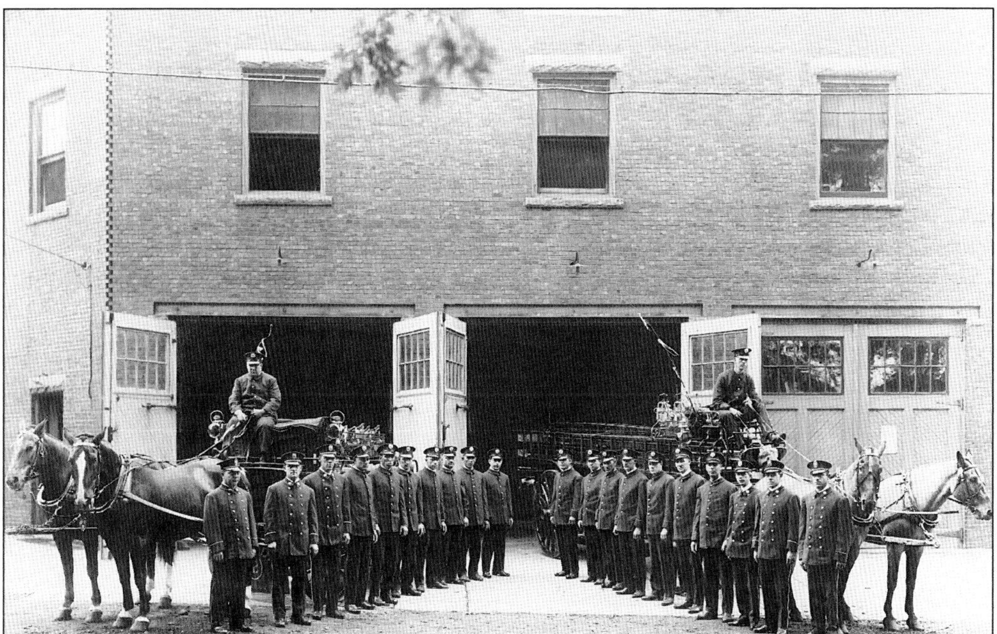

THE CRANFORD FIRE DEPARTMENT, 1920. Cranford's firefighters lined up in their new uniforms in front of the fire house. Horses "Dick" and "Dan" (left) pulled the hose wagon and "Nancy" and "Baldy" (right) hauled the hook and ladder truck. The brick fire house was erected in 1909 and razed in 1980.

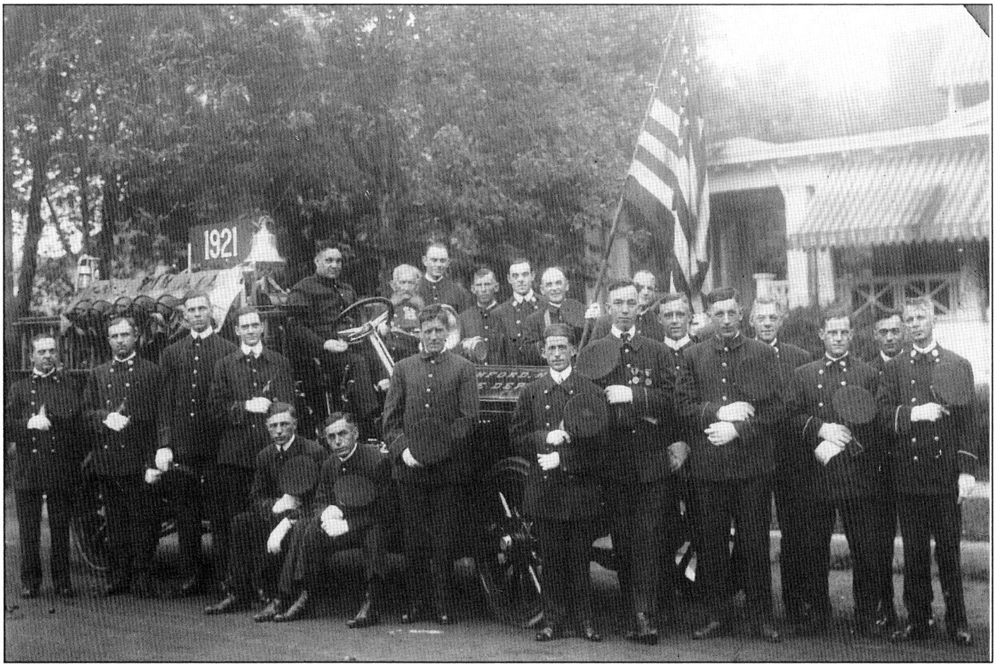

THE PROUD FEW, 1921. Cranford firemen pose with their new hook and ladder truck. Officers sport double-breasted jackets with twin rows of brass buttons, and the rank and file wear single-breasted coats bearing one row of buttons. The old gentleman with the whiskers (in the background behind the driver) is Gideon E. Ludlow, a charter member of the original Union Hose Company in 1892. He is wearing his red woolen fire shirt from that time.

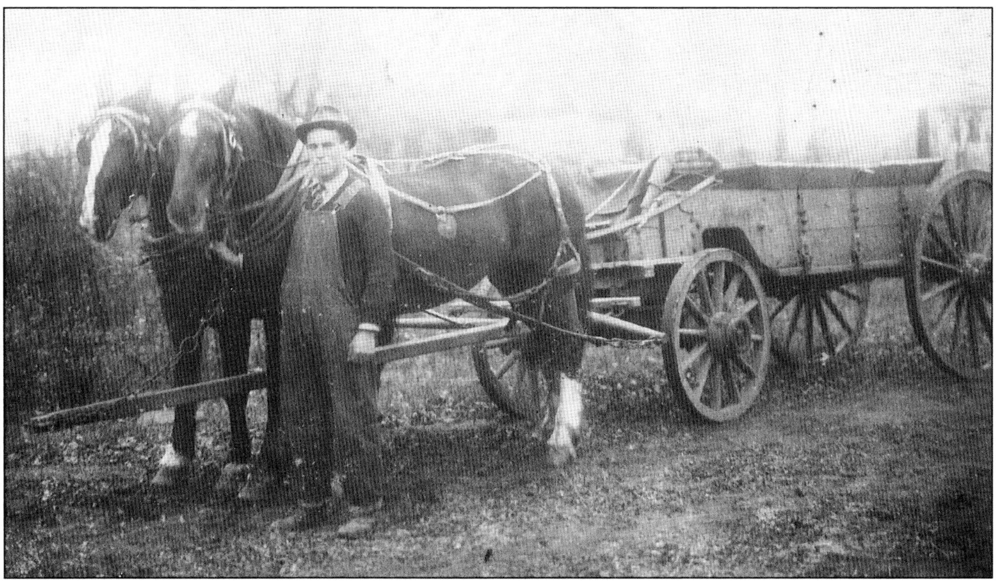

A WORKING RETIREMENT, 1921. Dick and Dan, two Cranford fire horses, became victims of technological unemployment when the fire department purchased motorized equipment. They were sold to Severin Droescher. They are held here by Rocco Della Serra, an employee of Droescher's. There was one problem: Dick and Dan would gallop back to their former home whenever they heard the firebell.

POLICE AND FIRE ALARM
TELEGRAPH ASSOCIATION.
SIGNAL CODE.

NOTICE —This instrument must not be meddled or tampered with in any manner. Do not unscrew the bell to clean it.

DIRECTIONS.

To give any Call, Alarm or Signal, pull the lever or handle of the box around until you hear it click or catch, at whichever name designated on the box is to be used, and let go

ONCE ONLY.

This will give your number on the bell, and also gives the signal or call at the Central Office. Then the Central Office, upon receiving the signal--which we will suppose, for instance, to be a Fire—will ring **5-5-5**, which is the general Fire Alarm, followed by your number, indicating where it is. This alarm or signal, and all others excepting the call for Doctor, will be repeated by the Central Office three times, thereby giving all subscribers on the line ample time to receive and understand the alarm.

THE DOCTOR'S CALL.—When the Central Office receives a call for the Doctor you will hear the call given by the Central Office, **2-2-2** followed by your number, upon which the Doctor, if he is in, will answer by giving your number, signifying that the Doctor knows where to go and will come immediately ; but if **1-2-3** comes back from the Doctor's office it will signify that the Doctor is away but will be back soon ; and if **2-3-4** comes back from the Doctor's office it will signify that the Doctor is out of town and another physician will have to be summoned.

SIGNALS

CAUTION.—Give the call or alarm ONCE ONLY, unless the Central Office should by some accident misunderstand the call, in which case you will hear 1-3-1 come back, signifying "Repeat call once more."

5 5 5	General Fire Alarm.
4 4 4	Special—Turn Out to Stations.
3 3 3	Police Call.
2 2 2	Doctor's Call.
1 2 3	Doctor is away—Will be back soon.
2 3 4	Doctor is out of Town.
1 3 1	Repeat Call once more.
10	Taps of the Bell signifies False Alarm.

THESE SIGNALS WILL COME FROM CENTRAL OFFICE ONLY.

MEMBERS' NUMBERS.

13	C. A. MERRITT.	**34**	WRAY, E. M.
14	ELY, G. G.	**35**	MARCUS, J. A.
15	DAMON, GEO.	**36**	WOOD, W. D.
16	HIBSON, J. A.	**41**	DRYSDALE, WM.
21	CLOSE, WM. H.	**42**	LITTELL'S PHARMACY.
22	DOCTOR J. K. McCONNELL.	**43**	MUNOZ, M. Jr.
23		**45**	
24	MENDELL, W. W.	**46**	CORDUA, F.
25	ADAMS, E. K.	**51**	MILLER, G. H.
26	PORCELLA, S.	**53**	BEADLE, E.
31	DERBY, J. L.	**54**	FERGUSON, J. W.
32	ISENMANN, J.	**56**	ABRY, C. L.
		61	

R. A. Bigelow, Printer, 75 Barclay St., New York.

A SIGNAL CODE CARD, 1887. The Cranford Thief Detecting Society was a vigilance society chartered by the State of New Jersey in 1869. In 1887, E.K. Adams Jr., then captain of the Society, installed an alarm system connected to the homes of various members. In his own home he maintained a 40-cell battery that powered the system. The signals were relayed by 6-inch electric bells. The first call went out on September 9, 1887. By a cruel twist of fate the call was for a doctor to treat Adams' father, who had been fatally injured by falling under a train at the Cranford station.

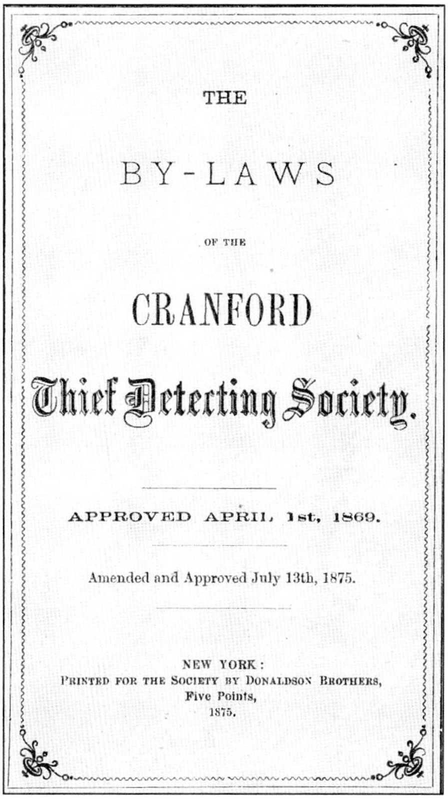

THE

BY-LAWS

OF THE

CRANFORD

Thief Detecting Society.

APPROVED APRIL 1st, 1869.

Amended and Approved July 13th, 1875.

NEW YORK:
PRINTED FOR THE SOCIETY BY DONALDSON BROTHERS,
Five Points,
1875.

CRANFORD THIEF DETECTING SOCIETY BYLAWS. This ten-page booklet contains the rules and regulations of the Cranford Thief Detecting Society, the amateur police force that was the forerunner of the modern police department. Chartered by the state, it operated from 1869 to 1889 and was composed of the leading men of the village. Armed with badge, belt, billy, and revolver, they pursued thieves and burglars but spent most of their time simply maintaining order.

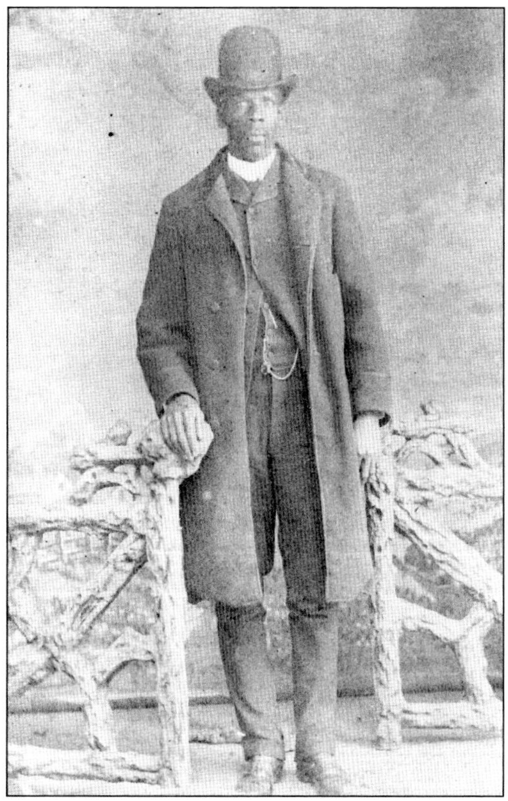

CONSTABLE JOSHUA BRYANT, c. 1885. In the nineteenth and early twentieth centuries, Cranford elected constables. Perhaps the best of the early ones was Joshua Bryant, who was also a leader in the local Republican Party. Elected four times, he served ten years between 1881 and 1893, longer than any other nineteenth-century constable. Bryant had one other distinction: he was the first African-American elected to public office in Cranford.

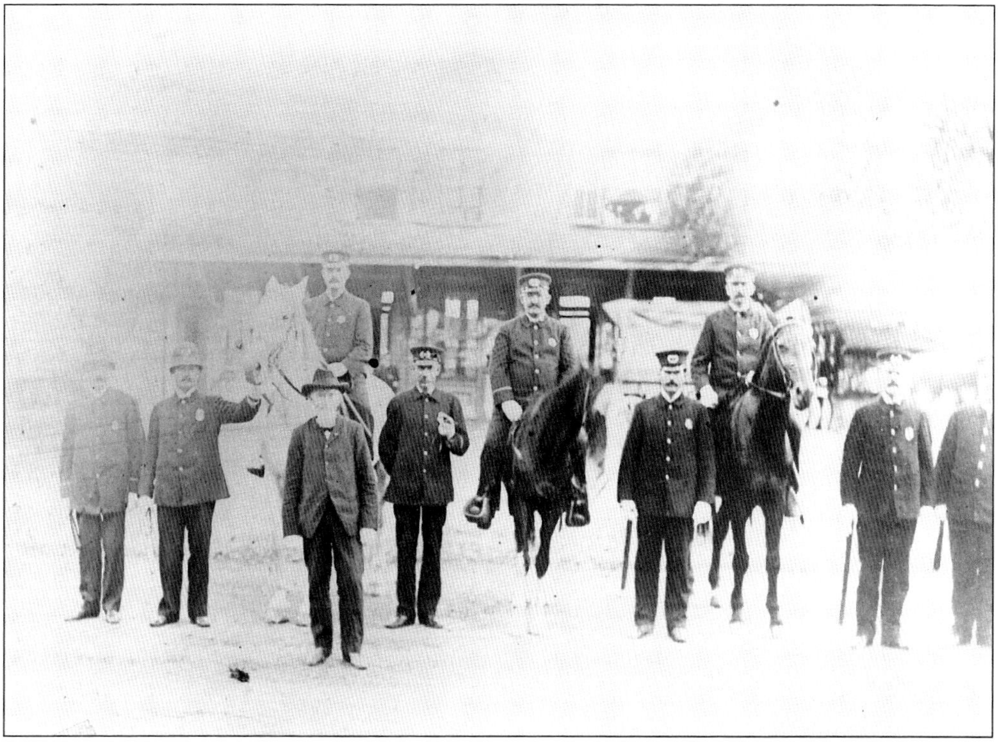

CRANFORD'S FINEST, *c*. 1910. Three types of officers are pictured in this faded photograph taken in front of the old railway station. In addition to the three mounted officers, two foot patrolmen on the left wear "bobby"-style police helmets, while the others have soft caps. The bearded man in front is Justice of the Peace W.W. Mendell. James Hennessey is the mounted officer in the center.

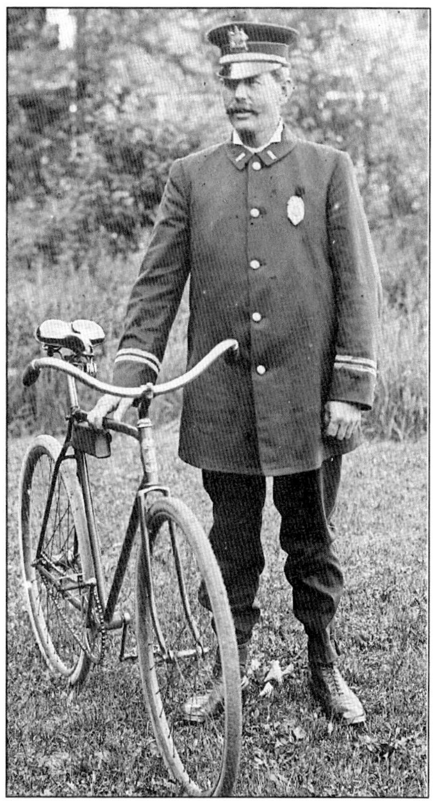

CRANFORD'S FIRST POLICE CHIEF. William Jennings (1869–1952) joined the Cranford Police Department in 1905. Five years later he was promoted to sergeant and made head (not chief!) of the department. He was also put in charge of all street and sewer repair. For this, he received a salary of $900 a year. In 1917 Jennings was appointed the township's first police chief. He resigned from the department in 1920.

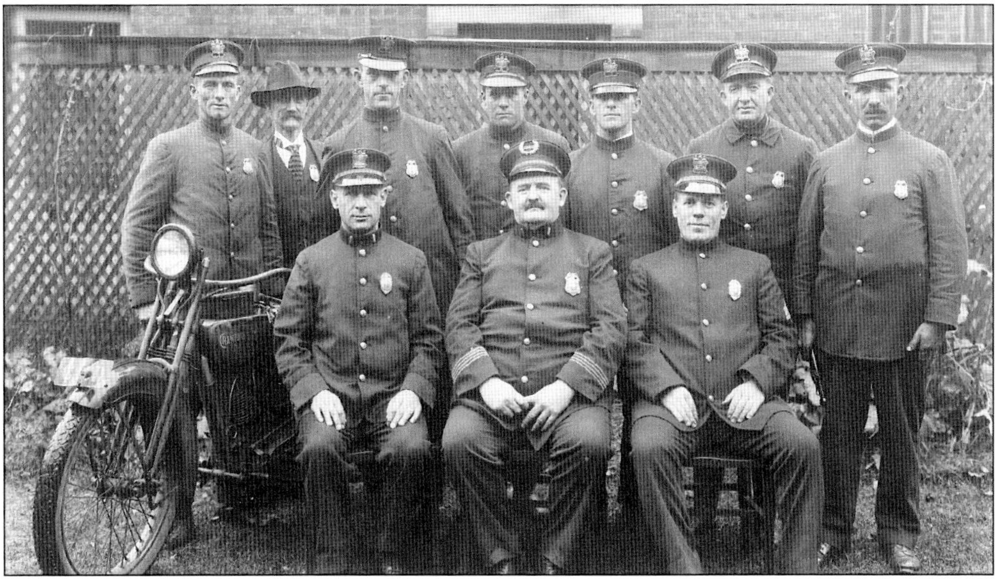

THE CRANFORD POLICE DEPARTMENT, 1921. Chief James Hennessey (seated in the center) is flanked by Lieutenant George Greiss (left) and Sergeant Carlangelo Massa (right). Standing from left to right are: Patrick Martin, Detective Joseph McCaffrey, Lawrence Bonnell Sr., two unidentified officers, David Winans, and Thomas Woods Sr. The motorcycle is a Harley-Davidson.

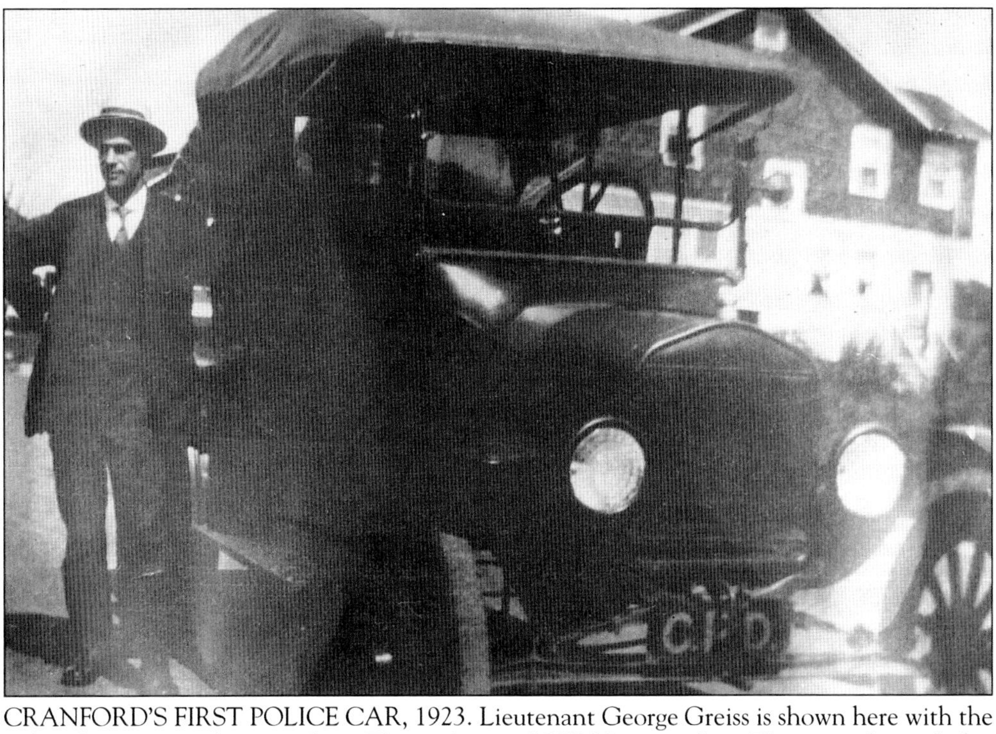

CRANFORD'S FIRST POLICE CAR, 1923. Lieutenant George Greiss is shown here with the police department's first patrol car. The car bears a "CPD" license plate. The man who took this photograph, Theodore A. Crane, remembered that the car was put into service on a Saturday. He snapped its picture the next day at the corner of Lehigh Avenue and Stratford Terrace.

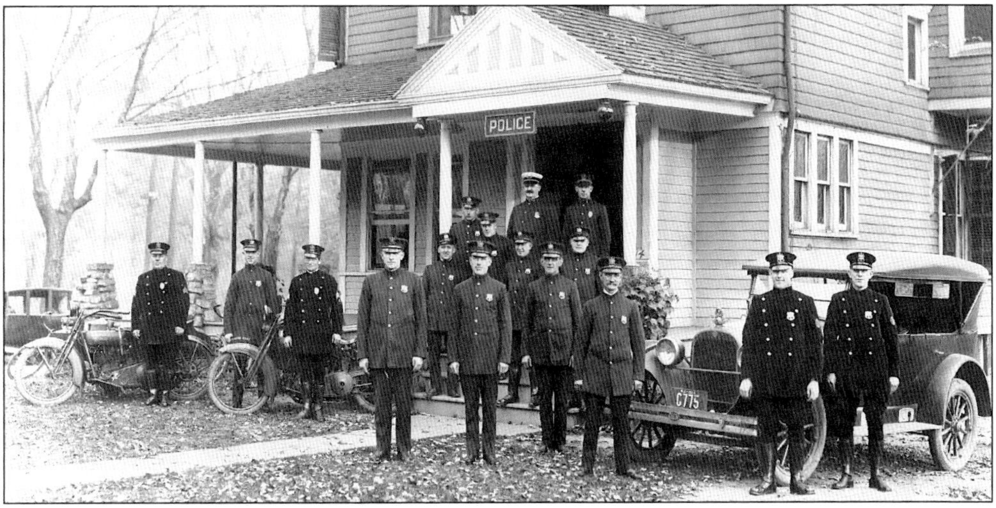

THE CRANFORD POLICE DEPARTMENT, 1924. Posing proudly in front of headquarters with their mobile equipment are, from left to right: (on the lawn) Sergeant Carlangelo Massa, Patrolman Lawrence Bonnell Sr., Sergeant Patrick Martin, and Patrolmen John McNerney, Harry Craig, Edward Coleman, Joseph McCaffrey, George Rosendale, and Edward Galvin; (bottom step) David Winans and Alex King; (on the steps) Edward Metzner, Thomas Woods Sr., and Edward Schindler; (standing on the top step) Chief James Hennessey (white cap) and Lieutenant George Greiss. Note the mobile officers wearing darker uniforms and leather leggings.

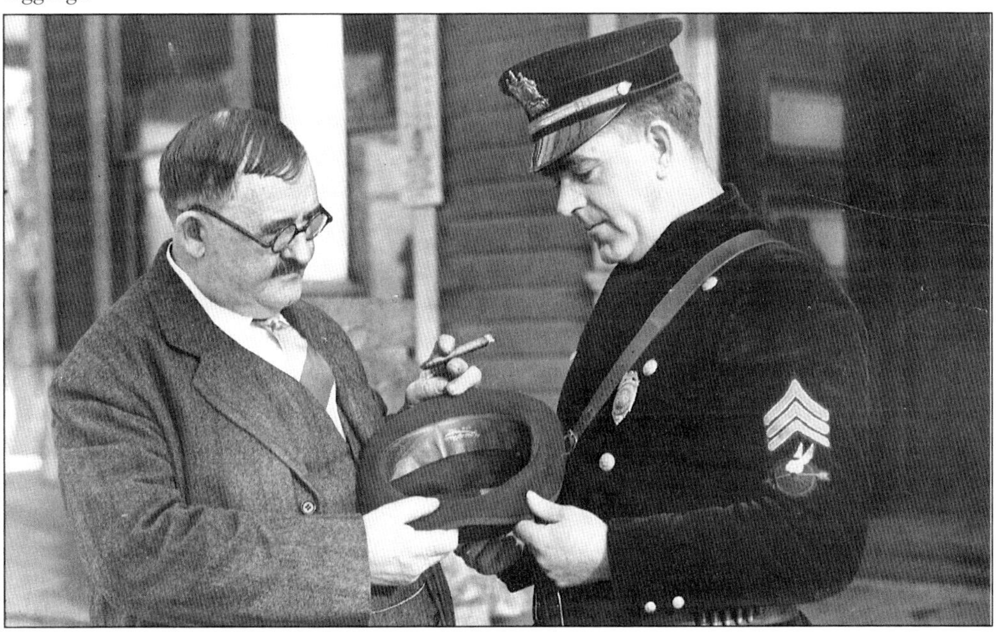

EXAMINING THE EVIDENCE, 1929. Police Chief James Hennessey (left) and mobile-patrol Sergeant Lawrence Bonnell Sr. (in his brown corduroy uniform) inspect a hat belonging to the bigamist torch slayer Henry Colin Campbell, alias Dr. Richard M. Campbell, of Westfield, N.J. The burning body of Mrs. Mildred M. Campbell was found on February 23, 1929, in a field off Springfield Avenue, near what is now Pawnee Road. The infamous case became known as the "Cranford Torch Murder." Campbell was caught, tried, and executed in 1929.

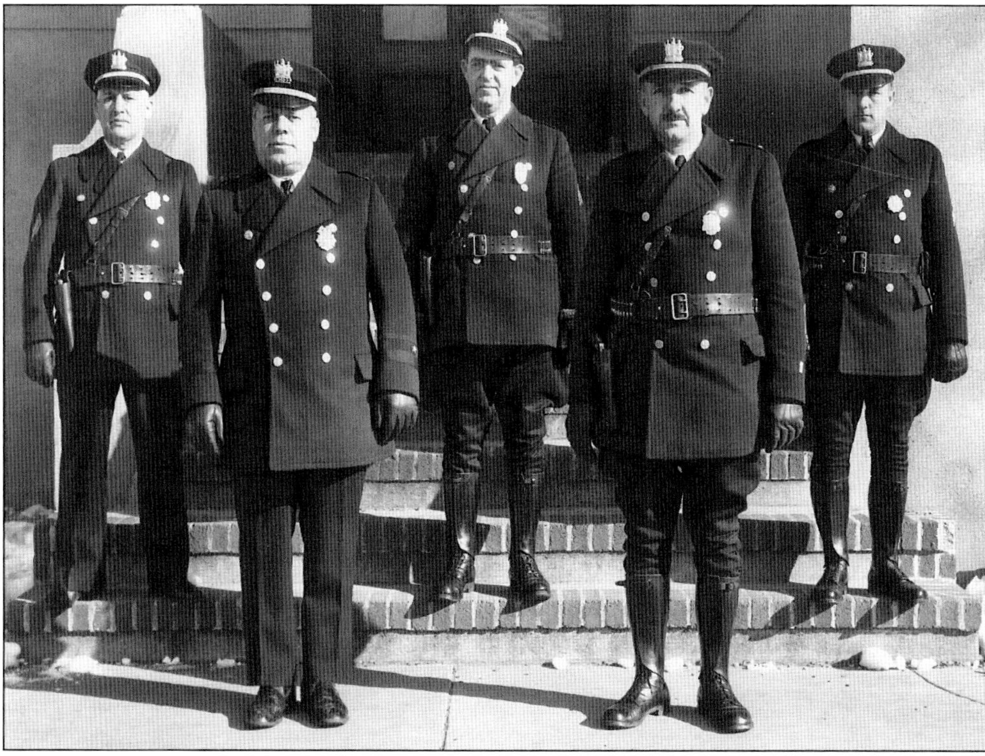

SUPERIOR OFFICERS, 1937. These were the men in charge of the police department in 1937. From left to right are: Sergeant Edward Metzner, Chief Carl Massa, Sergeant Lawrence Bonnell Sr., Lieutenant William Fischer, and Sergeant George Rosendale. Note that the three officers on the right still wear the old-style buckled leather leggings and jodhpur breeches.

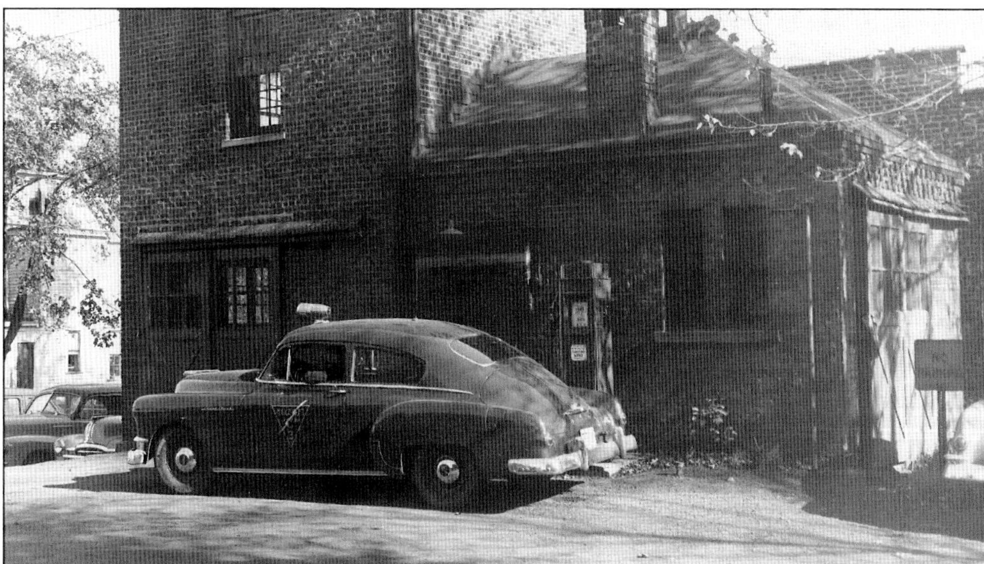

CRANFORD'S "BASTILLE" IN 1950. The township's sleek Pontiac radio car No. 2 sits in front of the police garage, formerly the department's headquarters and jail. The fortress-like brick construction of the building led local wags to dub it the "Bastille."

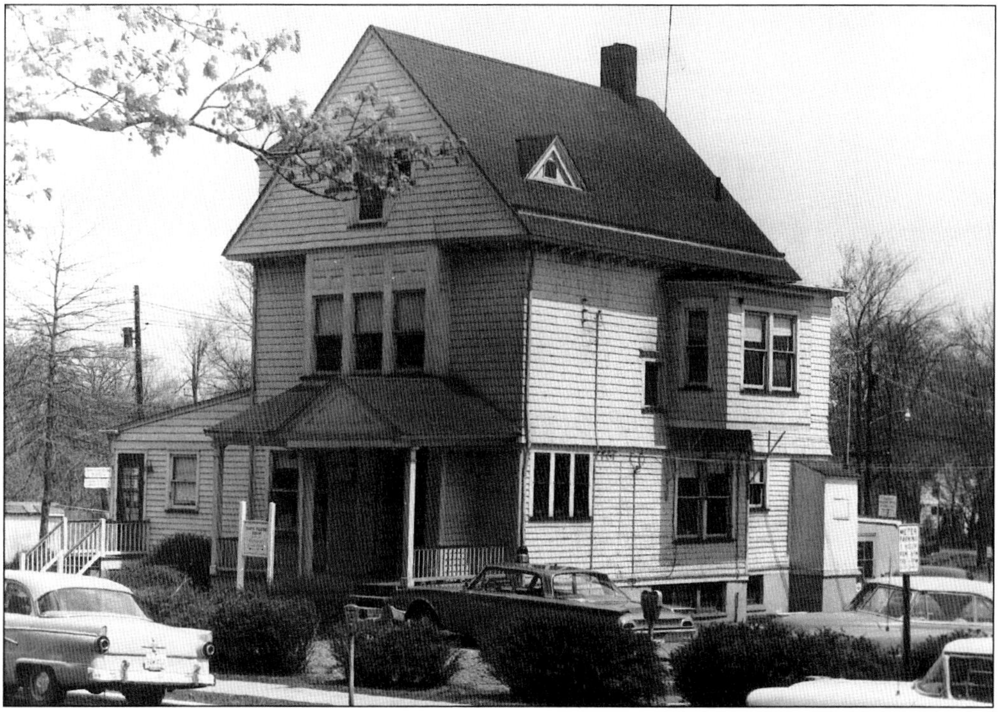

THE CRANFORD POLICE HEADQUARTERS IN 1961.Originally the Charles Day house, this building was located on the east side of North Union Avenue near the corner of Springfield Avenue, where a municipal parking lot now stands. From 1925 to 1962 it served as police headquarters and violations bureau. The house was torn down on April 17, 1962.

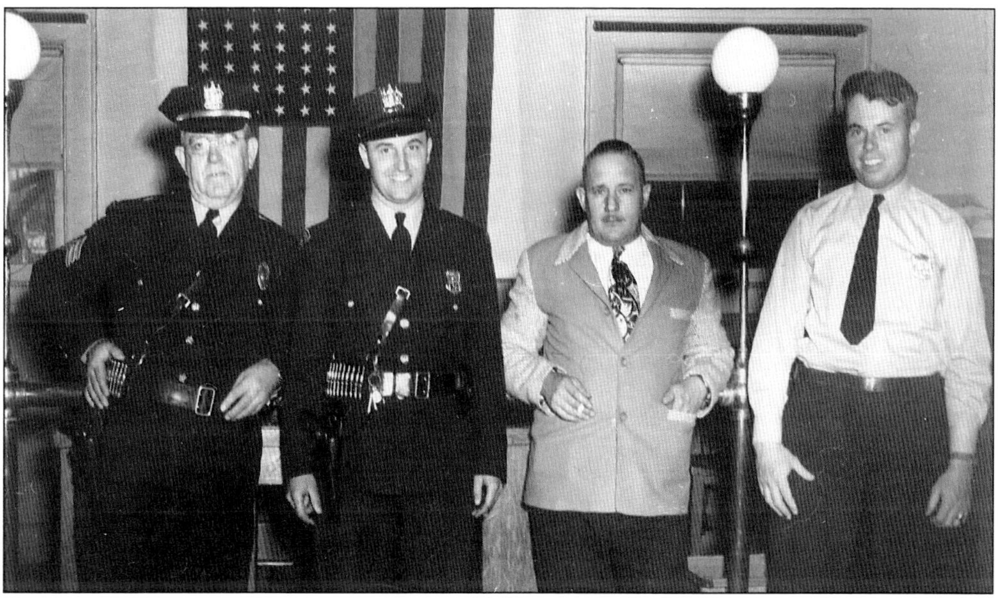

AT THE SERGEANT'S DESK, *c*. 1950. Leaning against the brass rail in front of the sergeant's desk at police headquarters are, from left to right: Sergeant Lawrence Bonnell Sr., Joe Kovacs, Thomas Woods Jr., and Lester W. Powell (who later became the police chief). Uniformed officers at this time wore Sam Browne belts with a double row of .38 caliber ammunition.

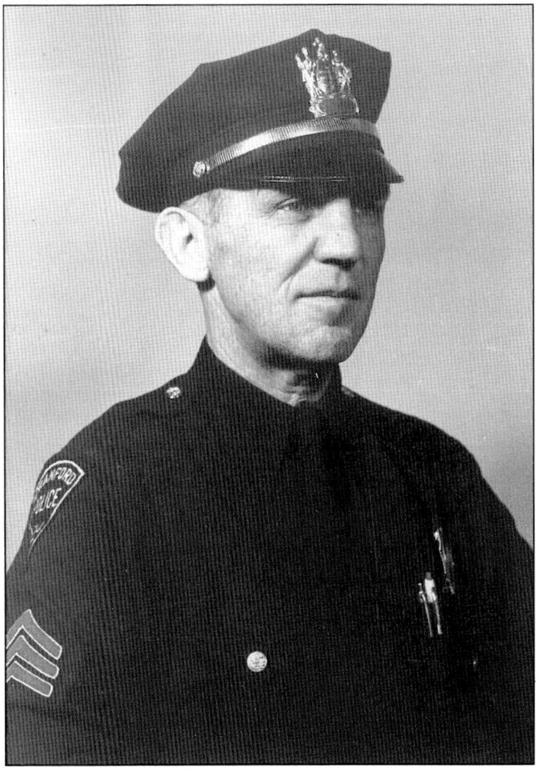

GEORGE CHARLES WARD, 1957. "Gentleman George" was an outstanding welterweight boxer during the 1920s, and fought 115 professional fights. The most memorable were two no-decision bouts with Mickey Walker, a one-time Cranford resident, who during his career held both the welterweight and middleweight championships. In 1939 Ward joined the Cranford Police Department, where he served for twenty-one years, retiring as a sergeant in 1961.

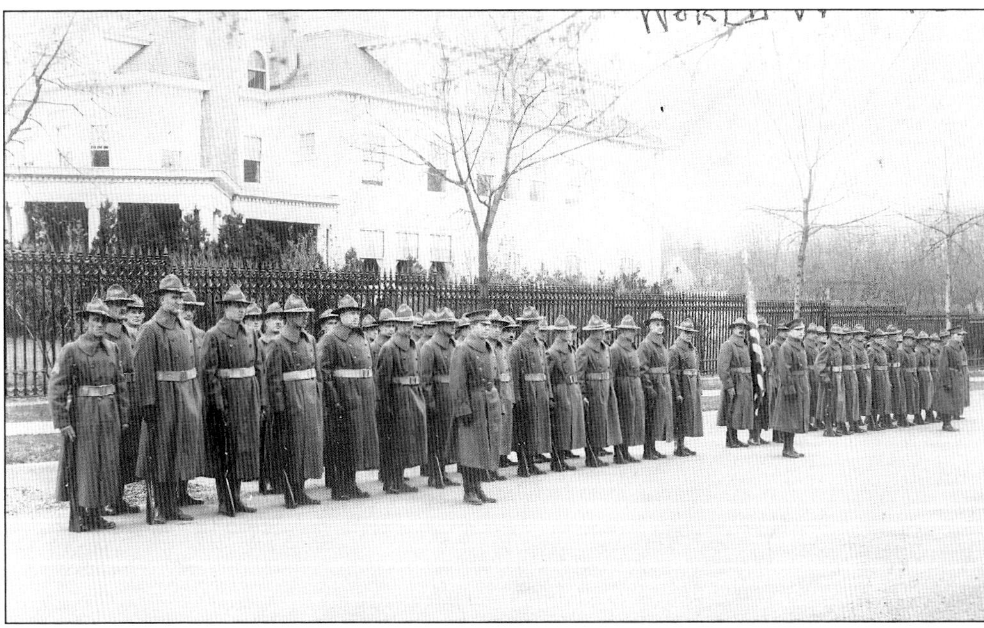

THE CRANFORD HOME GUARD, 1917. When the United States entered World War I, many local men enlisted in the Home Guard, a reserve organization for civilians. Cranford had two companies of regular Home Guards and, in an era of rigid segregation in all things military, one company of "Colored" Home Guards. Here a company of the Home Guard stands at attention beside the home of Thomas Sperry Sr., at Prospect Avenue and Claremont Place.